LITERATURE, AMUSEMENT AND ᴛᴇᴄʜɴᴏʟᴏɢʏ
IN THE GREAT DEPRESSION

Literature, Amusement and Technology examines the exchange between literature and recreational practices in 1930s America. William Solomon argues that autobiographical writers like Edward Dahlberg and Henry Miller took aesthetic inspiration from urban manifestations of the carnival spirit: Coney Island amusement parks, burlesque, vaudeville, and the dime museum display of human oddities. More broadly, he demonstrates that the literary projects of the period pivoted around images of grotesquely disfigured bodies which appeared as part of this recreational culture. Figures of corporeal fragmentation also proved important to novelists such as Nathanael West and John Dos Passos who were concerned to resist the ideological force of spectacular forms of mass entertainment like the World's Fairs, Hollywood film and military ceremonies. Psychic, social, aesthetic, and political tensions were thus managed in Depression-era American literature in relation to communal modes of play. This study will appeal to scholars of twentieth-century American literature and culture.

WILLIAM SOLOMON is Assistant Professor in the Departments of English and American Studies at Stanford University. He has published essays in *American Literature*, *Texas Studies in Language and Literature*, and *Style*. This is his first book.

LITERATURE, AMUSEMENT AND TECHNOLOGY IN THE GREAT DEPRESSION

WILLIAM SOLOMON

Stanford University

CAMBRIDGE
UNIVERSITY PRESS

CAMBRIDGE UNIVERSITY PRESS
Cambridge, New York, Melbourne, Madrid, Cape Town, Singapore, São Paulo, Delhi

Cambridge University Press
The Edinburgh Building, Cambridge CB2 8RU, UK

Published in the United States of America by Cambridge University Press, New York

www.cambridge.org
Information on this title: www.cambridge.org/9780521120913

First published 2002
This digitally printed version 2009

A catalogue record for this publication is available from the British Library

ISBN 978-0-521-81343-3 hardback
ISBN 978-0-521-12091-3 paperback

For Michael Sprinker

A piece of the body torn out by the roots might be more to the point. As it is, though, I'll do what little I can in writing.

James Agee, *Let Us Now Praise Famous Men*

One must learn *how to read* books, not *how to fear* them.

Kenneth Burke, *Attitudes Toward History*

Contents

Illustrations

Acknowledgments

My mother's uncle was a pilot, a reporter, and probably a member of the Communist Party. He was also the first American killed in the Spanish Civil War. While on a mission, his plane was disabled by ground fire. Struggling to return home, he died in the crash.

To honor his memory, my maternal grandparents helped organize the Joint Anti-Fascist Refugee League, the purpose of which was to collect funds to aid those fleeing Franco's forces in Spain. Many years later, my grandmother and step-grandfather were brought before the House Committee on UnAmerican Activities and told by the court that if they refused to reveal the names of those who gave contributions to the League, they would be imprisoned. When my mother graduated from high school, her parents were in jail.

My grandmother had it tough; she went in alone. My grandfather was more fortunate; he soon had the Hollywood Ten for company. Upon his release, my grandfather, who at the time of the trial was chair of the German Department at New York University, was promptly fired. He never worked in academia again. Blacklists can be tough too.

I began this project with the hope of re-establishing contact with a radical heritage from which I felt quite distanced. I set out to research and write about work and social protest in the 1930s – serious business by all previous accounts. Yet I became distracted by the proliferation of grotesque bodies in Depression-era prose. Attending to these figures of physical disfiguration drew my attention to the interaction through-out the decade between American literature and assorted recreational practices. Depictions of torn bodies and mutilated faces turned out to be a means of gaining interpretive access to the radical artist's intense involvement with urban manifestations of the carnival spirit, with the dime museum freak show, Coney Island amusement parks, American burlesque and vaudeville, and slapstick cinema. It then became evident to me that images of corporeal fragmentation had proved indispensable to dissident writers concerned to contest the ideological effects of the period's mass spectacles: its World's Fairs, Hollywood films, national holidays, and military ceremonies. Left-wing politics turned out to be a laughing matter.

To the degree that these forms of popular entertainment were mechanized, artistic interest in them led writers into an ambivalent engagement with modern technology. To manage the excitements and anxieties these public attractions produced, as did domestic devices like the phonograph, the predominantly male authorial subjects on whom I concentrate consistently turned to gender. Mass amusements were eroticized and made to embody the thrills and terrors conventionally associated with the feminine. In sum, my scholarly labors gave way to a fascination with the ways in which psychosexual, aesthetic, social, and political tensions were negotiated in the Depression era in relation to collective modes of play.

I take no responsibility for my deviation from orthodox literary history. I blame the following individuals: Renée Fox, Michael Pinkus, David Riggs, Bryan Wolf, Al Gelpi, Eric and Irene Solomon, and Molly Hutton. Unlike my grandparents, I am willing to name names.

Sections of the "Intermission" and Chapter 4 appeared in a different form in *American Literature* (68:4) and a portion of Chapter 1 appeared in *Texas Studies in Language and Literature* (43:4). I appreciate the permission of these journals to reprint these materials.

Introduction: Disfigurations

> ... disfigured and eternalized by the hieroglyphics of sleep and pain.
> Djuna Barnes, *Nightwood*

When Edward Dahlberg reappeared in 1941 after a five-year publishing hiatus with *Do These Bones Live*,[1] his once promising career as an autobiographical American novelist over, he did so as a decidedly eccentric and harsh critic of native literary traditions. Disgusted with what he felt to be an obsession with the grotesque body in contemporary prose fiction, he located the origins of this trend in the naturalism of the 1890s. He asserted, for example, that Frank Norris "set out to strip man down to a mechanistic integer and to despoil him of all human residue and emotional elixir. McTeague is not a character, or a person, he is a Male Digestive Tract mechanistically reacting to the most rudimentary stimuli."[2] According to Dahlberg, the predilection for degrading corporeal imagery emerged around the turn of the century and had persisted through the 1930s. "Today, the modern novelist, announcing a frankly realistic physical man, has spawned a fetal thing whose brains and bones cause us . . . to put rue into our nostrils. We are, finally, so defiled unto ourselves that we have to shriek at the Uncleanness of man's organs and functions out of the ugly cloaca of the naturalistic novel" (51).

Looking further into the past, Dahlberg considers the Depression-era perpetuation of this fascination with the nauseating aspects of the body as the logical consequence of the mid-nineteenth-century American writer's flight from the physiological. "Refuse the bones and the worms of the body as Hawthorne and Poe did and what is ultimately begotten is the contemporary underground biped, brain-spawn of the same flesh and bone denial" (47). Past rejections of natural processes amid the quest for spiritual transcendence have caused the present preoccupation with the conventionally overlooked parts of seemingly monstrous bodies. Preceding denials of "the male and female as they are, eating, sexually throbbing and giving off dense physical emanations" have resulted in a compulsive attentiveness to "the subterranean pores, valves and orifices of the hair, the nails, the teeth, the mouth." Repudiations of the more or less "classical" body – clean, healthy, self-contained, and inviolable – have pushed its grotesquely fragmented counterpart – impure, diseased, fluid secreting, and permeable – to the center of the literary stage. Previously subject to idealizing acts of repression, the material body has returned with an obscene and determinist vengeance. The effect has been to transform the mainstream of American writing into a putrid "allegory of human ordure" (52).

By the 1930s this loathsome trend had, as Dahlberg saw it, reached a feverish pitch. In a section of his study entitled "The Proletarian Eucharist," he produces a pseudo-anthropological critique of left-wing novelists like John Dos Passos, James T. Farrell, and Erskine Caldwell – in the process lending new meaning to the concept of a *mass* culture. The work of these three exemplifies a strain of literary primitivism in which working-class bodies serve as fetishistic objects. Caldwell, for example, seeks to find "medicinal deliverance in the people." Carrying the naturalist's "necrophilism," his "bitter corpse-lust," forward by sadistically amusing himself with "the dismembered cadaver of the stricken masses; the 'converted' author can now at will dissever a head, a finger, a leg." As compensation for the debilitating impact of urban-industrial modernity, such novelists participate in a kind of sacrificial rite, savagely mutilating and then consuming the proletarian populace ("the ritual bull") in the deluded hope that the writer will in the process "be reborn" (60). Physical reinvigoration and emotional redemption are unwittingly presumed to follow from the eating of "the cadaver flesh of the masses." Therefore it is "the worker's body that is dismembered in a remorseless Class dervish" (60). The commitment to social protest notwithstanding, the desire of the radical writer has driven him or her to perform a perniciously culinary task, to transform oppressed bodies into the main course of an authorial feast. The "great poems of slaughter and horror, like Marlowe's *Tamburlaine* or Goya's Saturn eating his son not only make man's man-eating nature known to him, and so purify and appall him, but they also gratify his nethermost lusts" (61). In contrast, proletarian literature fails to lead to the sublimation of cannibalistic impulses to devour (images of) the social other.[3]

Dahlberg's attraction, however, to the literary practices he characterizes as savagely repellent is palpable. Not only does he employ the offensively graphic imagery he claims is the distinguishing and intolerable feature of the novels he detests. He does so with great enthusiasm, as if the energetic vigor of his critical style were derived from and dependent on the vile imagery contained in the works he denounces. Placing Dahlberg's ambivalence in the context of the premature truncation of the initial phase of his literary career makes this ambivalence more comprehensible.

In 1936, Dahlberg abruptly decided to quit work on what would have been his fourth novel. By giving up on this project, provisionally titled "Bitch Goddess" and intended as a satire of the politicized literary scene in New York, Dahlberg unexpectedly terminated his career as a novelist. His potential had been immediately recognized upon the publication of *Bottom Dogs*, his first book. Appearing in print in the United States in 1930, it was reviewed favorably by Edmund Wilson, who praised it as a work bearing "the stamp of a real and original gift."[4] The book would soon be hailed (albeit in retrospect quite imprecisely) as an exemplary product of a developing movement in American literature: the proletarian novel. In addition to earning Dahlberg a reputation as one of the most talented of the new generation of radicalized authors, *Bottom Dogs* helped introduce the use of grotesque rhetorical strategies into the left-wing writing of the period. Though failing to register the humorous dimensions of the work, D.H. Lawrence's introduction (which infuriated Dahlberg) nicely evokes the book's degrading impact on idealized notions of human existence. In *Bottom Dogs*, Lawrence declares, "the human psyche" strips "itself to a sub-brutal condition of simple gross persistence. It is not animality – far from it." "They [the youthful protagonists] are cold wills functioning with a minimum of consciousness."[5] So unpleasant is the book's depiction of debased minds that it can be said to constitute "the last word in repulsive consciousness." For Lawrence, the principal virtue of *Bottom Dogs'* stark revelations is that they save "one the necessity of having to follow out the phenomenon of physical repulsion any further, for the time being."[6]

One of the critical targets of *Do These Bones Live* is thus an earlier incarnation of its author. Standing behind the hostile denunciation of Dos Passos, Caldwell, and Farrell is a version of Dahlberg himself. As a distinct period in literary history, the 1930s has until recently suffered from similarly dismissive treatments. Critical scholarship has repeatedly disparaged Depression-era radical writing in general as exceptionally naive and woefully misguided. The question is what of value to us today gets lost due to such acts of rejection? Recognizing that the use of images of the grotesque body was a distinguishing formal feature of the literature of the period furnishes a useful point of departure for an inquiry devoted to answering this question. To follow out this at times repulsive phenomenon requires, however, that it be comprehended as the manifestation of a more fundamental cultural process: the exchange between literature and an array of recreational practices. The recurrent appearance of the grotesque body directs attention to the otherwise difficult to perceive turn on the part of several Depression-era writers toward what may be called a carnivalized set of American amusements or forms of entertainment.[7] An interpretive encounter with images of corporeal disfiguration therefore leads toward a better understanding of the social and political significance of modes of collective play in the thirties. This is the aspect of the decade that deserves to be unearthed. To accomplish this task it will be appropriate to concentrate on the rather small area of the field constituted by such radicalized American writers as Dahlberg, Henry Miller, Nathanael West, Dos Passos, and Nelson Algren.

CARNIVALIZED AMUSEMENTS

A preliminary sense of the meaningful interaction between literature and amusement in Depression-era American prose can be secured by looking at a passage from James Agee's *Let Us Now Praise Famous Men* (1941). The passage appears in a section of the text entitled "(On the Porch: 3" and describes an overwhelming experience Agee and Walker Evans had while engaged in their documentary endeavor.

Lying on the porch of one of the Alabama tenant farmer families with whom the two men were staying, they found themselves listening in silence and delight one night to the repetitious call and response from the distant woods of two animals, perhaps foxes. The reciprocal sounds, "like the exchanges of two mirrors laid face to face," gather those attuned to them into a single, gigantic body part: "we now engaged in mutual listening and in analysis of what we heard, so strongly, that in all the body and the whole range of mind and memory, each of us became all one hollowed and listening ear."[8] After exhaustively elaborating a musical analogy, describing at length the acoustic effects of this phenomenon by referring to it as the sustained succession of almost "identical notes," Agee turns to a comic theatrical practice further to specify the quality and impact of the natural event. The interchange between the two creatures is, he asserts, comparable to "an old, not specially funny vaudeville act in which the whole troupe builds up and burlesques a dramatic situation simply by different vocal and gesticulative colorations of the word 'you'" (465–66).

Agee then expresses the miraculous effect of this performance on himself and Evans. Initially, it presents the "sort of mystery, we should run against in all casual experience if we found ourselves without warning possessed of a new sense" (466). Then, at the culminating point of the semi-humorous series of addresses, the aurally and visually transfixed spectators ("the ear always needs the help of the eye") undergo a shatteringly cathartic, ecstatic release of emotional and somatic tension. We "broke open, silently, our whole bodies broke open into a laughter that destroyed and restored us more even than the most absolute weeping can" (467). The violently regenerative, joyous force of the parodically mimetic routine which "turned out to have been the most significant, but most unfathomable, number in the show" (470), is articulated through the symbolic use of an image of physical collapse and dispersal. The figure (of corporeal disfiguration) is a fully ambivalent trope: the puncturing of fragile flesh allows for a spiritual commingling and psychic renewal on a more collective scale. The negative tearing apart of the vulnerable, isolated body communicates and facilitates the positive construction of a larger, more resilient communal entity – though in this instance the expanded social body is thus far composed of only two persons.

That the figure of the wounded body serves as the means of transgressing the limits of private identity suggests that Agee is participating in the construction of what has recently been termed the pathological public sphere.[9] An image of the vulnerable, painfully exposed body triggers the coalescence of individuals across physical boundaries. Yet the expressive use of the trope of somatic shattering is linked here, by way of the allusion to vaudeville, to a carnivalized form of entertainment. It is the joyfully violent experience of laughing that symbolically unbinds the men and conveys an unusually intense and intimate mode of contact.

Whereas Dahlberg was distressed by what he took to be the sadistic manipulation of the worker's body for the benefit of the middle-class novelist, Agee's masochistic capitulation to the experience of being rent apart evokes the socializing force of humor. The ecstatic dismemberment may even imply an identification between the documentary observer (and his photographer) and the traumatically victimized tenant farmers whose fate he has been reporting on with staggering precision.

The most pressing concern of the present study will be to disclose the significance and function of the unusual ways in which Depression-era American writers integrated images of somatic trauma into their radically motivated rhetorical projects. I intend to investigate the politicized deployment in the thirties of images of the mutilated, diseased or oddly shaped body as a vehicle to undo and refashion private and public identities. As an interrogation of left-wing insertions of the fragmented body into literary discourse, my inquiry stands as a complement to recent work across the disciplines on the ideological or compensatory usage of images of well-proportioned and whole bodies. In addition, the interpretive analyses carried out below seek to conceptualize grotesque figurations in relation to the mechanized condition of leisure (and labor) in urban-industrial modernity. For the unorthodox compositional strategies in question are most comprehensively understood when the corporeal imagery appearing in them is taken as a means of grasping the productive connection established at the time between American amusements and Depression-era techniques of writing.

The overarching thesis of the present study is therefore that grotesque figures of bodily disfiguration made up one of the vehicles through which energies derived from the cultural institutions and practices of American entertainment were transferred into the formally inventive prose of the thirties. These amusements, which began to emerge in the United States around the turn of the century, include the dime museum display of human oddities or freak shows, Coney Island amusement park rides and other attractions, vaudeville, burlesque, and early film genres like the newsreel and silent slapstick comedy. The relatively vulgar status of these various recreational pursuits, their association with the working class in terms of patronage, helps account for their viability as a resource for subversively oriented literary activities. Marginal fun became the basis of social protest. However, as will become evident below, the writers with whom this study will deal tended to condemn other, arguably more mainstream forms of collective entertainment such as Hollywood film and the World's Fairs as serving predominantly conservative or reactionary ends. Such antipathy alerts us to the complexity and heterogeneity of the body of amusements as a whole. Paying close attention to the diverse responses such amusements engendered enables the retrieval of a sense of the politicized tensions circulating across the cultural field throughout the early decades of the twentieth century.

My book constitutes an intervention into the ongoing debate within contemporary cultural criticism as to the progressive virtues and drawbacks of festive revelry. This is a topic that Mikhail Bakhtin's *Rabelais and His World* helped open up for critical discussion. As is well known, for Bakhtin the temporary suspension of repressive behavioral codes and authoritarian social relations continually supplied, from antiquity through the Renaissance, the basis for humorous acts of symbolic revolt.

Subversively inclined writers have been drawn to the carnival tradition because it was during these sanctioned breaks from normal everyday life that the subversive energies of the oppressed were unleashed in politically productive manners. Hence Rabelais's exemplary investment in the popular culture of his and previous eras. Yet for some time critics have been scrutinizing communal modes of play as merely licensed expenditures of potentially revolutionary energies. The effect of carnival from this point of view is to pacify potentially rebellious social agents by distracting them. Offering only diversionary relief from the rigors of the world of work, collective fun often appears as a reinforcement of the status quo through indirect methods of emotional and physical manipulation. The result of indulging in the commercially arranged pleasures of modernity would be, for instance, the maintenance of a docile and humble work force.[10] From this perspective, literary fascinations with mass entertainment should be approached with critical caution rather than enthusiastically greeted as the mark of inherently progressive embraces of the interests of disenfranchised persons.

One compelling version of the skeptical stance toward carnival and aesthetic appropriations of its symbolic imagery and structural motifs is Peter Stallybrass and Allon White's *The Politics and Poetics of Transgression*. Shifting the terrain of discussion away from arguments about the subversive or conservative nature of carnivals, the critics attend instead to the role the systems of grotesque imagery associated with festive practices have historically played in the construction of bourgeois identity. At the end of their inquiry, the authors convict both the modernist appropriation of carnivalesque repertoires and the poststructuralist fascination with transgression as being politically romantic gestures. The appeal to the putatively authentic cultural practices of "low" social groups by avant-garde artists and contemporary theorists alike is nostalgic and idealist. Those adopting such approaches are guilty of projecting the sensuous pleasures that have been historically eradicated from bourgeois existence onto socially marginal communities. Like Dahlberg, Stallybrass and White understand this process as the ritual staging of a festival of the political unconscious. Critical thinkers and their creative precursors wish to inhabit a liminal position beyond prohibition; they desire to squander the symbolic capital their class has accrued in the deluded hope of finding salvation in the undifferentiated, imaginary realm of the grotesque "Other." In offering temporary release from the repressive constraints of bourgeois subjectivity, such descents into the sphere of the crude and unruly serve to maintain the existing social system. Fantasy investments in the low tend to reinforce existing hierarchies. Thus Stallybrass and White remain wary of (though not absolutely hostile to) affirming the carnival-grotesque as a politically progressive force in the world.[11]

The first half of this inquiry tends toward a more Bakhtinian stance on these matters, though I adopt a tempered version of the utopian enthusiasm informing his outlook. This is in part because the authors to be studied were in fact from marginal communities (Dahlberg, Miller, as well as Algren).[12] But my project does not consist of a straightforward application of a Bakhtinian point of view to the radical literature of the thirties. For while the Russian scholar was busy rectifying a diminished cultural awareness of the importance of folk traditions of humor to European literature, American writers were busy fabricating a modernized version of the carnival-grotesque. Many of the amusements that caught the attention of writers in the thirties were mechanized, and the literary engagement with these technologically mediated recreations had as its logical corollary a shift in somatic imagery. Images of the grotesque body came to function as the site (and sight) mediating human beings and machinery.

Whereas Bakhtin studied the use of tropes of organic embodiment to reconcile individuals with their natural environment (and to incorporate persons into social formations of a [grotesque] body politic), the object of my investigation is different. The problem confronted by certain Depression-era artists was to forge links between the modern self and its urban-industrial setting. Consequently, the image content of the tropes they marshaled to accomplish this task switched toward the technological. By the thirties, the machine had replaced nature in the figures of embodiment designed to facilitate relays between individuals and their altered surroundings. "No one now," Dahlberg wrote in 1929, "would write a pastoral. It would be ridiculous and seem very much affected." To produce a grotesque aesthetic suited to the machine age one must register, as Baudelaire had started to do, "the mechanical note in nature." Today, when "everything is artifice," the "metaphysics which arise from machinery and mechanism has more aesthetic value than one which has its roots in naïve phenomena."[13] The developing literary interest in attending to the impact of inorganic milieu on bodies and minds did not simply consist, as Dahlberg eventually came to feel it had, of the reduction of the human to the level of the mechanical. On the contrary, the ambivalence Bakhtin has located as the essential characteristic of carnival-grotesque imagery was on occasion manifest in Depression-era writing. Although bodies were indeed throughout the period depicted in shattered conditions, at times this negative expression (and thus the emotional experience to which it corresponded) functioned as the prelude to a positive, even liberating reconstruction of the body as a hybrid or amalgamation of the organic and mechanical. The aesthetic fashioned by Henry Miller is a striking example of such a genuinely regenerative, albeit masochistic approach to the rapprochement of bodies and machines. And to the degree that the grotesque imagery he deployed in this process was technologically mediated, his approach may be characterized as the emergence in American literature of the technocarnivalesque.

If the painfully dismantled body remained at the forefront of his and other literary strategies of the period, radical writers inscribed such images of physical violence in various rhetorical contexts, and this aspect of the topic requires preliminary commentary.

THE RHETORIC OF THE FRAGMENTED BODY

We are never whole again, but living in fragments, and all our parts separated . . .
(Henry Miller, *Black Spring*)

The images of corporeal damage the present study exhumes from the graveyard of literary history for (postmortem) examination present an initial challenge to interpretation in that their extra- and inter-textual derivations may be variously understood. For instance, the depiction of the shattered body may be utilized as part of a representational enterprise aimed at disclosing the devastating effects on human beings of participating in mechanized warfare. The fragmented body also plays an important role in Marxist attempts to theorize the physical experiences of the modern worker under conditions of economic rationalism. Here images of corporeal disintegration serve to register the somatic and mental effects of the organization of the labor process in capitalist industry, effects that the rise of scientific management intensified. Such historically specific uses of the fragmented body have as their referent the state of bodies and minds within urban-industrial modernity. Modern psychoanalysis has also addressed the question of images of corporeal fragmentation. In this context, the body-in-pieces has been asserted to be a corollary of extreme conditions of subjective anguish. Images of somatic shattering are symptomatic expressions of the private fear that one's identity is collapsing. Similar figures have, as mentioned above, also been a constitutive aspect of the formal repertoire employed in festive celebrations and in the literary styles derived from these events. Lastly, within the realm of literary theory the egregiously damaged body has occupied center stage on numerous occasions. In the work of Paul de Man, for example, images of defacement, dismemberment, decapitation, and the like constitute a set of strikingly "lurid figures."[14] In these cases, however, the "imagery of bodily mutilation" is claimed to function in the texts under examination as a reflexive trope that makes the dismantling of abstract linguistic structures perceptible. Corporeal dismemberment makes the process of undoing textual models visible. An inter-textual process of disfiguration in the rhetorical sense of the term appears in the form of the taking apart or disfiguration in the physically referential sense of actual bodies.[15]

This list identifies some of the main discursive settings in which images of corporeal fragmentation have made their presence felt.[16] The language of the grotesque body has thus been spoken in a diverse range of literal and figurative idioms and the literature of the thirties draws on all of them. Depression-era American writing therefore constitutes a cultural space in which images of severely injured or misshapen, anomalous bodies proliferated in an array of representational and critical discourses. Physiological aberrance made the mechanically determined existence of the inhabitants of urban-industrial modernity perceptible. Somatic freakishness functioned as a means of expressing the psychic distress attendant upon a technologically determined life (Dahlberg). Imaginary depictions of the comically monstrous augured a utopian future where the distinction between men and women and human beings and machines would be obsolete (Miller). Visions of the gigantically diseased or painfully damaged body contributed to the negotiation of authorial identifications with economically devastated persons (Algren). The progressively dismantled living body was deployed to contest the rhetoric of native brands of fascist propaganda (West). A mangled corpse was mobilized as a challenge to militarism and the nationalist rhetoric of patriotism (Dos Passos).[17] A primary ambition of my study then is to grasp the meanings attached to images of the grotesquely fractured or disassembled body in the writing of the thirties and in so doing retrieve a sense of the social and political effects such shocking anatomizations aimed to produce.

To achieve this end, commentary must pass back and forth between disparate critical perspectives (historical materialism, psychoanalysis, and deconstruction will alternately be brought to bear on the literary materials). If the multiplicity of contexts in which images of the grotesque body appears requires the interpreter to move from one point of view to another, this requirement reveals that such corporeal imagery is one of the areas in which various contemporary theories overlap. Moreover, if to comprehend the poetics of the grotesque in the thirties demands a good deal of hermeneutic flexibility, one of the singular virtues of the decade in this regard is that the political forcefulness of the imagery of fragmentation under investigation is unmistakable.

The peculiarity of such compositional strategies as a form of social protest becomes evident when these are situated in relation to more traditional responses to the widespread effects of industrialization and empire building. The aggressive deployment of the fragmented body contrasts starkly, for instance, with the iconography typically produced by the Industrial Workers of the World – a political force that emerged in this country shortly after the turn of the century. A swift glance through the visual art of the political organization reveals its substantial investment in enormous, classically proportioned bodies as pivotal figures in the construction of a working-class identity, in efforts to build one big union (see figure 1). The intent behind encouraging enthusiastic identifications with powerfully mammoth figures was to promote a reassuring sense of wholeness, totality, and even indestructibility, while gathering together dispersed individuals to form a collective self. Charismatic images of corporeal hugeness were created inside the movement in the hope of injecting confidence and courage into an emotionally devastated and physically fatigued proletariat and in order to bind workers into a coherent, solidified entity.[18]

Reading the Statue of Liberty, Lauren Berlant deftly articulates the procedural dynamics whereby a gigantic body comes to perform reassuringly ideological tasks. Here too the function of the seemingly unassailable, whole icon is to fashion or reinforce a collective identity. The specular identification with the massive figure provides "a passage for the individual subject to the abstract identity of 'citizen.'" (Mis)perceiving the Statue's stability and indivisibility as personal attributes facilitates the insertion of individuals into the nation. They now experience themselves as members of a powerful body politic. By seeing themselves in the Statue, subjects feel elevated; they reach "another plane of existence" upon inscription into what Berlant calls the National Symbolic. Feelings of somatic fragility and psychic helplessness are overcome by virtue of this fantasy investment; the illusion that one possesses "a whole unassailable body" grants the subject a sense of public belonging and in the process gives him/her the impression of being corporeally invincible.[19]

The Certain Means Of Rescue

Fig. 1 *Solidarity.* September 16, 1916

In "Gigantomachia," Wallace Stevens evokes a comparable transformation in a military context: "Each man himself became a giant, / Tipped out with largeness, bearing the heavy / And the high, receiving out of others / As from an inhuman elevation / And origin, an inhuman person, / A mask, a spirit, an accoutrement." The soldier gives up his personal ego for the reward of becoming a "braver being." Immersion in the mass provides him with a belief in his physical resilience and immortality. The soldier comes to occupy a solid "body that could never be wounded" and partakes of a "life that never would end." The difficulties of a particularized existence are eliminated as the general abstraction crystallizes. That Stevens characterizes the experience of being "increased, enlarged, made simple, / Made single, made one" as "not denial" suggests his support of the process. For him, the burdens of war make libidinal investments in a "magnified" physique necessary.[20]

Within the logic that accords such functions to monumental figures, their disruption may generate widespread uncertainties. Visions of bodily fragmentation on a grand scale will augur the collapse of collective moods of well-being. If entrance "into an 'Imaginary' realm of ideality" allows the subject to become "whole by being reconstituted" as a citizen,[21] images of corporeal dismemberment may register fears of and even pre-cipitate the deconstitution of collective identities. Writers like West and Dos Passos, in addition to furnishing critical illustrations of the process of "citizen" formation, enable us to interrogate the political ramifica-tions of its negative counterpart. Their radical imperatives drove them to present their readers with devastated individual bodies *not* sutured to a body politic. West's depiction of an egregiously dismantled protagonist in *A Cool Million* (so severe are his injuries that Lemuel Pitkin can be eulogized as follows: "His teeth were pulled out. His eye was gouged from his head. His thumb was removed. His scalp torn away. His leg was cut off"[22]) and Dos Passos' portrayal of a shattered corpse rotting on the ground at the end of *1919* are methods of resisting the coercive force of discursive enterprises whose material effects derive from the use of attractively embodied figures.

We are approaching an understanding of such gruesome sights as crit-ical responses to persuasively totalizing constructs.[23] In the first instance it is the Horatio Alger "type" that the writer analytically dissects; in the second it is the Unknown Soldier that is demolished. Images of somatic mutilation counteract (ironically in West's case) the mystificatory reassur-ance such icons furnish in relation to the brutal agonies of rationalized labor and the violence of technological warfare. By exhibiting the soldier and the worker as the wounded waste products of modernity, the two writers tap the psychosexual and social anxieties that the heroic models, of moral fortitude and sacrificial heroism respectively, seek to alleviate. The traumas that imperial spectacles and popular fictions repress by pro-ducing and putting into circulation images of the healthy, perfect body return in the form of the individual as wrecked commodity or cannon fodder. Taking aim at dominant political and economic ideologies at the level of the corporeal imagery these persuasively utilize, West and Dos Passos helped introduce a critical practice into the American novel.

Justifying the coordination of literary images of bodily mutilation with sociological transformations will be a concern of the next section of this introduction. As a way of negotiating this transition while also locating West's and Dos Passos' methods as compatible with the image repertoire of the European avant-garde between the two world wars, I turn to the concise, summary account Hal Foster provides in "Exquisite Corpses."

In the early years after World War I, the becoming machine and/or commodity of the body was focused in the figure of the mutilated and/or shocked soldier. Then in the 1920s, with the spread of Taylorist and Fordist disciplines of the industrial body, the worker became the epitome of these processes. Finally, with the fascism of the 1930s a new figure, the Jungerian worker-soldier, the armored body become weapon-machine, emerged to overdetermine the other two. Together these figures form the dialectical object of attack of the mechanistic grotesques that surrealism developed, after dada, to contest the modern cult of the machine – a cult variously promulgated not only in technophilic movements such as futurism, constructivism, purism, and the middle Bauhaus, but also in the everyday ideologies of the Fordist state, whether capitalist, communist, or fascist.[24]

BODIES AND MACHINES AT PLAY

A is for amusement; and in the interests of many of the millions of Fair visitors amusement comes first. (Official Souvenir Book, The New York World's Fair 1939–40)[25]

The spirit of play enfranchised the mechanical imagination. (Lewis Mumford, *Technics and Civilization*)

Registering and reacting to the anxieties and enthusiasms generated by living in the second half of the period Siegfried Giedion has called the time of full mechanization (1918–39) was one of the central problems Depression-era writers confronted.[26] As the First World War demonstrated, the combination of modernized weaponry and rationalized methods of slaughter had greatly increased the efficiency with which human beings could be injured or killed. Writing partly in response to such a historical catastrophe, Lewis Mumford argued in 1930 in an essay entitled "The Drama of the Machines" that the balance of power between humans and technology must be reversed. The proper hierarchy, man as the master of the machine, must be restored in the wake of the disastrous outcome of its inversion. "It [the machine] has conqured us. Now our turn has come, not to fight back, but to absorb our conqueror."[27] What is required to put things back in place is a "fine machine ideology," by which he means a more profound understanding of the social purposes that technology serves and a clearer vision of the collective goals that machines might enable us to attain.

Hart Crane articulated a comparable perspective on the matter in "Modern Poetry," a critical essay published in the same year. As he sees it, the main threat of mechanization is that it can lower the sensory threshold of pleasure, the technologically induced over-stimulation of our nervous systems decreasing our ability to appreciate art. The "menace [of machinery] lies in its capacity for facile entertainment, so easily accessible as to arrest the development of any but the most negligible aesthetic responses." According to Crane, the task of the "machine-age" artist, given technology's "firm entrenchment in our lives," is to make us more familiar with the machine, to reduce its strangeness. Rejecting the technological sublime, Crane refutes the notion that mechanical apparatuses should inspire awe in us, asserting instead that the challenge poets must meet today is to render the machine *less* perceptually striking. The function of art is not to speculate "on the power and beauty of machinery" but to bring the human and the mechanical closer together, adapting one to the other so that they may coexist harmoniously. The practical contribution poetry can make to everyday life, then, is to subdue the machine by assimilating it to the human, coupling the two so that the former virtually becomes a kind of prosthetic attachment, an artificial addition that we no longer think about. The machine "can not act creatively in our lives until" our contact with it has become so automatic, so habitual that its effects are "like the unconscious nervous responses of our bodies."[28]

A few years later the planners of the 1939–40 New York World's Fair, the most extravagant and expensive of the international expositions held in the period, drafted a proposal for the event that expressed similar sentiments. The function of the fair, as its ambitious and optimistic organizers envisioned it, was to explain the utilitarian social role mechanization was to play in the future. In essence the fair (called by this group the "Fair of the Future") was designed to justify the ways of technology to man, to make it possible to comprehend the machine as a progressive force in the collective march toward an improved mode of existence. "Above all else," they wrote," the fair "must stress the vastly increased opportunity and the developed mechanical means which this twentieth century has brought to the masses for better living and accompanying human happiness." "We must demonstrate that supercivilization that is based on the swift work of machines, not on the arduous toil of men."[29] Whatever fears the machine had generated must be alleviated. Since terror derives from a lack of understanding, the task is to produce knowledge of the ways in which technology is less a threat to traditional patterns of existence than their benevolent complement. Paving the way for a more luxurious and leisurely existence, the mechanization of society would not only increase material abundance through more efficient production methods but in so doing free individuals to engage in more pleasurable, recreational pursuits.

A modernized striptease show (one of a half dozen at the fair) was the most popular (and semi-scandalous) attraction in the amusement zone of this last of the Depression era's numerous capitalist revelries. Alternatively referred to as the Crystal Gazing Palace, "Sexorama," a "Peep Show of Tomorrow," and the "Crystal Lassies" (its official name), the concession was designed by Norman Bel Geddes, who was also responsible for the fair's most celebrated corporate exhibit, General Motors' "Futurama." Whereas "Futurama" was a diorama that provided its visitors with the illusory sensation of flying in an airplane above an imagined, 1960s United States traversed by model cars speeding by on miniature superhighways, the "Crystal Lassies" offered its spectators multiple images of a dancing, barely clothed woman. At the latter concession, an elevator lifted the female performer onto a platform where, as she gyrated in a complexly mirrored room, hundreds of reflections of her body were made available to the viewer as he peeked in through a slot from the other side of the wall.

The construction and subsequent popularity of "Crystal Lassies" is especially telling given the thematic priorities of the fair: to solve the "problem of mastering our own inventions."[30] It is as if regaining control over the machine is here conflated with or displaced onto the task of gaining control over female bodies. Women and technology are substitutable because both in the logic of the World's Fair constitute a threat, presumably to the natural male body. The initial line of defence, the voyeuristic amusement concession suggests, is to frame the dangerous excess, to make the feminine form an object of knowledge that one can gaze at from a variety of angles while remaining safely out of sight. Moreover, if a reassuring knowledge of enigmatically mobile figures is at stake in the "Crystal Lassies," then a parallel can be drawn between the concession and the analytic procedures that had resulted earlier in the century in the reorganization of production methods in the industrialized workplace. I am referring to both Frederick W. Taylor's investigations of the work process, which led him to develop his system of scientific management, and to Frank B. Gilbreth's time-motion studies, which continued the rationalization of factory operations. First implemented more than two decades before the fair opened its doors, such attempts to improve efficiency and increase industrial productivity by scrutinizing physical movements and breaking them down into discrete elements employ vision, as does the "Crystal Lassies," as a means of maintaining control over bodies. While at the exposition it was the physical motions in space of female entertainers rather than the actions of bricklayers or steel mill workers that were surveyed, the kind of segmentation one set of bodies endured bears more than a passing resemblance to the fragmentation experienced by the other. An even stronger connection may be established between this striptease technology and the efforts of Taylor's and Gilbreth's precursors in this field of inquiry to observe and comprehend bodily movement. Eadweard Muybridge's photographic investigations come immediately to mind; but the more convincing parallel is with one of the experimental endeavors of the French physiologist: Etienne-Jules Marey.

As Bel Geddes and his partners put it in their application to the fair board, the amusement they hoped to construct would not only have the effect "of a ballet of several hundred girls working with the precision of the Rockettes." It would in addition offer the spectator the opportunity "to view her from all sides, from above, and from below, simultaneously." The idea, as one commentator has put it, was "for a machine-age dance that made a woman's body seem infinitely replaceable like the interchangeable parts on the assembly line."[31] Similarly, though more than a half century earlier, Marey had built in his laboratory a large hangar with black walls so that he could observe the flight of a seagull "simultaneously from above, from the side, and from the fore" (see figures 2 and 3).[32] Admittedly, whereas Marey (and Muybridge) were intent on recording their observations so that the various phases of bodily movement could be studied scientifically, Geddes' "Crystal Lassies" makes no attempt to offer a representational aid – graphic inscription, for example – to sensory perception. Still it remains feasible to argue that the concession is a belated and uncritical participant in the same cognitive undertaking famously ironized in 1912 by Marcel Duchamp. In other words, perhaps the most appropriate title for the multinamed, pseudo-cubist amusement would have been "Nude Ascending on an Elevator."[33]

The concession takes on additional meaning when we recognize its position in the social and political struggles being fought on cultural terrain in the thirties. In the years preceding the opening of the World's

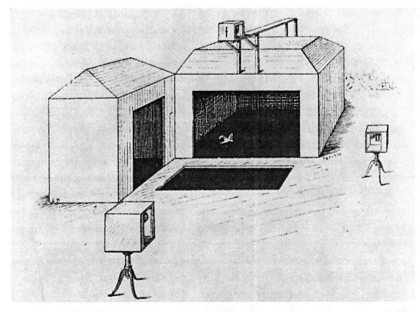

Fig. 2 Recording a gull's flight in three projections photographically. Etienne-Jules
Marey, *Le vol des oiseaux*, 1890

Fig. 3 Crystal Gazing Palace, New York World's Fair, 1939

Fair, New York City municipal authorities had been hard at work shutting down burlesque theatres. Deemed an indecent and salacious form of entertainment, one that "had contributed to the wave of sex crimes in the city," the amusement fell victim in 1938 to the ongoing war in New York "against the incorporation of filth."[34] The defeat of burlesque paved the way for the emergence of the officially acceptable strip shows produced by corporate America.

A writer like Miller firmly placed himself on the side of the filthy and indecent, and it is appropriate that burlesque emerges as a model for his aesthetic enterprise in *Black Spring*. Therefore it followed logically that the book and his other works of the period were all banned in the United States through the thirties. A comparable affiliation informs Algren's *Somebody in Boots*. Here the alliance is more explicitly cultural and sociopolitical. Defined as a member of the American lumpenproletariat, the novel's protagonist ends up working as the barker for a Chicago burlesque house. Moreover, Algren's cultural politics motivate his troping late in the book of the spectacularly decorated urban landscape as a syphilitic prostitute. The intent behind the obscene comparison is his desire to protest what he takes to be the further exploitation of the city's inhabitants at the time of the 1933–34 Chicago Century-of-Progress World's Fair. A class-based antipathy manifests itself in the form of a repulsive image of the grotesque body that can be correlated with a vulgar recreational practice.

In Depression-era rhetorical strategies, the grotesque body was frequently gendered female, as in fact was the realm of carnivalized amusements, even when associated with the machine. In other words, in the politicized dialogue between radical writers and American entertainment, sexual identity *and* the status of the natural body in relation to technology were also often at stake. It was not simply that a traditional model of the masculine artist was reinforced through the defensive rejection of two metaphorically conflated "others": the feminine and the mechanical.[35] On the contrary, just as writers were eager to put the autonomy of the literary at risk in the thirties, they were also willing to contest the stability of other conceptual oppositions (male/female; human/mechanical; natural/technological). In transgressing the boundary between literature and material culture, due to the fascinations of extra-textual amusements, radical writers forced themselves to renegotiate other kinds of differences. In the process of handling the excitements and fears non-literary modes of recreation provoked, writers found themselves interrogating with comparable enthusiasm and anxiety the possibility of inverting or even moving beyond conventional, hierarchical distinctions in other realms. This is to say that the challenge the textual materials under investigation pose stems from the complex ways in which the works conjoin social and political tensions with concerns pertaining to aesthetics, sexuality, and technology. If the grotesque body is the place where these multiple conflicts surface together, the interpretive task is to delve further into the politically charged energies that drove the production of such corporeal imagery.

If the radical writer's ambivalence toward mechanization was intertwined with his equally mixed attitude toward women, these volatile self/other dynamics were negotiated in the thirties in relation to modes of work *and play*. The potentially liberating aspects of technologically mediated amusement have been addressed less frequently in the recent critical commentary on machine culture than have its oppressive effects. And the tendency to conflate modes of work and play (or ignore the latter altogether) has diminished our sense of preceding investments in amusement as a creative, even a subversive force.

That one may discover homologies in modernity between mechanized forms of labor and mechanized leisure is not surprising given the possibility of tracing elements of both to their common origin in the experimental inquiries of Marey and Muybridge.[36] For instance, the latter's zoopraxiscope, the projection mechanism he invented to put back together synthetically the movements his serial photographs had analytically broken down, was recognized immediately, when displayed to the public in 1880, as laying the basis for new types of commercial entertainment. As he intermittently toured the country demonstrating his device in subsequent years, the images he showed, apparently to the dismay of some of the more refined members of his audience, often included "pictures of female dancers pirouetting" and even more scantily clad, virtually naked subjects.[37] A "cinema pioneer,"[38] Marey played an equally vital role in the modernization of the field of entertainment. His "chronophotographic gun," an apparatus that allowed its operator to record on celluloid objects moving through space, was a crucial technological precursor to the moving picture camera.

The work and ideas of both men then stimulated Thomas Edison (who met with each on separate occasions in the 1880s). And with the help of several assistants (W.K.L. Dickson in particular) Edison eventually managed to construct the viewing device that brought this inaugural phase of the history of modern motion pictures to a successful end:

the kinetoscope. Submitting a patent claim for the electric-powered machine in 1891, Edison hoped to have a demonstration model ready by 1893 to debut at the World's Columbian Exposition in Chicago but fell short of his goal. The kinetoscope was marketed shortly thereafter to amusement parlors, yet sales eventually declined after the novelty of the device wore off, and it eventually migrated to the urban "tenderloin" arcades and shooting galleries patronized predominantly by working-class men. Taking its place alongside the other mechanized attractions these establishments housed, the kinetoscope quickly became their most popular apparatus.[39] At the time the device was also known as "penny vaudeville," appropriately enough since vaudeville performers like Eugene Sandow, billed as "The World's Strongest Man," furnished the subject matter for many of the early films shot at Edison's Black Maria studios. It is to this amusement technology that Bel Geddes' World's Fair concession harks back, the kinetoscope entertaining the viewer by allowing him or her to look through a peephole at images of people (and other objects) in motion. And it was out of this "new mix of scientific will-to-knowledge and prurient show" that the cinema was born.[40]

In *Bodies and Machines,* Mark Seltzer has influentially examined the complicity of realist and naturalist discourse in the deployment within machine culture of visual strategies of surveillance as a means of disciplining individuals. The aspiration to comprehend and govern persons required that human beings be made legible; power relations (as well as erotic fascinations) were thus consistently exercised along lines of sight. Among other ways, such looking was facilitated by the construction of literary texts designed to function as seeing machines, realist and naturalist novels vigilantly gazing down on the city and its inhabitants while offering the observer the privilege of relative disembodiment. These discursive machines, though plagued by some internal resistance, worked steadily to convert individuals into statistics, to make them calculable abstractions. Moreover, what the reflexive attention to writing in turn-of-the-century American literary texts indicates is, from Seltzer's (avowedly Foucaultian) point of view, that they are virtually identical to contemporaneous procedures aimed at regulating persons and bodies in a thoroughly mechanized society. "What must be considered is a programmatic equation or identification: the perfect 'fit' between technologies of writing and the body/machine complex and the perfect 'fit' between the ontology of writing-in-general and an historically specific biomechanics."[41] The novels disclose that as acts of writing they participate in the same process they register: "the realist project of accounting for persons as effects of products of the machine" is an almost absolute duplicate of "accounting for persons and personation as effects of writing."[42] The representational enterprises the novelists pursue are motivated by the compulsive imperative to categorize or typify and thus control individuals, to render their behavior and the movements of their bodies predictable. Literary operations converge with social procedures: writing as calculation participates in the logistics of the body/machine complex and helps propel the rise of the emergent sciences of human engineering.

Paying close attention to the appeal radical writers made in the thirties to mechanical amusements helps reveal the socially and politically challenging, disruptive ways in which the natural and the technological may be coupled. So frustrated was he with the way this topic was being handled at the time in orthodox Marxist fiction and left-wing literary criticism, Robert Forsythe felt compelled to argue "In Defense of the Machine" (1935). Because the writing and reviewing of labor novels left him with "a picture of the man of labor tied to the wheels of industry until his brain reels with images of bolts and nuts," he insisted on distinguishing between machines and the way they are presently being used. The assembly line could thus be turned to human advantage under different circumstances; i.e., through a change in the social relations of production.[43] Attending to the intimate interaction of bodies and machines in the context of play in the period proves equally illuminating and in addition carries us beyond understandings of modernized recreation and modern literature as mere reflections of one another. If some writing strategies modeled on commercial entertainment are complicit with instrumentalized and rationalized labor, other compositional tactics derived from mass amusement decisively interfered with the disciplinary organization of work around repetitiously monotonous, sequential physical actions. Depression-era prose writers drew energy from increasingly peripheral forms of carnivalized entertainment to contest, from inside the general field of mechanization, the ongoing effort on the part of capitalist industry to accelerate production and thereby increase profits. Technologies of play became a resource for the development of a literature that repudiated the dominant values of machine culture.

In short, a difference within the category of machine aesthetics needs to be brought back into focus. The literary appeal to processes of modernization has customarily been framed as a quest for a maximally efficient, perfectly integrated, rationalized discursive system. The modernist writer idealizes the figure of the production engineer and intends formal innovation to serve the purpose of enhancing representational accuracy and clear communication. Cecilia Tichi's account of Dos Passos' method is a case in point. For her, the coherent organization of modernized labor supplied the analogies underlying his fictional strategy in *U.S.A.* The "synchrony of cogs, gears, shafts, bearings" in the machines used at the industrialized workplace "became the basis on which Dos Passos brought a fluctuant, unstable world into aesthetic order."[44] Such an interpretive perspective overlooks the critical resistance his texts pose to technocratic principles on the linguistic levels of semantic stability and referential certainty. Stressing the neo-classical dimensions of his machine aesthetic forecloses interrogation of the cognitively disorienting aspects of his undertaking, of the way his texts wreak havoc with signification. To recover the most radically subversive achievements of Depression-era writing, it will be necessary to attend to the conjunction of machine technology and *grotesque* compositional methods.

Miller's *Tropic of Capricorn* proves to be an extreme and therefore exemplary case in point. In the comic autobiography he affirms his unruliness and incompetence as a laborer, as well as his inability to hold a job. His incessant wasting of time functions as a symbolic repudiation of the priorities driving the rise of scientific management and assembly-line modes of existence. Similarly, his humorous expression of prohibited desires and praise of unconventional and spontaneous behaviors was intended to counteract the controlled and constraining manufacture of passively conformist persons and docile bodies. For him autobiography functioned as a perversely mechanized aesthetic process powered by the destructively excessive force of laughter. Diverted away from the serious world of discursive labor, writing emerges as a technologically mediated practice capable of wreaking havoc with verbal clarity. As he discloses in the latter portion of *Capricorn,* his ludic performances had as their precondition a reconfiguration of the author as an embodied writing machine. One day he "brought the machine to a dead stop" and "the other mechanism, the one that was signed with my own initials and which I had made with my own hands and my own blood slowly began to function." The first machine is clearly associated with the world of rationalized labor whereas its replacement is just as obviously plugged in to a form of entertainment. His miraculous experience of being reborn as a technological apparatus ("I heard my own cogs meshing") starts when he goes "to the theater nearby to see a vaudeville show."[45] In sum, the energies driving the most powerfully mechanized acts of Depression-era writing flowed directly from American amusement.

Much recent commentary on the impact of mechanical processes on the body and the psyche has relied on the notion of the double or paradoxical logic of technology as prosthesis.[46] It has been shown that the ambiguity of mechanization in labor and leisure elicits both positive and negative evaluations; technology has either been embraced as a welcome addition, as a complement to the organic body, or denounced as a dangerously invasive force. Film, for instance, like photography, has been frequently taken as a pleasurable tool that enhances our ability to see, that makes it possible to perceive phenomena that escape natural vision. Yet the still and moving camera may just as easily be accused of blurring reality, of yielding narrow, impoverished, and uninformed impressions of the world that in essence blind the viewer. Technological media may receive praise for augmenting optical and aural memory through artificial means; or blame for the decline of human capacity to remember sights and sounds.

James Agee (usually accused of being naive on such matters) articulates the ambiguous effects of the camera on the human eye in an exemplary manner:

Well used, the camera is unique in its power to develop and to delight our ability to see. Ill or indifferently used, it is unique in its power to defile and to destroy that ability. It is clear enough by now to most people that "the camera never lies" is a foolish saying. Yet it is doubtful whether most people realize how extraordinarily slippery a liar the camera is. The camera is just a machine, which records with impressive and as a rule very cruel faithfulness, precisely what is in the eye, mind, spirit, and skill of its operator to make it record. Since relatively few of its operators are notably well endowed in any of these respects, save perhaps in technical skill, the results are, generally, disheartening. It is probably well on the conservative side to estimate that during the past ten to fifteen years, the camera has destroyed a thousand pairs of eyes, corrupted ten thousand, and seriously deceived a hundred thousand, for every one pair that it has opened and taught.[47]

The list of such equivocal assessments could no doubt be extended at great length, yet the crucial point is to realize that modernized amusements generated similar anxieties. If the promise of these contrivances was that they would serve as beneficial attachments that overcome the inherent limits of human beings, such inorganic devices also seemed to contain the potential to diminish drastically physical and mental powers.

My twofold thesis in regard to this paradox is that the radicalized writer's engagement in the thirties with amusement technologies served as a stimulus to rethink the status of the body and psyche in relation to its urban-industrial surroundings *and* in relation to literature itself. The encounter with mechanical contrivances in the recreational arena triggered critical reflections on modernization's impact on bodies and minds *and* reflexive reassessments of the physical and psychic effects specific to writing. Put bluntly, writing, too, came to be treated in the thirties as if it were a prosthetic device, as a liberating and constricting force. Hence Dos Passos' reassessment of his commitment to literature: what "was to be an instrument to make you see more and clearer turns out to be blinders made according to a predestined pattern."[48] The significance of the period in this regard is that authors consistently tackled this problem as a political matter. For the time being, however, let me introduce the topic indirectly by focusing on the aesthetic uncertainties the newer media generated. My example, drawn from the realm of Depression-era popular music, also helps illustrate what proves to have been a recurrent gesture throughout the period: the condensing of sexual and representational dilemmas in tropologically facilitated collisions of natural bodies and mechanical contrivances.

Before he died in August 1938, reportedly as a result of drinking poisoned whiskey, Robert Johnson managed to complete two recording sessions in Texas, the first in late 1936, the second in mid 1937.[49] Relatively unknown at the time, his most commercially successful record was "Terraplane Blues." The song itself is notable in that lyrically it is organized around a body/machine metaphor: the singer's accusations against a sexually un-responsive woman are consistently figured as frustration with a poorly running automobile. More intriguing is his "Phonograph Blues," which figuratively conflates a domestic amusement and a human being. The song is thematically significant in that it addresses male impotence, an uncommon topic in an oral tradition in which the stress usually falls on boastful tales of masculine prowess. But more remarkable than the unusual confession of an inability to perform sexually is the equation the song rhetorically constructs between sexual complications and technological problems. The substitution of components of a recreational device for parts of the natural body is sustained throughout the song:

> Yes I love my phonograph, but you broke my winding chain
> And you have taken my loving and given it to your other man
>
> Now we played it on the sofa, we played it 'side the wall
> My needle has got rusted and it will not play at all[50]

The final line in the song, added only in the second version Johnson recorded, transforms the female as well as the male entity in the song into a technological device: "I am going to buy you another phonograph, just to hear your little motor moan." Rewriting eroticism under the conditions of gramophony[51] occurs in this instance as a mingling in the domestic arena of biological reproduction and a recreational activity involving mechanical equipment. As the pleasures of the flesh merge with the joys of technology, sexual dysfunction becomes a matter best referred to engineers.

The interest of "Phonograph" derives not just from the fact that it figures male genitalia as a mechanized instrument but that the trope implicitly links the mechanical reproduction of *sound* to the ability to copulate physically: "My phonograph won't say a lonesome word." The effect of the metaphor is to direct the listener's attention to the storage technology on which the experience of hearing the musical performance depended at the time. The reflexivity manifest here attends not to the material or physical circumstances of the song's production but to the conditions of reproducing the acoustic flow of data preserved on the disc. It is the contact of the needle with the spinning disc that retrieves or replays the live performance, rather than the guitar, vocal organ, and hands that the song self-consciously recognizes.

But Johnson's lyrics do more than acknowledge this shift; they also reveal the uncertainty it generated. On the one hand, access to technological media could be valorized as a prosthetic enhancement, extending the range of the voice beyond the inherent limits of the corporeal being; long after his death we can still hear his music. On the other hand, the supplementation of the human by an artificial contrivance involves a degree of disembodiment; as the voice is detached from its source, the machine replaces the body. And it is this physical loss that the song subtly comments on through the slippage between technological and sexual failure. The reliance on the phonograph enables the performer to transcend the inherent finitude of the natural body; he may be heard whether he is present or not, dead or alive. Yet surprisingly, this cultural achievement sparks a critical reflection on a recreational or procreative (the figure blurs the distinction) impairment. Undermining the boundaries between the organic and the inorganic, the lyrics at first glance appear merely to figure an erotic dysfunction as a mechanical malfunction, the broken technological apparatus a metaphor for a sexual breakdown, the phonograph a trope for a part of the human body. But the evocation of a fear of castration may itself be a displacement of a concern about a loss of voice in the wake of the development and application of a new storage technology in the field of popular music. Substituting an organ from the lower part of the body for one located in the head, the musician indirectly comments on his apprehensions about a device ostensibly designed to compensate for the limited extension of the human body but with the potential to do corporeal harm. The broken phonograph thus becomes, oddly enough, a literal reference to a perceived threat and, simultaneously, an element in a reflexive allegory that registers a crisis of faith in the mechanical reproduction of sound.

Johnson's song helps to introduce one of the central concerns of the following chapters, the superimposition of a representational ambivalence onto predicaments having to do with the precarious nature of sexual identities and correlative instability of gender distinctions. In other words, the security of the Depression-era male writer as *masculine artist* was consistently put at risk in his fraught exchanges with mechanized amusements. New technologies of entertainment produced dilemmas with aesthetic, psychic, and, ultimately, political ramifications.

Though attracted to the camera and phonograph as ideals in the effort to record optical and acoustic data, writers were also led by the emergence and proliferation of the new technological media to question with increasing severity the notion that printed words might serve as surrogates for perception. The phenomenality of the literary text, the notion that it could reproduce the visible and audible world, the sights and sounds of reality as they once appeared to the subject, gave way under pressure to critical examinations of the material specificity of the literary medium. Rather than continue to strive to preserve the voice and the image of the body in language, writers began to caution readers against such hallucinatory, imaginary responses to literary artworks on specifically politicized grounds. As the rise of mechanized amusements discredited the authorial ambition to achieve self-expression, as words ceased to seem the sensuous bearers of subjective experience, the radicalized prose writer's energies shifted in certain remarkable instances from representation toward criticism. The detour through still developing entertainment technologies thus led several dissident writers to approach an understanding of literature as a mechanized *critical* activity.

MAKING THE THIRTIES STRANGE

What is deadly about the interpretation of art . . . is that in the process of conceptualization it is forced to express what is strange and surprising in terms of what is already familiar and thereby to explain away the only thing that would need explanation. (Theodor Adorno, "Looking Back on Surrealism")

The conceptual terms most consistently used to characterize the thirties have been realism, customarily used in conjunction with documentary, and modernism, though recently a few critics have begun to unearth the roots of a postmodernist or poststructuralist sensibility in the Depression era. Of the numerous scholars who have employed these categories as a means to periodize the thirties, all rely with some nuances on the same developmental narrative of the history of twentieth-century American literary prose. Curiously, the decade has a different temporal status in each of the three stories that are usually told about the thirties and American literature. To those who see it as a moment of realism it is an end; for those who see it as a moment of modernism it is in the middle; for those who see it as a moment of postmodernism it constitutes a beginning.

The most familiar presentation of the period has been as a moment when left-wing writers committed themselves completely to conventional representational, mimetic procedures. Having rejected the aestheticism of their ostensibly formalist predecessors, Depression-era novelists and the documentary writers who followed them made referential accuracy their highest priority. The proletarian novel, which flourished during the first half of the decade, is customarily the focal point of such a view. Yet the apparent naivete of radically motivated writers is said to have persisted through the second half, as shifts in New Deal policy and changes in the Communist Party line combined to create the conditions necessary for the rise of a literary nationalism and its privileged genre, the documentary.[52] The transition from fictional narration to factual description amounted, if anything, to a further regression away from past literary ideals. That the two movements in the thirties were initially seen as logically continuous is apparent in Alfred Kazin's early study, *On Native Grounds* (1942). Although he classifies the "young novelists in the thirties," who "gave the new social novel its basic character" as guilty of an "abject surrender to *naturalism* [emphasis mine]," his main point is that what they in fact produced was "a literature of literal realism."[53] Similarly, the documentary writers who participated in the later "literature of social description" were passive empiricists, guilty of developing "a kind of sick pride" in "the fiercely objective 'realism' of the camera."[54] Striving to reproduce what the world looked like to the naked eye, dissident writers in the thirties failed to penetrate beneath the surface of visible reality. In short, "Everyone was writing documentary prose in the depression period" (368).[55]

In current scholarship on the period, the perspective Barbara Foley adopts in *Radical Representations* is closest to the traditional one. She evaluates the worth of her subject matter more affirmatively than did Kazin and those who followed his lead. By ceasing to consider Depression-era left-wing fiction as a vast mistake ultimately worth dismissing, she has helped re-establish the period's importance as a topic of critical analysis for those interested in the politics/literature conjunction. Her study stands out in its affirmative interest in the didactic aspects of the proletarian novel, and she acknowledges the persistence of modernist innovation into the thirties as well. But Foley distinguishes sharply between the present and the past on the grounds that we now possess greater sophistication in regard to the vicissitudes of representation than did thirties novelists. "Some [proletarian novelists] pursue," she writes in her introduction, "a transparent realism that seems aesthetically and philosophically naïve in an age of postmodernist self-consciousness. Others use experimental techniques that in hindsight represent the dead ends rather than the forward directions of modernism. If we look to these novels for models of oppositional discourses, we recognize an epistemological gap between their era and ours."[56] In narrative terms, then, the decade brought a certain stage of literary development to its logical conclusion; what comes next is the more advanced phase we remain in today.

More recently scholars have started to perceive the modernist aspects of thirties literature (though this is a perspective that has its roots in the 1970s). It has become since this time increasingly evident that the period may appear as a moment when formal innovations and a reflexive awareness of the medium were incorporated into more socially progressive cultural undertakings. As the editors of a book of essays originating out of a 1978 symposium on "The American Writer in the 1930s" put it in their introduction: "Modernism did not just die, however, when the bottom fell out of the stock market in 1929. The 1930s must be seen as an extension of the literary teens and the 1920s." "American intellectuals were aware of the modernist achievement as they faced depression America and sought to determine what their place and role ought to be in that grim environment."[57] One of the most significant accomplishments of this attempt at revisioning the period is that it helped break down the conceptual barriers between minority group writing and avant-garde literary priorities. Thus, in a collection of articles entitled *The Future of American Modernism*, Thomas Ferraro argues that "the politicization of American letters and the ethnicization of the *avant-garde* went hand in hand" in the Depression. Such an interest in the combination of aesthetic and political radicalism has helped maintain the status of Henry

Roth's *Call it Sleep* (1934) as an object of critical interest, his formal debt to James Joyce's *Ulysses* unmistakable.[58] The most important manifestation of this change in orientation has undoubtedly been Michael Denning's discussion of what he terms "ghetto pastorals." Characterizing proletarian literature itself as "an unstable, transitional modernism," as part of "a third wave of the modernist movement," Denning asserts that this proletarian avant-garde was responsible for "the emergence of a generation of plebian ethnic writers."[59] His claim is notable on three counts. First, his association of proletarian literature with modernism challenges received wisdom. Second, he cuts against the grain of past commentary when he argues that proletarian literature as a cultural phenomenon should not be viewed as merely an effort by a considerable number of middle-class intellectuals to integrate themselves into revolutionary politics by writing novels. Instead, Denning insists that the legacy of "the proletarian renaissance" of the 1930s was to enfranchise writers from marginal communities, enabling these "to represent – to speak for and depict – their families, their neighborhoods."[60] In so doing, these writers helped "stamp an indelible working-class imprint on American culture."[61] In the story Denning tells, the thirties marks the point at which the modernist movement reverses itself, abandoning its elitist pretensions and transforming itself into a populist cultural practice: the fall of the high to the low. Third, Denning is the only scholar to date to attempt to conceptualize the thirties as a whole from the perspective of the grotesque, alternatively characterizing the transitional modernism of the period as the "proletarian grotesque."[62] The claim is a provocative one. Yet it merely constitutes a starting point for further discussion, in part because his determination to organize a vast range of cultural materials into a comprehensible shape prevents him from engaging in detailed readings and also because his understanding of the grotesque remains undeveloped. Working primarily from the criticism of Kenneth Burke, Denning asserts that the proletarian grotesque consists of a "grim refusal of smiles and laughter." If so, grotesque writing in the thirties exceeds the proletarian version.

The extent to which aspects of the thirties anticipate either "poststructuralist" outlooks on representation or postmodern approaches to literary composition has also begun to become apparent.[63] This new approach to the decade has to this point been more concerned to recover individual artists than to revise our understanding of it as a whole. Appropriately, Nathanael West's fictions have been the subject of two exemplary returns to the period. Remarkably, one of the results of the critical analysis of West has been a revelation of the degree to which, as much as a precursor to postmodern artists, he now appears also to be a forerunner to attempts to describe and conceptualize postmodernism as a historically determined cultural phenomenon. His narrative fictions now seem to have anticipated the practice and the theory of postmodernism.[64] There are signs as well that Dos Passos, who has alternatively been considered a naturalist, a realist, and a modernist is on the verge of being recognized as a proto-postmodernist.[65] To characterize the thirties as the period when the essentialism of the high/low, art/mass culture binaries was contested makes the decade a point of origin for us. Looking backwards, we see, not as Foley would have it, "an epistemological gap" and difference, but similarity, the emergence of our present attitudes toward the relationship of literature to adjacent cultural practices.

My approach to the 1930s as an object of scholarly inquiry is to detach it from the assorted narrative contexts into which previous commentators have implicitly or explicitly inserted it. If the initial effect makes it more difficult to comprehend the decade historically, it is by way of this approach that its overlooked features may come sharply into focus. By removing the thirties from its familiar settings, it becomes possible to recover a sense of what others have noted only in passing: the varied use radicalized writers made of images of the grotesque body and the politicized interplay between literature and amusement throughout the period. By proposing to make the decade strange I do not mean to imply that it has yet to be depicted accurately. Rather, my claim is that past characterizations constitute partial and normalizing views of an object that, if looked at from other angles, appears as a much more confusing, peculiar phenomenon. The interpretive challenge will be to attempt to understand this literary curiosity without taking recourse to already familiar terms, without explaining away "the only thing that would need explanation."

What if I write circuses? No one says a novel has to be one thing. It can be anything it wants to be, a vaudeville show. (Ishmael Reed, *Yellow Back Radio Broke-Down*)

In the polemical conversation from which this citation is drawn, Loop Garoo, the hero of Reed's 1969 novel, is defending himself against Bo Shmo, leader of "the neo-social realist gang." Having "made a big reputation in the thirties," Shmo has, thanks to the funding of sympathetic liberals, built a huge neo-realist Institution in the Mountains toward which "trains of neo-social realist composers writers and painters" travel. He finds Loop to be "a deliberate attempt to be obscure. A buffoon an outsider and frequenter of sideshows." Most troubling is Loop's peculiar lack of interest in representational accuracy. Given "to fantasy," he is "off in matters of detail." He falls far short of the imitative ideal achieved by Shmo in "those suffering books" he has written about his old neighborhood and how hard it was.[66] Exasperated when Loop refuses to capitulate, Bo and his men decide to discipline Loop by giving him a version of "the Arab Death." They smear jelly on his neck, bury him up to the neck in the desert, and wait for the vermin to crawl across his face (37).

That Loop has the status here of an authorial surrogate is clear, for the aesthetic priorities he articulates are identical to Reed's. *Yellow Back* derives energy from and models itself formally on such non-literary amusements as the circus, vaudeville, and the dime museum display of human oddities or freak show – this latter form of entertainment alluded to on several occasions in the novel. Following Tom Gunning we might say that Reed's novel participates in the development of a "literature of attractions." For Gunning, what distinguishes early film aesthetics (up to around 1906–07) from subsequent narrative film is a commitment to entertainment through audience stimulation.[67] Instead of seeking to create an absorbing space through the construction of compelling plot lines and believable characters with whom one might identify, early filmmakers concentrated on shocking and astonishing the spectator. The serial presentation of a succession of disparate acts or performances took precedence over the pleasures of plunging into the apparently concrete depths of realistic illusions. Rather than a self-contained fictional world, the early film viewer encountered an aggressive cinema designed to generate powerful effects. Grounded in the late nineteenth-century variety format of theatrical entertainment as well as amusement park experiences, the genealogy of the aesthetics of the spectacle may be traced, Gunning claims, from its origins in American amusement through early film to the European avant-garde. With Reed, then, such an aesthetic would have finally made its way into American literature. Appropriately, Shmo accuses Loop of being a "Crazy dada nigger" with an annoying penchant for abstraction (35).[68]

The distinction Reed evokes between avant-garde experimentalism and the realist tradition reiterates a familiar dichotomy between the thirties and the sixties. With the example of the proletarian novel at the forefront of their minds, literary historians have tended to characterize the Depression era as a moment of aesthetic rigidity within the Left. No doubt the specter of proletarian fiction, notorious for its adherence to mimetic conventions, hovers in the background of Reed's critique of Bo Shmo. What therefore distinguishes Reed's method from his precursors in the field of radical writing is his willingness to allow collective modes of play to supply the basis for his own, non-realist compositional priorities. *Literature, Amusement and Technology* will demonstrate that Reed is in truth blind to the source of his insight, for in the period he mocks can be discovered the origins of his approach to radical writing. In sum, the openness of Reed and his contemporaries to the influence of (mechanized) American amusement has helped make it possible to unearth features of the literature of the thirties that have heretofore remained entombed.

Disinterring Edward Dahlberg

> I pose you your question:
> shall you uncover honey / where maggots are?
> I hunt among stones.
> Charles Olson, "The Kingfishers"

In chapter three of *Do These Bones Live*, Edward Dahlberg praises Randolph Bourne as a prophetic guide whose subversive writings retain the potential to lead the nation out of the political and cultural wilderness into which it has stumbled. It was the "raucous" voice of this physically "deformed but inwardly transfigured hunchback" that had spoken the "direful truths" the rest of the country refused to hear. "Bourne conceived such homely and radiantly mortal errors; this was his desperado impossibilism, and for this we remember him. We recall him to guide us . . . through the infernal limbo of American culture." What he saw was "the Cult of Politics that had dwarfed man down to the drabbest dimensions of the *homo economicus*, the 'ideational automaton'."[1] A fierce social critic who fell out of favor when he protested American involvement in the First World War, Bourne's dissenting opinions had caused him by the end of the 1930s to suffer the "grim and repetitious fate" of other equally committed radical intellectuals. He too now "lies in oblivion and is as unknown as our tradition," his marginalized writings buried beneath the highly esteemed "memorials" of respectable political figures. "The power of the State lies in the majesty of oblivion, in crypts, catafalques and mausoleums. The vaults in which the remains of the Presidents, those sacral ciphers of public chronicles lie, evoke no tears and laments." One will have to dig beneath these "canonical death-monuments" to catch sight of those unseemly yet impassioned creatures responsible for our populist radical culture, a powerfully moving tradition whose existence is hidden by "bureaucratic commemoration odes" (*Bones*, 22). It is below the magnificently constructed resting places of our past leaders that one encounters the challenging, assertive writings of those who have become in official history as frighteningly repugnant and unbearable to look at as a dreadful mythological entity. "We turn our back upon our own past as though it were as horrible to behold as Medusa" (28).

More than a half century later, it is Dahlberg who "lies in oblivion," unknown. His autobiographical novels seldom read and his criticism infrequently discussed, Dahlberg's decaying corpus has been deeply interred in the graveyard of American literary prose. Save for a brief resurgence of interest in him upon the publication of *Because I Was Flesh* (1964),[2] which makes use of the same autobiographical materials he used in his first two fictions (*Bottom Dogs* [1930] and *From Flushing to Calvary* [1932]) but in a rhetorically much altered fashion, Dahlberg has received minimal scholarly and critical care. The burden of this essay then is to determine what we have lost by turning our backs upon the creative and critical output of this peculiarly grotesque writer, one whose work may prove to be "as horrible to behold as Medusa."

The excavation of a portion of Dahlberg's corpus from its relatively unmarked place in the ground of literary history[3] brings into focus one of the first attempts in this country to formulate theoretically and develop a practice of a grotesque aesthetic suited to the machine age. The essential source of artistic inspiration for him in this regard was the field of carnivalized American public amusements. Dahlberg's turn to forms of entertainment for compositional guidance constituted a social investment on his part. Grounding his aesthetic appeal to non-literary cultural practices was his sense of connection to members of minority communities. It was his identification with the relatively disenfranchised persons in whose daily lives such popular amusements played a central role that spurred his interest in forms of entertainment. The traditional and modernized recreations that were condemned by "nice people" as "vulgar and naïve" yet that "millions of less pretentious people loved" and "flocked to" supplied him with a literary point of departure. It was out of the world that extends back from slapstick film to "the theatre: the barefaced honkytonk and the waltzes by Waldteufel, slammed out on a mechanical piano," and that includes as well "burlesque, vaudeville, [and] circuses,"[4] that Dahlberg the autobiographical novelist first emerged.

Like Henry Miller after him, Dahlberg's recollection of "the laughter of unrespectable people having a hell of a fine time, laughter as violent and steady and deafening as standing under a waterfall,"[5] helped initiate a radically motivated project. His rarely remarked upon status in the history of American literature may be marked as a precursor to postmodernism in the sense that his writing does not seek to seal itself off from the influence of non-literary recreational practices. Insofar as the distinction between high and low culture is inoperative in his enterprise, he appears to participate in the (postmodern) transition away from the high modernist aspiration to protect the autonomy of art. But he remained exceptionally ambivalent about the repercussions of his own project, and one observes in his early writing the recurrent impulse to reinstall the very distinctions he puts at risk. Dahlberg consistently retreated from the transgressions he required to get his enterprise going; and in the end, he desperately strove to expel technology from artistic realms. Thoroughly repulsed by what obviously attracted him, Dahlberg repeatedly sought to put the barriers back in place that he had helped dismantle.

His work manifests from this perspective the multiple crises the (male) authorial subject sought to negotiate in the Depression era. More precisely, the extreme anxiety apparent in his writing manifests the existential and aesthetic conflicts experienced with intensity in the 1930s by those interested in conjoining literature and amusement. The feminine, the machine, and commercial entertainment all rose up as objects of extreme fascination to the formally ambitious, innovative writer. Initially perceiving these as an exciting resource, Dahlberg eventually came to the conclusion that they constituted a debilitating danger. The completion of his career as a novelist coincided with his capitulation to "the double male fear of technology and woman."[6] We may trace this tension by following the paths of Dahlberg's traumatized autobiographical protagonists, who repetitiously encounter the machine as the cause of severe panic, as a kind of maternal force capable of enveloping the terrified individual. *Mimes*, a parodic autobiographical fiction he stopped working on in 1925 (though it would not be published for another half century), provides an introduction to this set of issues. A comic (self-) portrait of the anachronistic aspirations of a youthful, would-be transcendentalist poet, the narrative is designed as an illustration of a critical thesis. The comic presentation of the romantically inclined character's silly efforts to meet the challenges of his urban environment marks the obsolescence of pastoral aesthetics.

MACHINE-AGE MIMICRY

Mimes . . .
Mere puppets they, who come and go
At bidding of vast formless things
    Edgar Allan Poe, "The Conqueror
    Worm"

The ludicrous protagonist of *Mimes* is lodged firmly within the aesthetic ideology of Anglo-American romanticism, for Leonid Gottinger repeatedly attempts to evade the artistic and existential implications of life in urban-industrial modernity. The excruciatingly overwrought diction Dahlberg uses to convey the character's thoughts or direct speech establishes the work's critical frame. The following exceedingly ironic description of the solitary Leonid is typical: "In an open field he would lay, breathing in the aroma of new-mown hay and gaze into the heavens. Falling into a madcap vein he would luxuriate in the lugubrious droning of the crickets, wanton with the tapering shadows, mock the meditative night."[7] Leonid is most laughably misguided when striving to achieve an ecstatic union with nature. The next paragraph recounts the "mystic spell" that "the pure aeolian murmur of the trees" casts over the character.

Breathless, he halted for a moment and leaned against a large, gnarled oak; he became at one with it: with eyes fixed on the cold light of the stars, the snowy moon, the Milky Way, he poured forth the melody of all that had entered into the inner recesses of his self: nature's myriad forms were indelibly imprinted on his trembling soul – his pantheistic soul aquiver with rustling leaves, the droning of insects, geometric shadows, muddy blades of grass, the generative spirit of fecund earth! (*Works*, 16–17)

The target of Dahlberg's irony, however, is not the fundamental narcissism that sustains such an "insidious play between mood and matter" but the insistence on choosing pastoral landscapes as reflective surfaces. Thus the numerous, blissful mergers of self with nature the book describes are repeatedly presented as evidence of a deluded desire to convince oneself that one's mode of existence in the world is as stable as that of a tree or plant. Tellingly, Leonid is perennially evasive when it comes to acknowledging his own mortality. "The thought of death weighed him down; it was beyond his comprehension. He could not conceive of a still body, eternally breathless, spoiled of consciousness, laid in the cold, dank ground. He shuddered." "That one should suffer complete annihilation he could not brook nor understand. He could not resign himself to the existence of lifelessness" (30). The resistance to ontological insight gives rise to aesthetic foolishness. Nor can Leonid conceptualize adequately the temporality of human existence: "Time was such an incomprehensible thing to him [Leonid], he tried to understand it: he could not" (18). The character's unwillingness to acknowledge the difference between human beings and natural entities makes him a joke to author and reader alike, a ridiculous object they may laugh at together.

Given the rough yet unmistakable parallel between the events of the fictional character's life and those of the author's, it is reasonable to suppose that the ironic narrative is a form of self-mockery. Dahlberg's critical intention is to free himself from the desire to pursue romantic pastoralism. The interpolation of a manuscript – "Maurice Succumbs to the Malady" – confirms this hypothesis. It is a "burlesque brochure" by Leonid's "leman," a "young transcendentalist" who goes nowhere without a copy of Emerson," put together so "that he [Leonid] might better see and understand and laugh over . . . his own foibles and enormities" (49). Tellingly, it is stylistically indistinguishable from the main text itself, save for the fact that the vocabulary is even more pretentious and archaic in the inserted text, with diction like "sooth," "slewn," and phrases like "lavish main and purple choler." The significance of the title then is that Leonid and his friends are mere imitators, miming their precursors so completely as to remain (figuratively) mute; genuine expression is inaccessible to those who can do nothing but repeat conventionalized gestures.

The most significant scene in *Mimes* is its final one. Set in a New York subway station, it depicts Leonid undergoing an experience resembling what Fredric Jameson has called the hysterical sublime and diagnosed as a distinctively postmodern predicament.[8] Here the suffering Leonid becomes immersed in the urban crowd and consequently loses all sense of personal identity, the terrifying perceptual overload the city generates causing an emotional breakdown. The immediate cause of his psychic despair and subsequent disorientation is a shattered love affair. Yet the interest of the scene exceeds its context in the story in that it links the character's collapse, his inability to organize the events of his life coherently, to an encounter with a threatening mechanized environment. Moreover, the crisis involves not only uncertainties about the relation of the human to the technological but also the difference between male and female. As the body/machine complex coalesces with a panic pertaining to gender difference, it becomes apparent that for Leonid (and on a more self-conscious level Dahlberg) the threat of the machine is indissociable from the threat of the feminine.

Fleeing "madly through the evil city" that appears "to him like a solid cube spinning on its edges," the amusingly agitated character arrives at the entrance to a subway. Dahlberg presents the character's descent to the platform as a journey to the underworld, emphasizing the psychically disquieting experience mechanized systems of transportation may produce.[9] Standing on the platform as the train arrives, Leonid perceives it to be a gigantic beast. Hurled into the midst of an agglomerated mass of humanity, the character's ability to demarcate the self from what is outside it vanishes. As the boundaries between his body, other bodies, and his mechanized surroundings erode, the panicked, insecure male loses his sense of agency and identity. All motive power now goes to the machine, Leonid having ceded control over his physical movement through space to the "neolithic colossus."

Reaching the platform he saw looming up before him a terrible monster with garish green, amber yellow, and brothel red eyes. As a black ichthyosaurus, it swung about the curb of the grottolike tunnel. The masses, with one collective instinct, fell upon one another and were pushed headlong through the doors by the guards. Losing all personal identity he became completely absorbed into the press of bodies, as a speck of consciousness into Nirvana. The doors being automatically slammed to, the huge train, like a neolithic colossus, was set in motion. (125)

The tiny Leonid is doubly immersed here. Uncomfortably trapped in the surging crowd, he is then engulfed by the monstrous machine. Dahlberg genders the "ichthyosaurus," its "brothel" eyes vaguely associating the train with female sexuality. Literally propelled into the subway car, Leonid figuratively re-enters the body of the mother. From this perspective the plunging of the character into the car evokes a forced reversal of the birth process. His loss of motor control at the door to the electrically powered beast is analogous to a state of fetal or infantile helplessness at the threshold of the maternal womb. As the car gets moving, Leonid experiences an equally undesirable mingling of his body with the feminized machine. The "horrific cacophony" produced by the grinding of "the prodigious wheels" of the train along the steel rails of the track engenders "on his brain tone clashes which welled up into a grandiose discord." "The wheels" seem "to be revolving within his febrile temples and constantly throbbing against his aching head." "His heart" pounds "up and down within his chest, wildly" pulsating to the "insensate rhythm" that "the terrific hammer blows" of the wheels on the rails smash out. Fatigued by the concussive, shocking assault on his senses, mentally and physically overtaxed by the unwanted, involuntary fusion with the train, Leonid falls "into a sort of feverish drowse" (126). Over-stimulation of the nervous system has led to a depression of the vital processes.

The agonized retreat from the impression of a technological intrusion into the natural body is associated here with a youthful male's anguished sense of being overwhelmed by the maternal. The character's feeling that he is being consumed by the mechanical entity is also experienced as an absorption into a feminized (albeit faintly), undifferentiated mass. When Dahlberg rewrites this scene at the end of *From Flushing to Calvary* the associations will be enriched such that the anxiety manifested will encompass not just the subway and the mother but an American form of public amusement too (Coney Island). In other words, his handling of the relation of literature to collective entertainment was consistently coupled with his handling of gender distinctions. To come to terms as a writer with technologically mediated entertainment was, for Dahlberg, to come to terms with the feminine. Aesthetics and sexuality commingle in the writer's struggle to establish a self in relation to two associated others (women and amusement). Complicating this arrangement further is his battle to ground his identity in relation to urban-industrial modernity. That Dahlberg condenses women, the city, amusement, and the machine in this manner allows us to correlate Leonid's concerns about his masculinity and his status as a lyric poet with the character's distress as he mimetically assimilates himself to his urban environment.

Leonid next proceeds to lose all perceptual control over his field of vision, those around him appearing as distorted versions of himself, the reflected images flowing into an undifferentiated, formless background. In this proliferation of mirror reflections, narcissistic delight gives way to paranoid terror. External reality is no longer a pleasing mirror of the self but a horrifying array of turbulently swirling, indistinct, and indistinguishable shapes that refuse to stop moving erratically.

His cheeks flushed with burning fever, his vision obscured, he saw those opposite him as through a convex and concave mirror. Everything before him became grotesque and unreal. The figures, the arms of which were suspended to fixed straps, became hallucinations, were as theatrical marionettes made animate through wires and ventriloquism. A veritable medley of tawdry colors, jaundiced, hectic and pallid placards, danced before his eyes like cowering Greek mimes. The waxen faces, become a series of masks, could no longer be differentiated from the splotched advertisements above them – a sepulchral madhouse in motion. They were as pigments that had mixed and run together. (126)

As the living, breathing body is replaced by the wires and wood of inanimate puppets or marionettes, and the human face turns into a wax replication or a paper mask, Dahlberg could be staking out a grotesque counterpart to more classically oriented strains of modernist art. Plagued by the rush of sensations in a crowded metro, Leonid does not turn to natural imagery to organize social reality: the apparition of these faces is *not* like petals on a wet, black bough. But he accomplishes this task by going backward in literary historical terms rather than forward. For the scene derives from Poe's "The Conqueror Worm," as does in a sense *Mimes* as a whole. Like his precursor, Dahlberg characterizes human existence as a "motley drama" in which persons are no more than puppets, mimes, flying "hither and thither," coming and going at "the bidding of vast formless things." By the end of the narrative, Leonid's self-knowledge has brought him to the point where he feels he is a "mere automaton" (126), his movements and thoughts driven by outside forces ("he no more understood how he lived or breathed"). As the train jerks to a halt, the protagonist, hurled against his seat, falls into a fit of convulsions, his body shaking "spasmodically" as if in the throes of death. Coughing painfully, he feels the vibrations of the subway ring through "his hollow chest like the fatalistic knocking of the Fifth Symphony of Beethoven" (126); he now moves with "absolute mechanical resignation" (126).[10]

At the end of "Mimicry and Legendary Psychasthenia" (1935), Roger Caillois comments on roughly the same type of phobic, depersonalizing experience Dahlberg represents at the conclusion of his first extended autobiographical fiction. Drawing insight from the behavior of insects, Caillois argues that the anguished perception of space as an overwhelming, devouring force expresses the "mimetic assimilation" of the "animate to the inanimate," which inevitably leads to a sense of lifelessness and loss of identity. Proposing that biological (and magical) phenomena have "a common root" with psychic experience, he speculates on the possibility that the transgression of the boundary between living beings and their environment is a process comparable to Freud's concept of the death drive. This *"attraction by space"* is, Caillois suggests, "as elementary and mechanical as are tropisms," and its effect is that "life seems to lose ground, blurring in its retreat the frontier between the organism and the milieu."[11] Human beings and other animate entities have an innate tendency to renounce feeling and consciousness by assimilating themselves to their inanimate surroundings. The relationship of imitation, mechanization, death, psychic and physical dissolution that Caillois posits discloses a conceptual constellation of negativity that compulsively recurs in Dahlberg's literary theory and practice. It is as if his critical impulses continuously pushed him beyond his aesthetic principles so that he repeatedly interferes with the self-preservative aspirations of his own autobiographically expressive undertaking.

In *Mimes*, the corollary to Leonid's spatial disorientation, to his sense that he has been overcome by his oppressive surroundings, is a temporal breakdown. Leonid's hysteria involves a loss of historicity on a personal level: he can no longer organize his past experiences into a coherently substantive, narrative form. "Fixedly he [Leonid] contemplated his life as a series of disconnected, isolated moments without meaning or sequence – mere nothingness" (125). But on a more reflexive level, Dahlberg too has yet to resolve this problem. All he has done thus far is to copy and restate Poe's critique of American transcendentalism. The composer of *Mimes*, like his characters, has yet to invent an appropriate way of handling his mechanized surroundings and in so doing make a genuine contribution to the growth and development of literary history.

Four years later, in "Ariel in Caliban," Dahlberg articulates explicitly the challenge *Mimes* communicates implicitly; and in the process begins to construct a lineage of artists who have successfully confronted a changed environment. It is as if an act of self-mockery, in allowing Dahlberg to overcome his old-fashioned artistic tendencies, cleared the ground for a theoretical articulation of a more up-to-date aesthetic. Though published in 1929, before his first autobiographical fiction *Bottom Dogs* appeared in print in the United States, "Ariel in Caliban" was almost certainly composed after the novel.[12] The critical essay formulates in positive terms the artistic task *Mimes* outlines negatively: the burden of the artist in the machine age is to renegotiate the relation of the self to his urban, mechanized surroundings, a transaction in which grotesque amusements may play a significant role.

The essay situates historically the aesthetic and philosophical burdens of the contemporary artist, identifying the ontological and representational or expressive predicament of the American writer as particular to modernity. Mechanization remains at the forefront of the discussion while the feminine recedes into the background. Yet we might say that the latter's place is taken by the freak; the replacement of one by the other is justified in the logic of Dahlberg's discourse by virtue of their common existence outside the dominant (masculine) norm and their shared affiliation with artifice. Thus his autobiographical protagonists yearn for but remain wary of human oddities, women, and technology (in the form of mechanized amusements).

First published in the magazine *This Quarter* in 1929, "Ariel in Caliban" strives to formulate an aesthetic that will reconcile the self with its urban-industrial surroundings. Dahlberg calls for the development of a grotesque expressionism that will project the spiritual (Ariel) outward into the monstrous urban landscape (Caliban) and disclose the degree to which the city has penetrated the human. The grotesque body becomes a crossroads or relay point between the self and its mechanized environment. And American mass amusements like the dime museum display of human oddities, Coney Island amusement park attractions, vaudeville, and slapstick film furnish the basis for this nascent aesthetic.

Dahlberg begins "Ariel in Caliban" by identifying the writers, mostly European, who have set the stage for the development of what he calls "an aesthetic of diablerie," one that takes as its point of departure the fact that today "life and nature [are] thoroughly mechanized."[13] Flaubert and (with qualifications) Oscar Wilde are cited as important precursors, for if "too many things disgusted" the latter, and he often failed to "realize the lyric possibilities of the commonplace," he did on occasion "sense the unreality of a wet street or a city gas lamp" (*Samuel Beckett*, 3). Baudelaire is a more essential forerunner, his awareness of "the mechanical note in nature" and preference for "rouged women and metal trees" is a step beyond "sentimental and insincere," ridiculously affected attempts to "write a pastoral" today (3).[14] Poe is mentioned in passing, while Sherwood Anderson is praised with reservations. His work is "too reportorial and has nothing of the grotesque that arises from artistic monism. The emotions and the objects upon which it impinges are too separable" such that "he never enters into the life of these inanimate things" (6). Too objective and realist and therefore insufficiently subjective and expressionist, Anderson has not fused the inside and the outside, has not set up a system of circulation such that the attributes of the animate person pass into the impersonal city.[15] More impressive is Joyce's achievement. He has "done with ordinary Dublin what no artist has with the subway and surface cars of New York" (5), making the city give perceptual shape to what would otherwise remain invisible: "modern experience."

Surprisingly, Dahlberg clarifies the significance of *Ulysses*, Joyce's "intense personalization of Dublin life," by comparing his literary accomplishment to what amusement park and dime museum attractions have done. *Ulysses* is "like Coney Island where the scenic railway, the waxen figures lying in state, the merry-go-round which seems to move in a void and whose jangling music creates the illusion of a vacuum, like Noah's Ark in which the tragedy of machinery is bodied forth by an ingenious materialization of biblical symbols – like Hubert's [sic] Museum whose freaks and hermaphrodites by virtue of their unquestionable reality shadow forth an imaginary world" (6). Dahlberg draws on the imagery of human oddities not to reinforce mainstream notions of normality but to contest these. The metaphorical use of the body of the freak as a figure for a general psychic predicament unsettles the reassuring spatial separation and correlative difference in identity the dime museum displays often worked to stabilize.[16] To the extent that we are spiritually penetrated by our artificial surroundings, we are as internally unnatural as a human oddity appears to be on the outside. Dime museum freaks are representative because in the machine age we are all aberrant or anomalous, at least when measured against obsolete notions of what it means to be a human being. Noting the allusion to the fairgrounds is especially crucial not only because Dahlberg will soon attempt to reproduce the sensory appeal of the place in a section of *From Flushing to Calvary* but also because Coney Island stands "as America's first and probably still most symbolic commitment to mechanized leisure."[17] From Dahlberg's perspective, then, the American amusement park was ahead of the American writer in the quest to fashion a critically expressive aesthetic that will be adequate to "the social and economic conditions of a life and nature thoroughly mechanized" (4).

The essay also tackles the problem of how one should represent characters under such circumstances, and here forms of public amusement are most valuable. Two recent films from the German UFA cinema, shown at the Fifth Avenue Playhouse, provide some useful clues. Anne Boleyn in their production of *Henry the Eighth* and the maidservant in *Backstairs* are significant because their gestures "suggest a puppet – but a puppet bent and gnarled by suffering. Here, tragedy, in its true Greek sense has transmuted the face into a mask and the body, its twists and contortions, into a marionette" (4). Since the lamentable truth about contemporary existence is that individuals lack agency and are at the mercy of their setting, they are most accurately depicted as spiritless automatons, things without human volition. An equally worthwhile resource for the writer in search of an appropriate technique is "the American Vaudeville Theatre." The entertainment (as Nathanael West also realized) is "a rich library" where "a speculative mind interested in the comedy and mechanics of gestures" can find much to observe and learn from, especially by "watching the puppet-like movements of the jiggers" (8). Dahlberg offers one other cultural practice as a model for aspiring, machine-age artists: silent screen comedy, where one can observe the "inelastic jerks and movements" (4) of Harry Langdon.

Henri Bergson's theory of comedy is a precedent, as Dahlberg acknowledges, for the aesthetic emphasis on the inanimate and the involuntary in depictions of persons. In "Laughter" (1900), the argument is repeatedly made that "the attitudes, gestures and movements of the human body are laughable in exact proportion as that body reminds us of a mere machine."[18] What Dahlberg has done then is radicalize this thesis into a philosophy of modern existence and in the process brings out its more mournful aspects: "there is another element upon which Bergson has not touched and that is the tragic suggested by the mechanical" (4). Any aesthetic that proposes to do justice to the material conditions of existence in the machine age must adapt to this change in circumstances:

The metaphysics which arise from machinery and mechanism has more aesthetic value than one which has its roots in naïve phenomena. Philosophy and art, like all physical processes, are ever becoming, and must of necessity move toward a nature with mechanical and industrial encrustations than return to one with a pastoral décor. (8)

In "Ariel" Dahlberg articulates and affirms two seemingly contradictory processes. On the one hand, he praises under the aegis of "an intense personalization" anthropomorphic embodiments of external reality. We might call this a grotesque prosthesis in that the apparent effect is to extend the scope and power of the collective body by attaching to it the inorganic world. The animated city becomes a part of the people who live in it, making up for the physical deficiencies of its inhabitants. On the other hand, Dahlberg remarks repeatedly on the unsettling intrusion of the outside world into the mind and body of subjects, urban, industrialized reality penetrating and disabling the human being. As the city and the machine come inside, persons are transformed into things, reified. If the end result of moving in one direction is a grotesquely embodied city, the effect of traveling in the other is the grotesque caricature of persons as puppets or marionettes.

This process of exchange may be described in rhetorical terms. The relationship between the city dweller and the urban landscape is narcissistic in the sense that it involves the projection onto external reality of emotional properties of living, human beings. In addition to being invested with a grotesque body (Caliban), one's inanimate environment is also personified. The relay also occurs in the opposite direction: the qualities of objective reality are transported into living persons who can thus be conceived as dead matter or machines. The end result of this much less desirable, reverse aspect of the dynamic process is reification: human beings are degraded to the status of mere things. The myriad, systematic crossings Dahlberg's aesthetic theory calls for (yet which his practice also reacts against) are facilitated through the use of two tropes. But the transfer of attributes from one place to another and vice-versa may be accounted for more comprehensively in terms of a different figure of speech: chiasmus. It is the structure of this linguistic figure of reciprocal circulation that governs the numerous transactions (self/world; male/female; human/mechanical; natural/artificial) Dahlberg's early writing ceaselessly enacts. (It may even explain the basis for his literary enterprise as a whole: the transference of aesthetic traits from American amusements to the autobiographical novel is a crossing of sorts.)

It remains unclear whether the artist merely records or helps enact these two processes, but the interplay between the two is evidently asymmetrical. The insertion of the external into the internal and consequent emptying out of the substance or spirit of the living is more prominent in the essay. Caliban tends to obliterate Ariel. This is the condition that elements of American amusement make perceptible and intelligible. (The waxen figures "lying in state" are imitations of death, the merry-go-round moves "in a void," its jangling music creating "the illusion of a vacuum," and the biblical figures of Noah's Ark materialize, "body forth" "the tragedy of machinery.") The Coney Island exhibits and rides render in visible form the technified condition of human existence in the machine age, the depersonalized state of nothingness from which we all suffer.

The novel Dahlberg would soon set to work on constitutes a practical corollary to the theory articulated in "Ariel in Caliban." *From Flushing to Calvary* is additionally important in that it broaches the possibility that the emptiness of the subject can be determined in a more precise sociological manner. This sequel to the autobiographical *Bottom Dogs* concerns itself with the purposelessness impoverished and excluded individuals feel, in part due to their lack of political awareness. Rather than characterize collective spiritual despair as a general problem, in this book Dahlberg points to the absence of class-consciousness as the cause of the disenfranchised individual's dejected state of mind. Still a couple of years away from joining the Communist Party,[19] Dahlberg had already begun to politicize his aesthetics, and it is on the threshold of his involvement (a short-lived one) with the political organization that he completed his most enduring novel.

Flushing is also a comically inflected analysis of the psychic dilemmas of Lorry Lewis, its profoundly troubled protagonist, who anxiously negotiates his vexed relationship to his gravely ill mother. This fraught familial relationship is densely intertwined in the book with the character's ambivalence toward mechanized recreation, a visit to Coney Island proving traumatic and precipitating an emotional breakdown. More intriguing, elements of carnivalized fun are oddly conjoined to maternal images in the youth's psyche, both alternately attracting and repulsing him. Put differently, mechanized recreation and the mother tend to merge in the text because both phenomena are phobic objects capable of triggering intense, symptomatic reactions in the shocked male subject. The oscillations of unconscious desire thus emerge as familial *and* social investments. Abjection is a private mental condition paradoxically alleviated and exacerbated by public modes of collective play.

We can catch a preliminary glimpse of Dahlberg's penchant for layering social, psychosexual, *and representational* anxieties onto twentieth-century entertainment technologies by looking at a short piece he composed with the intention of including it in *Flushing*, though he ended up publishing it (in *Pagany* in 1931) separately: "Graphophone Nickelodeon Days."

"GRAPHOPHONE NICKELODEON DAYS"

And I think it can be boiled down to one statement (first pounded into my head by Edward Dahlberg): ONE PERCEPTION MUST IMMEDIATELY AND DIRECTLY LEAD TO A FURTHER PERCEPTION. (Charles Olson, "Projective Verse")

A fictional reminiscence that compresses much of the autobiographical material Dahlberg used in his first two novels, "Graphophone" takes as its point of departure a three-term analogy between mental, literary, and mechanical recording processes. The analogy is grounded in the fact that the brain, printed matter or verbal discourse, and new technical media all share the capacity to preserve acoustic and optical information. The piece implicitly affirms therefore that autobiography, considered as a supplement to memory, may now take its formal cues from two recently developed storage technologies. The aim of Dahlberg's compositional experiment is to achieve the status of a media link between (silent) film, the graphophone, and writing. The implication of its title, which refers to a type of phonograph (see figure 4[20]) and to the theatrical venue where early movies were viewed, is first that human memory may be materially or technologically conceived of as a combination of celluloid and a record disc.[21] The psyche records aural and optical data, which are therefore available for future projections and playbacks. The literary text is designed to perform both these functions. And if writing is like a technologically mediated recording process, reading is comparable to the

Fig. 4 Columbia Graphophone. c. 1905. Advertisement in New York
Hippodrome Program

watching of a mental film with musical accompaniment. In Dahlberg's cinematic prose, the page is an internalized screen with sound. (That the remembrance exceeds the eye and ear and involves the perceiving body in its entirety is evident in that "Graphophone" is an attempt to reproduce the serial flow of olfactory, tactile, and gustatory data as well. It is the total sensory response to his outside surroundings that the autobiographical subject "could never erase."[22])

Yet the significance of the innovative piece is that in the end it empties the familiar comparison between literary and technologically mediated representations of its positive contents. In an oft-quoted formulation, Agee *seems* to support a more externalized variant of the analogy in question, affirming, in *Famous Men*, his faith in the representational abilities of the camera in relation to objective as opposed to subjective reality. If handled appropriately, the camera, a "some ways limited, some ways more capable, eye" is, "like the phonograph record and like scientific instruments:" "incapable of recording anything but absolute, dry truth" and both are therefore epistemological ideals for the documentary writer.[23] Dahlberg starts out with a related belief that writing modeled on the moving picture camera and the phonograph can record the rush of sensory impressions and in the process protect past subjectivities from vanishing without a trace. But he also unsettles (in frustration) this assumption. Beginning with the aesthetic intention of taking the media revolution of 1880 as a means of enhancing literature's power to recreate a visible and audible world,[24] Dahlberg's critical rigor pushes him to reject the idea that a literary text that can be read "as music is listened to or a film watched" (*Famous Men*, xv).

A personal recollection of the pleasures commercial entertainments provided the author during his youth, the highly crafted "Graphophone" alludes to a wealth of early twentieth-century cultural materials. For the autobiographical protagonist, "it all came back, the taste of it, the tang and brine of it." "All that he was and could never completely unknow all those down-and-out days went carouselling through his brain ragtiming through his head" ("Graphophone," 306; spacing in the original). The fond recollection conveys the essential role amusements played in his everyday life, forming a constitutive element of his existence as a member of a relatively downtrodden social group. The material artifacts mentioned appear amid a dizzying rush of remembered images – a kind of projective prose. The recollections include lyrics excerpted from popular tunes, the sports and political figures once found on the "oblong pasteboard pictures" accompanying the purchase of cigarettes, the "funnies," "penny arcade moving pictures," "slot machine phonographs," and a "one cent muscle machine." The character also remembers live forms of entertainment: "lyric moving picture house, open air tents, lawdie lawdie tabernacle sermons" and "pimpish gaslight joints" (308). The period of time the reminiscence covers stretches from the days of the "rough riders" and visits to the "ringling bros." and "barnum and bailey" circuses (313) to 1917, when America entered the First World War and "keith's circuit vaudeville [and] slapstick" were still in the air (317). That Dahlberg devotes an entire section of the prose poem to a live performance given by Lew Dockstader's minstrel troupe suggests the lasting impression it must have made on the writer when still a child. Reproducing the comic routine of the opening act, he remarks as well upon the audience's delighted response: as one jokester sings and the other mocks him, the "pulsing and motorthrobbing" crowd becomes frenzied; there is "stampeding of feet everywhere" and "thick yellow spudblocks of laughter jam the air" (314). Dahlberg then hints that the joys the show furnishes its overly enthused patrons had a politically subversive edge as well, hyperbolically characterizing the general impact of its central monologuist on the nation as comparable to social and political upheaval. "Lew Dockstader who shook the country like the russian revolution of 1905" (315).[25]

Immediately after this line, however, Dahlberg begins to put his representational undertaking into question. For example, the epigraph (from *Peer Gynt*) to the next section reads " '*layers and layers of sensation and no heart in it.*'" The shifting implication of the internalized museum that Dahlberg employs twice in "Graphophone" also marks the critical turn. Early in the piece the recollected cultural materials have constituted for the young protagonist "his boyhood louvre" (312). Whereas here the figure connotes the fascination of the objects the child found around him in the outside world, the later use of the trope frames the psychic return to the material past as the observation of relics on display in a deserted, barren cultural institution: "up the hall of the memory-membrane tissues of the nose, clinking, clinking against the metaphysical corridors and stirring up the museum – desolation in his blood" (316). No longer immersed in the animated world of amusements, the protagonist's mausoleum-like consciousness retains only the unsatisfying idea of the substantial things and persons formerly available for direct sensory contact. If the displacement from outside to inside and consequent loss of substantiality is a common motif in narratives of recollection, its presence here nevertheless clarifies the nature of "Graphophone" as an act of mourning. A personal expression of grief in the wake of the separation of the self from the milieu in which he once found sensual pleasures readily available, the piece also, in a crucial detail, suggestively registers referential absence as an inherent aspect of mechanized reproduction.

Having just characterized New York in the twenties as a "syphilitic body" decorated with "jaundiced electric lights diseasing the night," Dahlberg further qualifies the appearance of this object as "a cancerous blurred negative" (318). The effect of this last characterization is unsettling in the context of a work predicated on the virtues of *positive* images as the means of re-establishing contact with an original perceptual experience, of reinhabiting the body. By remarking upon, if only in passing, the stage during which the illusion that the referent is still physically present is temporarily displaced by an encounter with the materiality of the medium, Dahlberg reverses the thrust of his "intermedial"[26] analogy. Though adhering throughout to the implicit equation between literature, the psyche, and technological recording devices, Dahlberg ends up inverting the significance of the relationship. In the end, what the assorted media (writing, film, and the phonograph) are shown to have in common with the mind is that the traces they preserve all presuppose the irretrievable absence of the referential thing.

The brain, mechanized representation, and writing are like one another in that all fail to bring the world the body once inhabited back to life. Thinking autobiography and memory along the lines of technical processes has the unexpected effect, then, of drawing attention to the mechanical aspects of literary and mental processes of recollection. If the dialectic whereby the absence of the thing is the precondition of its illusory presence in a representation has been the theme of much critical discourse on the arts in the twentieth century, "Graphophone" suggests the contribution the rise of mechanical amusements made to this development. The writer's practical investment in new entertainment technologies stimulated a theoretical awareness of representational problems pertinent to autobiographical literary undertakings. The last feature of "Graphophone" I would like to take up is Dahlberg's use of oedipal motifs and tropes to account for his altered relation to the field of commercial entertainment over the course of the first two decades of the twentieth century. Early in the prose poem the cheap attractions surrounding him both excite and frustrate the child's libidinal impulses. For instance, an optical device gives him a goal without allowing him to reach it: "get a peep at *venus* through the telescope for only a nickle! cheap at half the price but why through a telescope" (307). In the same memory block, desire for the female star of the stage drama "*beverly of graustark*" plagues

the boy at night: "her talcum-powdered lotion-creamed breasts – a long
moving picture soul kiss   hot tossing nights, her thighs whorling like an
electric barber pole: the penny arcade automatic piano jangling away in
spasms" (307). The lusts American entertainment provoked in the boy
at the time are also evident in his memory of one of the women who
worked in his mother's barber shop as having "legs [that] were lost in the
amusement park grotto of her shroud-black clothskirt" (309). The incestuous dimension of the child's erotic passion for older women becomes
strongly apparent toward the end of the prose poem. While specify-
ing the First World War as the force that destroyed his initial cultural
milieu, or rather the legal sanctions on the entertainment field the war
precipitated,[27] Dahlberg figuratively conveys this repressive action as
the father reasserting his rights over the mother's body. In other words,
wartime restrictions on the nature of popular amusement in America
are characterized as the prohibition of a primary object of desire. The
following verbal compound establishes the conflation of the historical
and the familial in the protagonist's mind:

you goddam son of bitchin' bolsheviks, the big parades, the war, the War, THE
FATHER, SON, AND THE HOLY GHOST: THE WAR: *all ye millions I embrace thee* the
redlight districts were shut down, puberty skyscraper erections, tallest building
in the world, bigger and better wars, *all ye millions I embrace thee*, you goddam son
of bitchin' bolsheviks, *then what are you doing over here, over there, over there*
    The yanks are coming ... the yanks are coming, puberty skyscraper erections, the
vaginal walls of jericho are falling. (317–18)

If the capitalized liturgical phrase registers strikingly the paternal
dynamic operative here, the more surreptitious introduction of this relation in the oath ("*son* of bitchin'") does so in a more significant manner,
associating a political threat to authority (the Russian Revolution) with
the child's attempt at usurpation. The father's reassertion of his rights
then takes the form of an encircling ("*I embrace thee*") of the domestic arenas
of commercial entertainment from which all interlopers are henceforth
excluded ("the redlight districts were shut down"). And it is tempting
to read this as a drastically condensed allegory of the historical appropriation and transformation of vulgar working-class amusements into
forms suitable for more respectable audiences. In any event, it follows,
given the oedipal resonance of the passage, that these arenas are tan-
tamount to the maternal body. The discovery of the invading offspring
("*what are you doing over here*") leads to his expulsion, to his being pushed
"*over there, over there*," away from the tempting yet forbidden territory of

what we might call the national maternal entertainment body. Once he regains control over the sphere of pleasure, once he successfully defends his territory, the father as American military force will be free to return to and satisfy himself upon the domestic body of his wife. In the citation this task is both imminent and accomplished – the verb in the phrase "*The yanks are coming*" denoting approach yet connoting climax. Lastly, the conjoining of "puberty skyscraper erections" and "vaginal walls of jericho . . . falling" may be taken as an evocation of the threat of castration, this threat experienced in relation to the sight of the mother's genitalia.

The resolution to this crisis, which Dahlberg does not pursue in "Graphophone," would be for the maturing boy to recognize that he is on the verge of becoming a man. He may anticipate the acquisition of the phallus and the fixing, however precarious, of his sexual identity if he submits to the paternally imposed order and agrees to select a new object of desire. Given the evasive yet firm association between the body of the mother and the realm of commercial entertainment, the correlative burden placed upon the artist would be to find a replacement for the carnivalesque joy his original cultural milieu provided. However, it is quickly revealed in the following section that the twenties New York nightlife is an inadequate substitute as the character expresses his extreme loathing for the city by figuring it (with some help from the Bible) as a diseased female prostitute. After citing a passage from "the revelation": "BABYLON THE GREAT, MOTHER OF HARLOTS AND ABOMINATIONS OF THE EARTH," he begins the concluding section of the piece as follows: "NEW YORK, the syphilitic body of god, its jaundiced electric lights diseasing the night, welfare island, a cancerous blurred negative" (318). Where, then, is one to find a satisfying substitute for the pleasures of turn-of-the-century carnivalized amusement? Can formally inventive literature provide these same joys? Dahlberg allows the tensions this quest engenders to unfold in the latter portions of the novel he published in the following year where he again explores psychosexual matters and the field of mechanized amusements in conjunction.

CONEY ISLAND ABJECTION

A Coney Island of the mind. The amusement shacks are running full blast. (Henry Miller, "Into the Night Life . . .")

Throughout *Flushing* the barriers between bodies and machines, mothers and sons, persons and landscapes, life and death, the animate and inanimate, inside and outside are in a state of collapse. Julia Kristeva has approached the effects of these unwelcome yet longed for penetrations by way of the concept of abjection. The abject is what "the deject," the "I," desperately excludes, his survival seemingly dependent on the success of his demarcations. Yet the abject refuses to go away; it "beseeches and pulverizes the subject," contaminating him with what he perceives to be defiling and repugnant and in the process threatening to wreck his sense of identity.[28] The assault of the abject is comparable to the force of the grotesque in their shared tendency to transgress established limits. In *Flushing* Dahlberg situates the machine, often in relation to recreation, in this agonizing process of felt dissolution. Striking comic effects from the intercourse of people and things in the context of American entertainment, the book employs the grotesque not to erase the opposition between humans and nature (or animals) but to unsettle differences between persons and amusement technologies. The implications of this process in relation to autobiographical writing and its effects on the living body emerge near the end of the text.

Insofar as the subject matter of *Flushing* is the troubled existence of those at the lower end of the social scale in Depression-era America, the book explores the role that mechanized amusements play in the lives of the marginalized and impoverished inhabitants of the country. Focused alternately on Lizzie Lewis and her son Lorry, and set predominantly in two New York neighborhoods where, as the epigraph to part one puts it, "cheap peoples live," the novel also attends to the difficulties confronted by two recent immigrants to the country. Jerry Calefonia [sic], newly arrived from the Argentine, is a local bicycle shop repairman who briefly becomes one of Lizzie's numerous suitors; while Willie Huppert, a young German, who hopes to become a famous boxer, is taken in by Lizzie as a boarder. That Dahlberg affiliates himself with and feels compassionate toward his characters is evident throughout, though his sympathetic identifications are always tempered by irony.

The opening paragraph of the novel, by suggesting an analogy between the book and silent screen comedies, situates the literary text in the field of mechanized entertainment. The narrator describes the houses in Bensonhurst as "a makeshift stage-setting for a slapstick comedy."[29] Toward the end of the novel, Lorry, said to be staring "like a lowbrow heavyfooted comedian," catches sight of himself in a window and sees a "silly helpless Harry Langdonesque image" gaping back at him (244). (Early in the book before joining his mother in New York, Lorry [always Dahlberg's fictional counterpart] has been in LA struggling to become a successful screenwriter. He has failed, predictably since his ambition was to convince the main reader at Universal Studios that Oscar Wilde's *The Ballad of Reading Gaol* would make a swell "cowboy film" [79].)

For much of the novel the dependence of lonely individuals on mechanized entertainment is treated as a sad yet funny state of affairs. The pathos arises from the function of the machine as a substitute for physical contact between human beings. In the opening scene, Jerry sits in a Bensonhurst "moviehouse" watching "a very sexy picture," his head "partially dipped in the silver dust which tipped his ears and hair as it flowed river-wise toward the white sheet" (4) Then, after a Harry Langdon comedy, Jerry reaches over and tries to touch the leg of a young girl sitting next to him. Rebuffed, he moves on. Later, however, after pawing a "fourteen-year-old schoolgirl," he is arrested and convicted of child molestation. Willie too initially turns toward the machine for sexual excitement. In a penny arcade, having dropped his nickel in the slot, he begins to turn the crank of a "moving picture" machine. "Through stereopticon lenses he watched her undress. Each clockwork flap of a postcard picture progressively revealed new banks of foaming flesh. Willie brought the crank to a dead halt. He wanted to get his money's worth. Then it went blank with a machine-sprung thud" (180).[30] Mocked by a prostitute, who has been watching the autoerotic encounter, Willie accepts her invitation to obtain gratification in a more intersubjective manner and winds up with a venereal disease. Whether or not he would have been better off with the moving pictures is left open.

Her health failing, her financial situation dire, Lorry's mother is a bit of a medical quack who must also rely on a mechanized apparatus in her daily life. She has two principal sources of income, both of which are designed to end unwanted pregnancies. The second of these involves charging her distressed neighbors for "treatments" with her "violet-ray machine." She also uses the machine on herself to prevent "her bladder from coming down" (18) and as "a nerve tonic" that breaks "up colds, headaches, or rheumatic pains." Feeling "very scientific" whenever she manipulates "the *External*" or "the *Internal*" on the device, it functions as "a kind of mediumistic rattlesnake cure for all illnesses" (18–19). Two paragraphs later we learn that she regularly uses a work of literature as another way to alleviate her physical troubles. Locating the *History of Tom Jones* in the oven, where she had left it, she reads a few pages, as she does every day "after breakfast" as a digestive aid, the novel helping "to appease the angry gases and rumblings inside of her" (20–21).

The novel also helps her compose responses to marriage ads. *Tom Jones* is "handy to have around" because it enables her to "shoot the grammar" and furnishes her with "fancy phrases" to use in her business letters.

Halfway through the novel the focal point of the narrative shifts toward Lorry's increasingly agitated state of mind, and as the book's comic edge begins to fade the machine and the feminine rise up together as a threat to the male protagonist. Back from California and living with his mother in an apartment in Flushing across the street from Calvary cemetery, Lorry notices, much to his distress, signs of age and illness on his mother's face and body. Lizzie too is troubled by her appearance. "She didn't look in the mirror any more, for she was afraid to see herself. She was sure her face was falling away and that she was just skin and bones" (198). Lizzie's fears about her impending fate are also treated humorously. For instance, after she has finished reading the obituaries, hoping to reassure herself that only the elderly pass away, an oblivious Lorry comes home and much to her dismay puts Chopin's *Funeral March* on the phonograph. To convey further that the boy knows his mother is dying, Dahlberg extends the human/machine relationship to encompass the workings of Lorry's consciousness, producing an internalized figure of sensory perception as a technological process. "His eyes x-rayed her, passed through her, and somewhere inside of him there was an accurate photographic plate of her broken-winged mouth, her dead hair, the dye on it" and "her slick shiny embalmed chin. Vaguely, he knew; somehow, he saw her, the photographic negative of her, as if in running water. He didn't want to look too close; for he didn't wish his eyes to tell him anything more" (173).[31] The trope again registers the negative implications of his investment in the film/literature analogy. If the point of departure of the appeal to the technical media is to reinforce the illusory presence of the body in the literary work of art, the figure of seeing as the taking of an x-ray pushes in a different direction. Evoking procedures in which the flesh and blood of a human being are eliminated, made imperceptible, the trope reintroduces a tension that will erupt again at the end of part three, titled "Daily Graphic Slabs."

Perceiving his mother's eyes as "moving picture epitaphs in her head," Lorry, his fear growing that she is going to pass away, strives to hold on to her physically and emotionally. Presumably, his extreme anxiety is partly conditioned by a past trauma; her death would repeat the experience of separation he felt upon being sent to an orphanage as a small child.

(*Bottom Dogs* represses this event, passing over it with a single sentence.) In any event, when his mother emerges from her room, groaning and naked save for a white bedsheet she has wrapped around her, he wishes to "go to her, to comfort her." But ascertaining that the "knack of kissing and petting her was gone," he goes to bed, where he tries "to strain her back to him" in a dream (200–01). Discovering himself in a pawnshop where he is confronted by the body of his apparently deceased mother, "a skinny toothpick heap," he desperately strives "to get nearer and nearer to her," petting and fondling her. Realizing that "he couldn't mix his warm breath with hers, for she didn't have any," "she was a dead oilswamp sea" (201), he weeps until he has "cried himself out." However, as the scene shifts, his pain turns to pleasure, and he begins to delight in the separation. Watching a staged performance – perhaps a vaudeville show – in which his mother's teeth are the featured dancers, the dreamer is clearly enjoying himself. "Sitting alone in the audience he watched her front teeth dancing in the pit like a phalanx of robotian men. He clapped his hands to beat the band as he stared at her 14-karat solid-gold tooth tapdancing before the semicircular footlights of her false whiteteeth" (202). It is as if her (imaginary) death has furnished the conditions of possibility for the production of a spectacle, one that positions Lorry at a safe, reassuring distance from the engulfing or devouring (the presence of the teeth suggests that the stage is a mouth) event itself. In other words, the dream fulfills the character's wish to be rid of his mother who stands as a constant reminder of his own mortality.

But in the final paragraph of the section, Dahlberg indicates that the dilemma is also a representational one and that he, as the author, has yet to solve it. Jolted awake, Lorry dresses and rushes out of the house in a panic. "There ran through his brain, in a kind of litany: 'What shall I do? What shall I do?'" (202). He then turns a corner and is confronted by Calvary cemetery with its myriad tombstones, which the narrator oddly refers to as "daily-graphic chewinggum slabs" (202). On the one hand, this sight allows for an enhanced interpretation of the dream imagery. The vision discloses the dancing teeth as symbolic substitutions for the tombstones Lorry passes by daily, "chewinggum" arbitrarily linking the gaping mouth (the pit in which the teeth dance) to the graveyard. On the other hand, this last portion of the scene may also be read as an expression of a specifically authorial anxiety, the "slabs" grasped in turn as reflexive emblems, figures for the autobiographical novel in which they appear. The "slabs" (which also allude to the daily newspaper Lizzie has been reading) are an undesirable trope from the novelist's perspective because they characterize the text as an inscribed surface metonymically related to its referent, merely in its vicinity. Gravestones of course are placed next to or on top of the corpse they memorialize and neither incarnate nor preserve this thing against the ravages of time.

Thus death has been eliminated neither on the psychic nor the aesthetic level. The threat this poses to Dahlberg's aesthetic ambitions stems from his desire to incorporate the spiritual substance and thus protect from decay the referential objects of his autobiographical discourse. Dahlberg's interrogation of this problem consistently occurs in conjunction with forms of commercial entertainment (such as in the dream show), revealing the centrality of the latter in his thought. And the "robotian" men in the dream scene suggest that he is especially fascinated with the mechanical dimensions of contemporary amusements. We can pursue this cluster of issues further in the next part of the book, titled "Coney Island Angelus Bells," which recounts a trip Lorry and friends take to the park on mardi-gras night.[32]

The aesthetic aspiration of the book here is to reproduce verbally the onslaught of sensations a visitor to the park typically receives, to capture the somatic experience of being at Coney Island. The frequent interpolations into the narrative of song lyrics and the calls of the park barkers mimic the auditory impressions the place engenders. The anthropomorphic figurations powerfully convey the effect of visual hyper-stimulation, tropologically induced distortions recreating the hallucinatory impact of an overdose of seeing. The recorded sensations bombard the reader as the narrator's "eye," frenetically mobile, swinging in dizzying arcs as if in imitation of a ride on the merry-go-round or carrousel, makes one feel like part of the "jamming and oceanbillowing" crowd (217), rushing excitedly from float to ride to exhibit. As Lorry strolls along the boardwalk, the narrator characterizes "the evening" as "still young with dim blue circles around its eyes" (212). "Sight-seeing in Noah's Ark," the boys encounter a "stunt automatic giraffe, with a flagpole rigormortis neck" and "a macabre skeleton syncopated in lithographic blackness" (218–19). Dahlberg's technique is put to use in an especially energetic manner when Lorry and the girl he has just picked up arrive at the boardwalk dance floor. In this anarchic atmosphere everything is "going at high gear" (227), the jazz band is "going crazy," the "lamps gyrated" (229), the "partners shook against one another like an eruptive civil war" (230). When the music ends and the floor clears, its "varnished pompadour" slides "back off its receding idiot's face. It grinned inanely, masklike at the slippery steppers" (229). After a brief interval, the band starts up again, "the saxophone" taking "on swaddling clothes," going "clean infantile," the "smooth skin of the floor assumed a babyish stare" (229) and, after a tempo change and "a wild blast," the trombone starts "frothing at the mouth" (230). In this highly kinetic part of the novel, a dizzying series of perceptions rush after one another with remarkable swiftness.

The chiasmic crossing of self and surroundings, the exchange between the animate (human faces and bodies) and the inanimate (saxophone, the dancefloor), is embraced here as a means of communicating the nature of the perceptions being recorded. Positioned as a kind of "agentless sensorium," the reader identifies with a "subject that is all body" in an environment that has been fully embodied.[33] Yet Dahlberg's grotesque tropes also draw attention to the unsettlingly violent, murderous implications of this somatic experience. For example, when Steve and Slim pursue two "janes," they appear to do so as "though their heads had been decapitated" (212). And when the carrousel suddenly stops revolving and the music goes silent, "everything went hypnotically still, a lunatic still-life. Necks and cheeks distended like paradeday balloons blown up to the bursting point, and then popped and shriveled as if a pinpoint had been put into them" (224). Such images of bodily violence are complemented by images that transform human beings into inanimate artifacts. The whirling riders of the merry-go-round wooden horses appear to have "window-display dummy legs" and "freak museum faces with Modigliani endocrine necks" (223). The circulation of life outward is shown to have the reciprocal effect of bringing death inside the living person.

Caught up in the physical delirium, Lorry goes off to a sidestreet hotel and has sexual intercourse for the first time with his date (who turns out to be a prostitute). The act of copulation having been completed, perhaps feeling a bit ashamed, he soon becomes overwhelmed by the grotesque mingling of opposites, the fusion of contraries, that the amusement park experience enforces. This unsettling of difference reaches its peak intensity as he and his friends take an underground boat trip through the park's wax museum, "The Slums of Paris." It is at this point that another reversal in effect occurs, the excitement and attraction of transgression yielding to nausea at the sight of unnatural couplings, scenes of physical excess and ambiguity frightening the observer.

Featuring static, immobile and foreboding displays of murderers and a cocaine fiend's home, the subterranean ride functions as a counterpart

to the reckless mobility and thoughtless abandon the aboveground attractions cultivate. Whereas at the surface level people gather together
for noisy, exuberant, and public fun, in the nightmarish realm below
one looks at examples of private, domestic immoralities, of the secretly
illicit behavior that goes on behind closed doors: drug addiction, criminal activity. Resembling a drop into the enclosed world of the mind, the
trip has the effect of an encounter with the grotesque other of mainstream society, with the repressed contents of the collective unconscious.
Dahlberg compares the process whereby these materials take shape not
to the experience of a dream but to the watching of a film, again displac-
ing a psychic phenomenon with a technological one. Traveling "through
an artificial canal," in which intervals of darkness give way briefly to
lit sets, "projected and extinguished," "disclosed and then dispelled"
(234), the sordid exhibits appear and disappear as quickly as the images
that flicker across a movie screen. Thus an "underworld boudoir scene"
lies "exposed like a cinematographic projection of Plato's concupiscent
soul," and while looking at other "dim and luridly lighted" stages Lorry
is "forked and pronged [by] the photo-plate darkness" (234).

   Lorry nears emotional breakdown, however, as the boat passes by a
set of "freaks":

   There was Irene, the jolly fat girl, her bushman clack-clack laughter tripping
   up and down the gargantuan staircases of her throat; Hubert's museum trained
   mobocratic fleas; trained businessmen; Alzora, the turtle girl, a swiftian flesh-
   blob; Elsie-John, *The Enigma of the Human Race*, the hermaphrodite, a freakish
   spinozistic proof of a dualistic universe, the mysterybox. (235)

These sights are followed by "Woo Foo, the immune man," "the leprous
leopard boy," marvels such as the "World Wonder," which, if looked at
through a microscope, has the Lord's Prayer engraved on the head of a
pin, and "the maharajah mentalist" possessed of a "radio mind" (236).
Feeling physically ill, Lorry also falls into a vertiginous mental spin.
Able neither to comprehend the oddities he has seen nor to distinguish
between the natural and the unnatural, the character becomes panic-
stricken in his confrontation with what Miller would term a few years
later in "Into the Night Life . . ." as the "sovereign pasteboard power" of
the amusement park. "The faked-up grotto made of wood and canvas recalled Calvary cemetery, all those boulders which formed a wall around
the graveyard and which were so intensely natural as to suggest artifice.
All the desolation and dizziness of artifice, of contrived unreality swirling
in his brain and in the pit of his stomach" (236). Sexual indeterminacy,

the ambiguous mingling of humans and animals, and the sight of exotic persons' overflowing flesh threaten in combination to collapse the classificatory oppositions governing the subject's understanding and place in the world. This experience precipitates a kind of nervous breakdown. In *Flushing* the carnivalesque therefore manifests itself as a participatory activity and an objectified spectacle.[34] If in some areas of Coney Island socially inscribed differences are compromised (on the crowded dance floor, for instance), elsewhere the park works to reinforce culturally determined norms, placing the "exotic," "bizarre," "aberrant" other on stage so as to strengthen the visitor's sense of his or her own normalcy. Notably, however, the delirious mingling the carnivalesque produces at the level of collective performance carries over in the novel, collapsing the psychically reassuring space between the observer and the observed in the underground exhibitions.

Confronted by a series of perceptual and cognitive paradoxes, perplexed by the fluidity of demarcations, the boy's thoughts turn back to his mother; in his mind a "dissociated skull," her return thus precipitates another suspended difference: the living son is now penetrated by the image of the inanimate mother. "Death lay in his stomach . . . and he wanted to get it out. He wanted to be clear of her, to cut the material film-vision of her out of his brain" (237). Running in desperation to the subway, "the carrousel screaming, subway-expressing, and fleshblobbing in his ears," thoughts of his "mother's oatmealy, scribbled, and shriveled up throat" plaguing him, the boy suddenly vomits on the station stairs: "gardenseedcereal went pouring out of his mouth." "He didn't want to go back" (238). The semantic contents of this symbolic act of vomiting include the artificial, the feminine (maternal), the mechanical, and death – what the character must flush out of his system. Experienced as an assault by the outside on body and ego, these seemingly foreign elements must be expelled to preserve the fractured integrity of the frightened male subject. In that she is blamed for causing the loathsome, death, to enter into the subject, the mother is set up as a scapegoat. Lorry is caught up in the "transference of something deeply within" to another in the hopes of ridding himself of what he fears: mortality.[35]

Lorry's panic attack may be analyzed from the point of view Stallybrass and White set forth in their discussion of bourgeois female hysteria. As they see it, the middle-class woman is excited by and terrified of a set of imaginary figures in which distinctions of all sorts are canceled, and her condition is a result of her belonging to a class that has historically labored to detach itself from the low and grotesque.[36] But Lorry has grown up as a "bottom dog" and it therefore appears that the process of division or negation underlying "bourgeois" subject formation is just getting underway here. We are in fact witnessing the beginnings of the *author's* attempt to construct a self in opposition to the freakish body of the grotesque other. Moreover, if, following Kristeva, we define abjection as a force that also has the capacity to put the "I" at risk, then it becomes evident that Dahlberg is confronting a "horror" with the power to pull him back to his origins in a compost heap of inorganic and organic materials.

For Lorry to solidify his physical integrity and psychic identity, he must subdue this threat. What confuses and overwhelms is perceived as filthy and repudiated in the defense of body and mind. In the novel's next part Dahlberg interpolates the following memory into the narrative in order to display the character's strong reaction to such encroachment as a defense against incestuous longings: "when he [Lorry] was 9 he didn't want to sleep with his mother: in winter he didn't mind as much."

> but july and august were sticky months: days when he smelled his own nose and his own lips: all the swearword parts of the body fretted him like big hossflies and when he could not shoo them away he cried and goddamned and believed that the devil who he had seen in the cowboy and indian gillis theatre at a matinee performance had gotten a bearhug on him and was holding him as fast as the staves of a barrel and was trying to put him up to things he didn't want to do.
>
> Then he wanted icicle january back . . . then his thoughts could be as straight as trees and as white as clouds and soapsuds and his muscles as hard as the rocks of the baptist church. (242)

Here too an intolerable proximity to the mother ("he wanted a room and a bed for himself") and to mechanical forms of entertainment (one night "just before he awoke an *edison* graphophone disc was creaking through his head like the end of the world") again coalesces. The imagery of the second paragraph suggests that if the child is frightened, it is because he fears castration will be the punishment for his physical proximity to his mother. (That Lorry in a later recollection admits to having wished his father figure dead confirms the oedipal interpretation.) Kristeva also mentions food-loathing as a typical "seme" of abjection, alongside fear of death and incest (*Power of Horror*, 92–97). Earlier, during his visit to Coney Island, Lorry has remembered his youthful dietary predicaments as well: "he never could eat red lobster meat in the electric oysterhouse because of its smell. now it all came back and stirred in him: seaside oysterhouse brine curled in his nostrils" (*Flushing*, 220). Struggling against the drive to mingle the self with feminized entertainment machines, the desperate, nauseated character must sever his ties with two associated sources of defilement, must break free of a mother he finds repulsive and equally loathsome mechanized amusements. Previously drawn to both, Lorry now realizes that his subjectivity depends on his ability to keep technology and his dying mother at bay. This dilemma is simultaneously a psychic and a representational one. The author's ambivalent attitude toward the influence of American amusement on his expressive aesthetic is superimposed upon the character's ambivalence toward his mother's body.

The loathsome and vile attributes – maternal materiality and mechanical artifice – that put the subject at risk in the narrative turn out to be the attributes of writing that threaten the project of the autobiographical novelist. From one perspective, language abjects. As a rhetorical system of tropes it makes it impossible to maintain ontological, psychological, and cultural differences, causing life and death, mothers and sons, literature and carnivalized amusements to flow into each other. Yet from another angle, writing is itself the abject. Registering the materiality of writing has the effect of collapsing figurations and thus destroying the representational claims of the artwork altogether. In the reflexive imagery of the text, this amounts to the degradation of embodied souls to skeletal remains. The materiality of the medium is the encroaching, suffocating filth that the author strives yet fails to keep from ruining his expressive self-portrait. Much as the character's convulsive retching is a deluded attempt to expunge what refuses to go away (the feminine), the authorial subject realizes the impossibility of transcending the disturbing attributes of writing. The final sections of the novel, which address the problem of the father, constitute a desperate and ultimately unsuccessful yet still illuminating effort to resolve a complex predicament that is simultaneously psychic and literary.

AUTOBIOGRAPHY AND ENGRAVING

Record grooves dig the grave of the author. (Friedrich A. Kittler, *Gramophone, Film, Typewriter*)

The carnival was over and I had been picked clean. (Henry Miller, *Tropic of Cancer*)

When we left Lorry with vomit spilling out of his mouth he was dashing toward the subway. At this point an awareness of the other bearer of death who has been haunting him throughout the novel re-enters his consciousness. This is the recently deceased Simon Wolkes, an intimidating father figure from the boy's past. "And out of the bottomless pit to which he had no key, the orphanage superintendent Wolkes mouldered in his mind, the applecore bones of him haggling away in the wind of the earth's effluvia" (237). What is most curious is the boy's association of the older character with the materiality of language as writing, this connection already tentatively established in relation to Lizzie (her "scribbled" throat). Immediately after recalling the superintendent, Lorry enters a men's bathroom where "his eyes scanned homo geographical maps and inscriptions" (237). Such images of writing as the drawing or carving of lines on flat, solid surfaces, continue throughout the remainder of the novel, Wolkes' lips, for instance, later said to be "as awful as hebraic letters: how he feared the cruel pencil sharpening curl of them!" (258). The culmination of this motif is the reproduction on the final two pages of the novel of the sheet music to a hymn the boys used to sing in the orphan asylum. The ironic inclusion undermines the illusory presence of the speaking voice behind the narrative discourse. Acknowledging the materiality of writing in this manner compromises Dahlberg's aesthetic phenomenalism because the latter is predicated on the capacity of stylized novelistic discourse to approximate embodied perceptions and reproduce the sounds of (idiomatically) spoken words. Here we are left with the unnerving awareness that writing is in truth more like a musical score, like black notes on a white page.

Insofar as the ostensible function of the grotesque body within this aesthetic is to mediate between the self and a variety of others, acknowledging the fact of writing as printed matter disrupts this process. Focusing on the material properties of the medium of exchange itself hinders its usefulness as the means of maintaining contact between individuals and groups, persons and things, literature and amusement. The ramifications of the critical turn under investigation are developed in "J.O.A. Ja Wohl, Das Ist Das Weisenhaus," the fifth and next-to-last part of the novel.

Having decided to visit the orphanage in the hopes of reattaching himself to his social and cultural roots, Lorry's journey is an effort to halt the process of psychic fragmentation. He feels his identity is slipping away and he therefore returns to his Cleveland home. The character's desire to stave off the emotional experience of disintegration is inseparable from the writer's wish to maintain contact with his aesthetic origins. So when, upon his arrival, the taste of his chewing gum reminds Lorry of "Keith's Circuit," and is said to have a "burlesk theatre about it," Dahlberg is evoking his own yearning. The "spooning vaudeville jigging ragtime"

that once "lifted" the character up was what initially energized the artist
(244).

When Lorry laments the burden he believes the superintendent has
placed on him, it is as if Dahlberg, in displaced fashion, is formulating
the imperative governing his autobiographical enterprise. "Why," he
wonders to himself, had "the dead Wolkes singled him out? Why had
he chosen him, chosen him to transubstantiate his dryscraped straydog
buried bones back to their original warm walking substance?" (246).
Though expressed as a task the character must accomplish at the level
of consciousness, his memory the place where the dead father is to be
resurrected, the query articulates as well the duty the author feels to
resurrect his previous self. What both character and author wish is to
overcome temporal change and reunify the self with the dead other
(though in one case this other is an earlier self). Success in both instances
requires that the representational image coincide with the substance of
the represented entity, and for this to occur the body of the latter must
be put back together and revived, brought back to life.

With great sadness Dahlberg, speaking through his character, admits
that he has failed to achieve what he set out to do. Thus Lorry painfully
realizes that "except in his dreams he [Wolkes] was no longer whole: the
earth had raped his flesh, obliterated his thighs, made worm-arithmetic
tables out of his blueberry lips" (25). This critical turn leads to a negative insight, to a reductive awareness of the formal preconditions of
autobiographical discourses.

he [Lorry] wept because he could not bring him [Wolkes] back in entirety
again. now nothing was left but the dream, nothing left of him but a grammar
textbook substantive, a noun, a name in the brain, a noun without a copulative
verb *to be* (now he could not help but control himself; when he like wolkes was
an uncopulative substantive in the grave and in some unknown guy's mind, he
would control himself, too). (250)

Drastically reduced to the status of a linguistic category, to a substantive
without substance, this father figure survives after his death, in the brain
and on the page, as "nothing" more than a literal mark in a "textbook."
The written word, like the machine, enters consciousness and determines
a forgetting. Wolkes' status after death is that of either an empty, hallucinatory image (a dream) or of a grammatical subject with no predicate,
devoid of the spiritual or physical properties of an existential being. Both
options of course fall far short of the more desirable, satisfying experience
of a full remembrance or recollection. Wolkes is a displaced figure for

the self of the author in relation to a future reader: "he like wolkes was an uncopulative substantive in the grave and in some unknown guy's mind." Thus it becomes evident that what must be rejected is the notion that through autobiography one may achieve a degree of immortality, that language can serve as the site of the soul's redemption. Because paper and ink are material in the same sense that the earth is, Dahlberg can (a bit later) register the distressing outcome of his own literary undertaking (both senses of the word are appropriate here) in the form of his character's sadness over his lost memories. "Lorry smoothed the wolkesless earth with his shoes. And so he buried him, put him away" (268).

In an essay on reader-response theory, Paul de Man, alluding to Benjamin (and Hegel), offers a pertinent description of the critical process under investigation here as the precondition for the move toward allegorical modes of writing. Defined polemically and narrowly as "anorganic," as material in the same sense that "an inscription or a notation" on a "piece of paper" is, "allegory names the rhetorical process by which the literary text moves from a phenomenal, world-oriented to a grammatical, language-oriented direction."[37] If allegorical ruins are what are left behind after attractively beautiful aesthetic constructs have been obliterated, this process of destruction corresponds to the degradation of past experiences of consciousness to mere letters in a text.

The descriptive focus now falls on images of temporal decay – appropriately enough given the oft-noted thematic concern in allegorical narration with impermanence and transience. When the melancholic Lorry arrives back at the orphanage, he discovers that it has been boarded up and is for sale, the ruined buildings as subject to change as human beings are. The orphanage, site of his childhood, appears here as a "ramshackle sepulchre, dead and gaping," "a roomy battered cemetery out of use" (256). In sharp contrast to grotesque realism, in which recourse to natural processes often serves as a redemptive and therefore reassuring model of human existence as cyclically regenerative, death inexorably followed by renewal, Dahlberg, perhaps thinking of Whitman, figures the asylum grass as lying "scattered and dumped like bones" (255). The dejected fictional protagonist is as emotionally vacant as his surroundings. Despite the fact that memories of his youth do come hurtling back into his mind, he still ends up feeling cut loose, emptied out, without direction, and vulnerable to the forces around him: "He was in no place and no place was in him. He had nowhere to go." "He walked through the light and the light walked through him" (271). After wandering mournfully around the empty, forsaken grounds, Lorry sits down on the rim of the water fountain's "circular stone-ledge" and asks himself " 'Do these bones live?' " (269).[38] What is at stake in this question within the narrative is whether the punctured non-subject can secure a sense of who or where he is in the world by recollecting his past experiences. If the place has retained the essence of his youthful experiences, he will thus have located a substantial foundation for himself, a stable point around which he can orient his existence. Yet on a generically reflexive level, the query is concerned with the capacity of autobiographical novels to keep the perceptual lines of communication open between the living and the dead. The response the text delivers is unambiguously negative: the orphanage trees are "stone-deaf in the wind and the grass talkless too" (269). Writing puts persons and things in their graves.[39]

Flushing moves toward its critical insight by passing through the realm of mechanized American amusement. In "Graphophone," the burden of the implicit analogy between writing, the functions of the brain, and technological media was to reinforce the representational capacity of autobiographical discourse. Yet the ultimately disquieting result of comparing memory processes and an autobiographical discourse to the operations of mechanical contrivances was to strip away the assumptions on which the project had relied to get underway. At first, the rise of ostensibly superior storage technologies like film and record discs served as representational models for Dahlberg in his attempt to reproduce the visible and aural world. Eventually, however, he found himself forced to register the incapacity of his own medium to furnish the semblance of surrogate sensualities. Similarly, in *Flushing*, a visit to Coney Island is posited as a metaphorical analogy for an exhilarating, perception-based method of writing. But the novel inexorably moves toward a confrontation with the textual properties that cancel out the appealingly hallucinatory, intoxicating aesthetic experience of a visit to a popular amusement park. In the end he is left with is an internalized set of what Susan Stewart has called material souvenirs of death; and these serve only to mark disruption and discontinuity in relation to the meaningful experiences of the past.[40] Lorry turns to leave with "the orphanage tied up inside of him like a neat little bundle of old dated postcard views" (270).

In following the tortuous path that led him to undo the representational claims of his autobiographical discourse, Dahlberg brought himself to the edge of the rhetorical terrain Benjamin had (unbeknownst to Dahlberg) mapped a few years earlier under the heading of the allegorical.[41] In *Flushing*, the end product of this critical process is emblematized in the form of skeletal remains. The bones of a corpse are a figure for the literary artifact after its referential plenitude has been stripped away.[42] The image of the grotesque body has undergone a decisive rhetorical alteration. It has been removed from the fleshly realm of carnivalized aesthetics and relocated on the threshold of the more barren world of allegorical signification. Autobiography, which had seemed to be an expressive instrument designed to preserve the soul and restore the body to life, turns out to be a critical force that lays the dead to rest, that lodges them firmly in their graves. The critical drive that repeatedly makes its presence felt in Dahlberg's work has some affinities with the Freudian concept of the death drive, for both impulses, in their respective realms (the literary and the psychic), counteract efforts aimed at prolonging life. The analogy suggests the importance – in literary theory and practice – of continuing to go beyond the principles of (grotesque) aesthetic pleasure toward an understanding of what these principles conceal.

Though Dahlberg never develops the possibility fully, he does gesture toward a way of moving beyond the impasse he had reached, and commenting briefly on this aspect of the text will help pave the way for the discussion of the compositional specificity of Dos Passos' *U.S.A.* Of particular interest in this regard is Dahlberg's deployment of gender distinctions to negotiate a rhetorical transition. Whereas the bulk of *Flushing* is devoted to the transgression of differences, often through the use of grotesque imagery, the text retreats from this endeavor in the end. The book concludes by acknowledging, mournfully, the need to respect established divisions. It does not do so in the insistent manner of an enraged prophet (the Dahlberg of *Bones*). Instead it articulates the need to adhere to culturally prescribed oppositions from the perspective of a devastated youth preparing to accept the oedipal authority of a figure associated with religious codes of behavior.

As Lorry's return to the orphanage – an institution devoted, however ineffectively, to producing socially respectable individuals – precipitates a series of recollections of embarrassing incidents from his past, we have the sense that he is preparing for a move into adulthood. What he remembers most vividly is the stress at the orphanage on the importance of disciplining the self and training the body, maintaining a habitual commitment to cleanliness of particular importance. The model for such civilized, correct behavior is of course Wolkes: his "popish nose dilating with ministerial refinement, his breath pure from ablutional gargles" (246). But as a boy, Lorry, though desperate for Wolkes' approval, found himself in one humiliating situation after another. In the chapel, for instance, he was unable "to control himself," to "stop his disgusting throwing-up," so he "puked all over the chapelseats," which led to his being ordered out by the furious Wolkes. Significantly, in the next paragraph of the text (set weeks later), Lorry finds redemption amid the supply-room writing materials. Helping the superintendent "stack and load and carry out textbooks," the boy feels that his sins are washed away by the instruments of composition: "the tiny pyramidal pencil sharpenings piled up next to the ink-bottle were as sweet and slender to the balls of his fingers as an easter rabbit's back – the waterman's blue-black fountainpen ink, rows and rows of unthumbed erasingum, all as neat and clean as the lord's paschal lamb. his nose still hungered for the supply-room which seemed to cleanse and obliterate everything else" (247). Whereas Dahlberg's autobiographical discourse has consistently mocked such appeals to moral purity and the sacred, treating with compassionate humor the repugnantly filthy, unhealthy conditions his downtrodden characters endure, a shift in tone or mood begins at this point in his career. This is the first indication of what will become his pronounced commitment in *Bones* to literature as a means of overcoming or sublimating a fascination with base physiological functions. The comic deployment of the grotesque body ceased to be a constitutive aspect of his art.

It is revealing that the author's departure from a grotesque aesthetic coincides, in terms of the book's themes, with the character's detachment from his mother. Appropriately, the epigraph to this pivotal section of the book and of his career is *"father, see thy suppliant children"* (239), and we soon learn that as a boy Lorry "loved wolkes more than his mother" (248). The identification with a paternal authority allows at the end of "J.O.A." for an initiation into the knowledge that leads to maturity. Thus the narrator informs us that the forlorn character repeats his "church responsives: *thy commands shall be engraven / on the tablets of our hearts*" and in this manner ends "his puberty confirmation hymn" (269). Lorry's capitulation to the law would seem to augur Dahlberg's acceptance of writing as a violent practice that marks and assigns a position (in the social order) to the individual, that forcibly positions the subject in a pre-existing system of relations. Such a concept of writing (which does not have a formal corollary in the text) stands as a rejection of grotesque methods modeled on the spoken word, on orality, and the perceiving body. The thematic emphasis on the necessity of the son separating himself from the mother corresponds to an authorial recognition of the necessity of words separating themselves from things. The boy's unhappy submission to a patriarchal mandate matches the author's anguished acceptance of the linguistically determined requirement (the law of the signifier?) to relinquish his aesthetic dream of achieving (re)incarnation through representation.

In the final sentences of "J.O.A.," thoughts of Lizzie come back to trouble Lorry: "Then his mother, a dark cataract aura, densely, thickly, webbed his eyes. What had become of her?" (271) In the novel's next and final part, the title of which, "Kentucky Blue Grass Henry Smith," refers to another father figure for the boy, this threat to vision is shown being cut into and then dying on the operating table. "He [the surgeon] touched her arm. It went numb, lifeless flesh that wasn't hers. The touch sawed her." "Then she was strangely and medically divided, one part of her trailing away from the other. She was being unribboned, physically unravelled. She floated away from herself" (288). So too does she float away from her son. This process of division may be read as an allegory of the autobiographer's loss of contact with his experiences as a subject in the world. "Lorry was out there and she could not reach him. Dimly she could hear circles and figures of talk. But their voices were distant, the wiry bass barranging cello echo running through telegraphpoles" (289). For Dahlberg, the desire to become an author demanded that he extricate himself completely from the temptations of the feminine and the referential (and from the seductions of carnivalized amusements).[43] Ultimately, the successful resolution of their respective predicaments required character and author to strive toward the (ultimately unattainable) position of authority marked out for them by the absent, dead father. "Once imaginary effects and real inscription have been renounced, what remains are rituals of the symbolic."[44]

Ultimately, the intention does not faithfully rest in the contemplation of bones, but faithlessly leaps forward to the idea of resurrection. (Walter Benjamin, *The Origin of German Tragic Drama*)

In his famous manifesto, "Projective Verse," Charles Olson attributes his belief in the necessity of developing an alternative, non-traditional set of poetic priorities to the aesthetic convictions of his mentor, Edward Dahlberg. But at no point in the manifesto does Olson mention a non-literary model for this new, rapidly paced method, in which "the *kinetics* of the thing" is essential. If the aims of verse are henceforth to be to "keep moving, keep in, speed, the nerves, their speed, the perceptions, theirs, the acts, the split second acts," then this compositional ambition, one that makes its strongest appeals to the body rather than the intellect, must have derived from somewhere. If the task of the writer is to produce a "high energy-construct," one that would transfer to readers "at least the equivalent of the energy which propelled him in the first place," then there must be an original source of power somewhere.[45] The "Coney Island" section of *Flushing* suggests that this high-voltage compositional inspiration was located outside literature in the realm of American amusement. The mechanized rides and uncanny displays of human oddities at a thoroughly modernized site of mass recreation provided the initial stimulus for the sort of forceful approach to writing that would resurface long after the Depression had ended.

Nevertheless, I have attempted to show that Dahlberg's Depression-era autobiographical writing manifests much ambivalence in regard to the relationship between technologically mediated forms of entertainment and literature. Even in *Flushing* he rejects immediately after deploying a somatically oriented sensationalism (one quite similar to the aesthetic Bill Brown has characterized as "a modernism of special effects.")[46] By the end of the book all traces of a carnival-based approach have vanished, as if the formal experiment has failed.[47] At the end of the decade he adopted a willfully anachronistic critical stance predicated on the repudiation of industrialized fun in favor of a new pastoralism. What had previously been an object of desire became an artifact of great disgust. It is this authorial or rhetorical tension that he superimposes in *Flushing* onto his protagonist's emotional predicament. This reflexive supplement to the narrative representation of a psychic uncertainty helps in turn to disclose the extent to which in the thirties femininity and mechanized pleasure combined to form a complex object of fascination for male writers, especially those with an interest in grotesque aesthetics. A stimulus of formal innovation, such entertainments also threatened the autonomy of the literary text, a frightening dilemma Dahlberg provocatively intertwines with the autobiographical subject's concerns about his corporeal and mental integrity.

Dahlberg's eventual reaction away from the exhilarating if unnerving intrusions he initially embraced is strikingly evident in *Bones* as a passage from a section of the study entitled "Ezekiel's Valley" demonstrates. His antipathy to all kinds of mechanized urban entertainment – the cinema in particular – is now fully developed. He therefore distinguishes these, to him, imitative undertakings from an oral-based literature devoted to cultivating and augmenting the natural body. The rigidly inflexible position he has decided to adopt, after switching from autobiographical fiction to literary history, from creation to criticism, is unmistakable.

The lonely city biped is rifled of flowers, fields, hills, of all spatial mead; chained to the machine, celled in the mechanized room, immured in the theoretic sidewalk, he stalks his vasty Asias and Indias upon a sieved screen, gazing on dithering, husked heaths, travelogue terrains, Himalayas. Denied replete and rondured vistas, he is given instead the bogus "audioscopic" dimension, an interior which is added *on* to drained, splayed objects, figures, skies, houses; cozened of pigments, his thirsts are slaked upon "Technicolor," reds, greens, ambers, spilled, painted *on*. The automobile, the radio, the ventriloquistic "Talkie," are mechanical anesthesia-horrors which give man all the counterfeit moods of travel, sound, *acting*, vocal utterance, while insidiously depriving him of motion, energy, act, human speech, animate contact. (*Bones*, 73–74)

American civilization is "deanimated" and "metronomic," is a grotesque enlargement of that "gap between touch and thing."[48] A superficial impression of having conquered space and time belies the modern city dweller's sensory enslavement, his perceptual confinement. By offering cheap, artificial substitutes for genuine experience, technological amusements have robbed him of his proper capacity to expand outward toward the world and other persons. Onanistic filmmakers indulge in a wasteful, non-procreative activity in which fluids are "spilled" or artificially "added *on* to drained, splayed objects." The deceptive imposition of color contributes to the construction of an illusion of spatial depth that replaces the use of art as a means of enlarging persons and bodies through the achievement of contact (or copulating) with external reality. His desire for movement and expansion gratified by the fake substitutes that the cinema furnishes, the momentarily pleased spectator is further separated from living things – animate entities – than before he entered the theatre. Obeying the "first commandment of the manic, machine age" (*Bones*, 74), "Thou shalt not TOUCH," "the Human Hand" has "become impotent, maniacal," and is therefore no longer the origin of creative, carefully crafted labor. Guided by "the myth of progress" in the area of commercial entertainment, we have been led "far underground, where we wander over flowerless and treeless plains of macadam, feeding upon the ruby leakages of neon lights" (74). The substitution of artificially reproduced landscapes for natural ones has numbed our perceptual capacities.

In the years preceding his re-emergence as an aesthetic Luddite, however, Dahlberg had responded in a more compellingly progressive manner to the infiltration of cultural practices by machine processes. The firm structural oppositions he insists on throughout *Bones* between humans and machines, literature and amusement, orality and writing, nature and technology mark his retreat from the complicated interrogation of these distinctions he had pursued earlier in the Depression era. The autobiographical novelist's initial flexibility on the relation of writing and communal modes of play calcified over time into the literary historian's vehement and absolute repudiation of one in the name of the purity of the other. As he began his literary career, Dahlberg (equivocally) approved the newer entertainment media as sources of artistic inspiration. At first he evinced a willingness to suspend the categorical distinctions structuring the cultural field, and in so doing he participated in the process of rethinking the relations of bodies, psyches, and literature in the machine age. Then he stepped back in horror from his remarkable accomplishment.

2

Laughter and Depression: Henry Miller and the emergence of the technocarnivalesque

... out of music halls, burlesque, vaudeville, circuses and limbo ... he tapped in on that great pipeline of horsing and miming which runs back unbroken through the fairs of the Middle Ages at least to ancient Greece.

> James Agee, "Comedy's Greatest Era"

Many of the statements made in my story [should] be taken somewhat "tropically."

> Kenneth Burke, *Towards a Better Life*

Speaking in *Tropic of Capricorn* of the diseases that bring about "a condition of misery which is irremediable," Henry Miller identifies Bloomingdale's as his "special sickness," his "incurable obscure malady." Whenever he enters the department store – a symbolic center of consumer culture (and perhaps associated by him with the feminine) – he has a phobic response. So intense is his fear that "I fall apart completely: I dribble onto the floor, a helpless mess of guts and bones and cartilage."[1] With help from Neil Hertz, we may diagnose this extreme reaction as a case of male hysteria under economic pressure.[2] Corporeal fragmentation figures the mental collapse of the autobiographical self, the unbinding of his fragile ego. The physical disintegration or experience of de-partment is a visible trope expressing a mental breakdown. The anxiety the panicked subject feels is conveyed through the rhetorical use of an image of his body in pieces.

The psychic and economic anxiety the passage manifests occurs, however, in a humorous vein. Miller is playing the role of the emotionally distressed male hysteric for laughs. Moreover, the event depicted is by no means an entirely negative one. His loss of wholeness clears the ground for a positive renewal on another plane, for a spiritual rebirth. In fact, Miller even seems to desire masochistically the destructive shattering of his body because it paves the way for emotional rejuvenation. The ecstatic and emancipated Miller post-collapse is now free to "become a real schizerino," to "fly with the etheric body," leaving behind on the store floor the "sack of bones, guts and cartilage" previously weighing him down (*Capricorn*, 206). Now a transcendently fluid, freely soluble self, Miller is delighted to learn how simple it is to achieve liberation, to take wing from what society praises as a strong, fixed-in-place ego. "As the Bloomingdale experience goes to prove, this whole self, about which so much boasting has been done, falls apart very easily" (206).

The grotesque rending and tearing of the body Miller depicts may be located as the point of intersection of two distinct (and relatively contemporaneous) theoretical accounts of the significance of images of corporeal fragmentation: Lacanian psychoanalysis and Bakhtin's model of the carnivalesque.[3] That the passage deals with a case of personal shock, of a clinically definable mental illness, suggests the feasibility of interpreting the scene as the pathological manifestation of aggressive intentions. Miller communicates a private crisis (undergone in a public place) through the symptomatic use of "*imagos of the fragmented body*."[4] Alternatively we may read the event as a comic performance whose social meaning is comprehensible in light of the carnival-grotesque tradition of festive behavior.[5] From this interpretive angle the collective ramifications of the shattering of the ostensibly autonomous ego and seemingly biological body come into focus. The autobiographical representation of corporeal dispersal is inscribed in a system of symbolic imagery that expresses a populist, utopian faith in "the historic, progressing body of mankind" in its entirety.[6] The laughter engendered by the sight of somatic mutilation and dismemberment functions to reintegrate persons into a ceaselessly developing communal entity: the grotesque social body.

Rather than insist on one of these two competing interpretive perspectives at the expense of the other, I suggest that acknowledging the validity of both as conceptual frames helps circumscribe the specificity of Miller's Depression-era enterprise. Because Miller's writing hovers between a fascination with his own emotional anguish and an anarchic commitment to wreaking social havoc, understanding Miller's autobiographies requires commentators to draw on psychoanalysis *and* politicized theories of the carnivalesque.[7] To grasp the significance of Miller's imagery of bodily fragmentation, we must borrow from these two relatively discrete interpretive systems, thus complicating without eradicating the difference between them.

The interpretive confusion his work induces does not exhaust the pertinence of his accomplishment. Miller's writing also carries us beyond the Bakhtinian model of the carnivalesque. As is apparent throughout *Rabelais and His World*, it is the links between the self, society, and the *natural* environment that the Russian scholar investigates. In folk-based systems of corporeal imagery, grotesque tropes mediate between these three terms. Admittedly, in the Bloomingdale's scenario, Miller appeals to the natural as the desirable alternative to his forced attachment to the artificial. "Man, the miserable alchemist, has welded together, in a million forms and shapes, substances and essences which have nothing in common" (*Capricorn*, 205). And it is the corporeal permeation (through the senses) of the man-made that triggers his decomposition. "The smell of linoleum, for some strange reason, will always make me fall apart and collapse on the floor. It is the smell of all the unnatural things which were glued together in me, which were assembled, so to say, by negative consent" (206). Yet there is a contrary impulse that can be traced through Miller's thirties writing. Frequently, he embraces the mingling of the mechanical and the natural and he even valorizes the heterogeneous entity one such crossing forms as the condition of his emancipation from the disciplinary thrust of capitalist industry. Miller opens up our understanding of the way the grotesque can be used to respond to the oppressive conditions of urban-industrial modernity. His aesthetic enterprise helped bring into existence a technologically mediated version of the carnivalesque.

Moreover, examining his writing will enhance our awareness of the political implications of systems of imagery that facilitate relays between humans and machines. The figurative mixing of the organic and the inorganic is a complex cultural phenomenon that may be interpreted in two opposing manners. Such strategies may sustain radical enthusiasms or they may serve conservative ends. In *Capricorn*, the tension between different ways of imagining the intimacy between bodies and machines is correlated with a distinction between work and play. Modernized recreation revitalizes or regenerates those locked in the battle against the "monstrous death machine" (289). American amusement became for Miller an affirmative life "force strong enough to whirl" him "out of this mad stone forest." Without this source of inspiration, not one page could be written that "would have meaning" (69). Constituting a kind of mechanical "lower bodily stratum" (Bakhtin), American entertainment supplied the artist with the aesthetic energies he needed to cure his historically determined ills.

SHOCK THERAPY

When I was asked later why I had killed myself I could only think to say – because I wanted to electrify the cosmos! (Miller, *Tropic of Capricorn*)

Mark Seltzer's inquiry into realist and naturalist novels at the end of the nineteenth century has powerfully and influentially broached the topic of literary preoccupations with the problem of the body in machine culture. For him, the excruciated project of turn-of-the-century American novelists was to bring bodies and machines into alignment rather than merely to degrade human corporeality to the status of a mechanized thing or simply to anthropomorphize machinery. Such intertwining of nature and technology induced an ambiguous combination of excitement and fear; it was alternately seen as desirable and distressing. And the role of writing in the nexus in question is more often than not in Seltzer's analyses complicit with the dominant discursive practices of machine culture. For him, literary undertakings tended to employ representational strategies that conformed to the imperatives of economic rationalism. For example, Stephen Crane's emphasis on the relation between seeing, vigilance, and power dovetails with the deployment of the methods of scientific management technologies in factory settings.[8] The decomposition and calibration of corporeal movements as a means of maintaining control over the work process join seamlessly with the compositional compulsion to account for persons as statistical abstractions. Visual surveillance in both functions as an instrument of social control. In sum, there is a "perfect 'fit' between technologies of writing and the body/machine complex," and it is along these systematizing lines that "writing and mechanics" communicate with each other in circular fashion.[9] The *work* of mechanized writing is to perform the discursive tasks of machine culture.

The present chapter argues that Miller adds a grotesque twist to the notion of a mechanized literary practice. Emphasizing the dimensions of unregulated play informing his performance-based autobiographical prose, I examine the analogy he establishes between technologically induced physical thrills and the shocks provocative literature generates. His carnivalized approach deviates from the logistics of machine culture without retreating into an obsolete pastoralism. Inhabiting the body/machine complex in a humorous manner, he affirms mechanically produced laughter as a force of radical liberation. The intimate coupling of nature and technology in his writing, his biomechanics, culminates in the grotesque vision of the author as a writing machine capable of channeling comically disruptive energies into mainstream society. But he can only construct himself in this manner by modeling his enterprise on an array of twentieth-century American amusements.

Surprisingly, Miller's efforts to construct a technologically mediated repertoire of carnivalesque imagery bears some resemblance to the kind of radical project influentially theorized by Donna Haraway under the aegis of the notion of the cyborg.[10] Miller too was bent on evoking, at times humorously, our current status as hybrid entities *and* on recognizing this condition as the possibly progressive basis for an improved collective future.[11] For Miller, to achieve this end we must overcome lingering fears of the machine, envisioning instead the positive implications of supplementing the body with mechanical attachments. Embracing available prostheses will alleviate mass despair and fatigue. By joining "the great circuit which flows through the subterranean vaults of the flesh" the artist will re-electrify "the creaking machinery of humanity."[12] Radical writing was to be an act of applying high-voltage wiring to readers, and if contact with this wiring was bound to hurt, enduring such pain was seen as the precondition of achieving bodily and spiritual ecstasy.[13]

Near the beginning of *Tropic of Cancer*, shortly after asserting that because the "world is rotting away, dying piecemeal," "it needs to be blown to smithereens," Miller proudly declares that he has successfully fused the human and the technological. Part organism, part apparatus, he has become "a writing machine. The last screw has been added. The thing flows. Between me and the machine there is no estrangement. I am the machine" (28). This is the entity that will help produce *The Last Book* that he has been planning to compose in collaboration with his friend Boris and publish anonymously. This book, when completed, will be a seminally explosive device, will be "a vessel in which to pour the vital fluid, a bomb which, when we throw it, will set off the world" (26). It is toward a fuller understanding of the formal and functional imperatives behind Miller's grotesque mingling of natural bodies and mechanical devices that the following section of this chapter is oriented.

Understanding modernity, as was already becoming common at the time, as the traumatic subjection of persons to an endless series of shocks, Miller commits himself in this text to counteracting the debilitating effects of his mechanized environment.[14] If the relentless buffeting and jolting of the tormented inhabitant of the modern metropolis leads to fatigue and extreme nervousness, Miller's response, metaphorically echoing the practice of nineteenth-century physicians, was to combat psychic suffering and dwindling physical energies by *painfully* shocking his audience. Observing what he took to be the spread of neurasthenia due to the assault of external forces on bodies and minds, due to mass over-stimulation, he turned (figuratively) to mechanical and electrical devices as instruments that might revitalize the weakened and dispirited.[15] The images of somatic fragmentation and gaping interiors on display in his thirties output were a constitutive aspect of his effort to heighten his audience's awareness as to the physical dangers their environment ceaselessly posed to them. It is as if he felt that society had begun to take corporeal vulnerability for granted, as if repeated subjection to the sensory onslaught of everyday life in the city had left individuals numb to the threats of their milieu. So overwhelmed that they were on the threshold of becoming automatons, his devastated readers needed to have their mental and physical suffering rendered and thus restored to consciousness.

His representational stress on the ease with which the body could be painfully mutilated and the psyche breached was intended, then, to make the capacity of one's historically specific surroundings to cause extreme injury perceptible again. The violent cruelty with which he treated his own body and the bodies of others was meant to express a collective experience, to furnish knowledge of a widespread condition of wounding. Cognitive aims motivated the grisly figurations of his confessional discourse. In addition, his emphasis on the mortification of the flesh was also driven by a therapeutic aim, his peculiar conviction that dramatic scenes of intense agony might have the effect of curing contemporary illnesses, might bring the spiritual and somatic malaise to an end. In sum, he reconceived autobiography as a kind of mechanized Theatre of Cruelty, as the cultural site at which "the endlessly renewed fatigue of the organs" would receive the "intense and sudden shocks" required in order to "revive our understanding."[16]

Two scenes taken from *Cancer* allow for a preliminary marking off of a literary undertaking worth exploring in much greater detail. In the first, he insists that a part of the body be reinserted into an overly mechanized realm of pleasure, corporeal pain proposed as a necessary prerequisite to the restoration of human passion. In the second, he appeals to obsolete forms of punishment as a public spectacle, setting the brutalized artist up by way of this analogy as a heroically masochistic figure, his self-inflicted wounds a means of saving others.[17] In both cases, then, communal regeneration follows from the exhibition of the somatically traumatized individual.

The first scene involves a liaison Miller and his friend Van Norden have with a Parisian whore. Having brought her to their apartment, the men watch "as she goes about her preparations mechanically" (*Cancer*, 142).

Then she "works" over Miller (or the narrator), presumably engaging in an act of oral copulation. As she struggles "to blow a spark of passion" (143) into him, he oddly compares their exchange to "a state of war." Once transactions between people become economic, the aggressive battle to conquer the enemy is on, "the fifteen francs" they paid the prostitute for her services "like the primal cause." Inevitably "one surrenders to the situation, one goes on butchering and butchering." Then comes "a day when the bottom drops out and suddenly all the guns are silenced and the stretcher-bearers pick up the maimed and bleeding heroes and pin medals on their chest" (142). In the end one is left a blind, mutilated torso, without "eyes or arms or legs." If commercially obtained pleasure is analogous to a military conflict that brutally dismembers the body and causes a loss of organs, paying for sex also makes it into a thoroughly mechanized process. His turn over, the curious Miller now observes with great interest as the well-trained but poorly functioning Van Norden fights to get sufficiently aroused to achieve penetration. "I'm looking at a machine whose cogs have slipped. Left to themselves, they would go on this way forever, grinding and slipping, without ever anything happening. Until a hand shuts the motor off." Physical copulation is like a war between two motorized machines. Sitting on a chair nearby "watching their movements with a cool, scientific detachment," Miller adds that it is similar to "watching one of those crazy machines which throw the newspapers out" (144). The impersonal struggle between Van Norden and the prostitute, a "performance" devoid of "human significance," is intriguing because its repetitive meaninglessness is emblematic of the print media's transformation of lived experience into an endless and efficient flow of recorded information, into a mass of facts without substance or significance. Thus the "machine seems more sensible, crazy as it is, and more fascinating to watch, than the human beings and events which produced it" (144). The best one can hope for under present circumstances is to be able to afford to buy a few prosthetic devices, "a pair of artificial lightweight limbs, aluminum preferably" (150).

This is a vision of sexual activity as a reflection of the routinized drudgery of everyday life in modernity, of the elimination of physical desire, even when engaged in erotic pursuits, due to one's adaptation to the regularized, monotonous rhythms of the work process. So powerful is the force of rationalization that leisurely fornication becomes the mirror image of rationalized labor, both boring, serialized operations devoid of human affect or purpose: automatized screwing. That Van Norden works at a newspaper (where Miller soon secures a job as a proofreader) draws the connection between the two activities. Caught up in recreational and media technologies and therefore thoroughly subjected to the mechanization of everyday life, Van Norden's lack of passion may be figured as the loss of a body. While he was asleep his "body was stolen" (145). (Previously Miller remarks that in a dream he saw Van Norden's detached penis lying on the sidewalk, "about the size of a sawed-off broomstick" [127]. In short, castration has been played for laughs.) Victim of an undesirable prosthesis, plugged into a machine that robs the individual of desire and leaves him nearly immune to physical sensation, such a deanimated person could continue (mal)functioning eternally as a lifeless thing. "If somebody doesn't turn the switch off he'll never know what it means to die; you can't die if your own proper body has been stolen" (145). The solution is to reinsert a human, somatic element into modern technology. Such an intervention, apparently the task of the autobiographical writer as "mechanic" (144), involves the irrational (albeit metaphorical) sacrifice of a body part, corporeal pain a necessary counter-force to the mechanization of pleasure. "Somebody has to put his hand into the machine and let it be wrenched off if the cogs are to mesh again" (145).

The passage is meant to register and protest against the disturbing aspects of existence in the machine age, somatic dismemberment paradoxically a consequence of and defense against the effects of industrialization. In the next scene, Miller articulates a peculiar philosophy of autobiography as a mode of literary resistance that consists of a series of torturous acts of (figurative) self-mutilation. Putting radical energies in circulation via confessional writing appears to require the author to fragment brutally his body in public.

Miller begins his euphoric discourse on aesthetic revolution by alluding to the chronic physical and mental exhaustion of those around him; then he asserts that it is necessary to bring about an emotional resurrection in these neurasthenics by showing them a human being "in the grip of delirium." Appalled by the "feeble" lifeless bodies he sees – "Are these men and women, I ask myself, or are these shadows, shadows of puppets dangled by invisible strings" (245) – he argues that somehow these "human sparks," whose pathology is similar to his own, must be energized. His own personal revitalization occurs while staring at the crotch of a trollop, her "dark, unstitched wound" opening up a "deep fissure in his brain." The collapse of his psychic system of classifications is conveyed through images of corporeal evisceration, the destruction of his "laboriously or absent-mindedly assorted, labeled, documented, filed, sealed and stamped" "images and memories" troped as the spilling out of his "guts." Confronted by the vagina, to him a materialized image of "the Absolute," from which issues a "wild, utterly uncontrollable laughter," he then reflects on the First World War, one of his main obsessions throughout the period, ironically characterizing it as an event designed "to further the cause of plastic surgery" (247). Miller identifies this "sink of abomination" as the birthplace of "a clown" who possessed the power to overcome widespread exhaustion. Were he to dive down as he wishes to into this "crack" he would hear Dostoevski's words, which tell the "story of art whose roots lie in massacre" (248).[18]

Miller then proceeds to figure confessional discourses through analogies with more public rituals of torture and execution. Limiting himself to physical terms of comparison for the act and effect of writing as the tearing open and exposure of the body and mind, he now characterizes it as a theatrical spectacle in which the artist barbarically butchers himself. The punished body displays for everyone to see the truth of the dissident writer's criminal transgressions. Corporeal mutilation, of a ruthless and atrocious sort, marks him as guilty, proving his engagement in illegal behavior. Miller admires most those who have aroused hatred and disorder, who overthrew "existing values" by willingly going "again and again to the stake and the gibbet" (252–53). He then draws upon theatricalized modes of punishing criminals (in this peculiar case an act of self-evisceration) as a literary model:

> I see that when they [his "old idols"] bellow like crazed beasts and rip and gore, I see that this is right, that there is no other path to pursue. A man who belongs to this race must stand up on the high place with gibberish in his mouth and rip out his entrails. It is right and just, because he must! And anything that falls short of this frightening spectacle, anything less shuddering, less terrifying, less mad, less intoxicated, less contaminated, is not art. (255)

When he contemplates Stavrogin (in Dostoevski's *The Possessed*) for example, it is "of some divine monster standing on a high place and flinging to us his torn bowels" that he thinks. We may locate the origins of Miller's startling reliance on a historically obsolete system of punishing malefactors as a figure for literary expression in what Foucault has called the "gallows speeches" of men before their executions. Such speeches gave birth to a "'last words of a condemned man' genre," the significance of which is that it indicates the ambiguous effects of the ritual event itself. Granting the criminal a final opportunity to accept responsibility for his illegal conduct and acknowledge the justice of his conviction had the potential to undermine rather than reinforce the power of the sovereign. Scenes of spectacular pain threatened to turn into acts of carnival dissidence. Combined with an exhibition of his ability to endure physical torture, the abominable criminal might be transformed into a glorious hero, one with whom the people readily identified in opposition to the King, the law, the wealthy, magistrates, and so forth.[19] Drawing on such a perception of the condemned as a victim of the struggle against social and political domination, Miller compares his autobiographical discourse to that of a man on the verge of death, about to be killed in public. His "back up to the wall" (*Cancer*, 98), with nothing left to lose, the writer may speak as freely as he wishes, seeking in so doing to sow strife, cause discord and rancor (252). The connotations of his predecessors' actions as illegal extend to their undisciplined infractions of formal conventions, "the monstrous styles they chose," and the morally abhorrent qualities of their disgustingly unsanitary and depraved work. All of them "mired in their own dung," the words they leave behind mark a trail of lust, crime, evil, and sorrow (252).

The force of Dostoevski's art, its capacity to "turn the world upside down" via pages that "explode," that "wound and sear," that wring "groans and tears and curses," derives in the figural logic of the passage from a technological system or apparatus. The "scorching light, the radiant light" resounding from the Russian writer's work is a result of his understanding how to make "guinea pigs squeal," of knowing "where to put the live wire of sex": "right between the legs" (249). Despite Miller's lament at our collective need to compensate for physical disabilities by attaching artificial devices to our bodies, his rhetoric is prosthetic: writing appears as a kind of literary "electrotherapy" aimed at curing modern ailments. Characterizing his potential audience as neurasthenics, Miller proposes that if they accept the submissive position in a masochistic scenario, their reward will be "ecstasy" and "joy" (252). To endure physical anguish as the author willingly does will revitalize their chronically fatigued bodies and reanimate their emotionally drained personalities. Identifying with the self of the artist will enable readers to reverse the process of spiritual and corporeal degeneration from which they have been suffering.

Fearing that his natural attributes are insufficient to bring about the sexual conflagration he desires, that he may not be able to rise to the task of scorching "the gizzards," the artist "hitches his dynamo to the tenderest parts." Hoping to end the inertia and paralysis of contemporary existence by shocking persons, the electrified writer aims to trigger a violently immediate reaction of some sort, if only to cause his readers to twitch in pain as he makes their "blood and pus gush forth" (250). The prosthetic analogy facilitates an understanding of writing as a torturous practice, the effect of which is to cause revitalizing harm to exhausted bodies. To bring thrills, excitement, and intoxication back into the world the writer must sing "with burning sparks" (251). Previously "a zero," dizzied by "the fizzing lights," "chewed to a frazzle by the spiked mouth of the machines," dwarfed by the skyscrapers in which "the lights shoot up between the ribs of the skeletons like rockets," Miller finally found literary self-expression as an energized form of "emotional release." Writing, as the application of high-voltage wires to persons, produces the requisite charge such that the "dead may be restored to life" (253), "body and soul" resuscitated (257). When Miller proudly declares that he is *"inhuman,"* he means to say that he has returned to nature, that he no longer has anything "to do with the creaking machinery of humanity" and now belongs "to the earth" (254). Yet his tropes suggest otherwise, for to generate "natural fury" it is necessary to rely on scientific invention, or rather, to attach technological devices to human sex organs: "Let us have a world of men and women with dynamos between their legs" (257).[20]

The motive behind Miller's somewhat perverse affirmation of a highly charged sadomasochistic aesthetic is that social redemption will follow from extremely painful corporeal experiences. He reconceives the literary text as a thermodynamic machine that puts energy to use in acts of extreme cruelty. Writing is figured as the application of an electrical current to the flesh of fatigued persons. But where does the artist as therapist find his energy supply? What source does he draw upon to power the instrument of his audience's salvation?

The virtue of *Black Spring* (1936), the collection of short pieces Miller published between *Cancer* and *Capricorn*, is that it clarifies the vital importance to him of an assortment of American amusements. Complicating without eradicating his claim to be part of a lineage that stretches back through Dostoevski, Whitman, Shakespeare, and Dante to "the mythological founders of the race" (*Cancer*, 255–56), Miller's reliance on city-based forms of entertainment has been insufficiently recognized. Modern recreations like the Bowery dime museum, Coney Island amusement parks, burlesque, and vaudeville served as the cultural touchstones of his comically aggressive endeavor.[21] Recollecting the communal pleasures he enjoyed in the United States before leaving the country, Miller took these, as Dahlberg did before him, as models for his aesthetic enterprise. But in contrast to Dahlberg, whose ambitions remained expressive or representational, Miller's interest in non-literary influences led to the incorporation of more performance-based priorities in his autobiographical project.

BURLESK DREAMS

We wait that writhing pool, her pearls collapsed,
– All but her belly buried in the floor;
And the lewd trounce of a final muted beat!
We flee her spasm through a fleshless door . . . .

Yet, to the empty trapeze of your flesh,
O Magdalene, each comes back to die alone.
Then you, the burlesque of our lust – and faith,
Lug us back lifeward – bone by infant bone.

Hart Crane, "National Winter Garden"[22]

Yes sir, *laughter.* A new and vitalizing dimension for me. I could easily have ended up a neurotic like most youngsters today. Thanks to the filth, the vulgarity, and the humor of the burlesk I was saved. (Henry Miller, *From Your Capricorn Friend*)

The epigraph above taken from Hart Crane's *The Bridge* suggests a still inadequately appreciated reliance within avant-garde American literature on "low," sensationalized genres of cultural entertainment.[23] For Crane, burlesque – generally considered a vulgar amusement – possesses redemptive potential, the shame it induces notwithstanding. Though the embarrassed spectator takes flight while observing the female performer's crude display of corporeal ecstasy, sexual and spiritual desire drive him to return to this fascinating scene. The religious allusion invests this "degraded" cultural practice, organized around the exposed woman's body, with a capacity for salvation that may reach beyond the individual and achieve a collective function ("us"). Drawn toward the disturbing sphere of the grotesque body, the "belly," the audience is shattered and reconstituted, the negative experience of death (and apparently physical fragmentation) the prerequisite for a positive resurrection, a physical rebirth. The indispensable outcome of the repulsive and attractive performance is to "Lug us back lifeward – bone by infant bone."

Crane's lyric, in that it discloses that burlesque excited formally inventive writers and evoked desirable social functions, puts us on track to answer the question one of Miller's exegetes has posed: "the source of his [Miller's] strength – where does it come from and how does he retain it?"[24] Once we realize the degree to which the lines of communication

ESM

between avant-garde writing and American *amuse*ment remained open throughout the Depression, it becomes clearer that "the birth of artistic perception"[25] in Miller's case had its genesis in his youthful experience of modern recreations. If registering the political significance of the aesthetically invigorating exchange between popular entertainment and autobiographical literature is the primary aim of the present chapter, *Black Spring*, Miller's second book-length publication of the thirties, is a valuable object of inquiry.

Despite its loosely autobiographical frame, *Black Spring* owes formal and thematic debts to the *variety format* utilized by a range of commercial amusements thriving at the turn of the century. Miller's compositional model for putting together the collection of ten diverse pieces of varying lengths was the structural organization of the type of show eventually codified by vaudeville but also a distinguishing characteristic of early burlesque. His rapid, discontinuous stringing together of an assemblage of heterogeneous selections that feature the use of an assortment of genres and expressive styles, in which the moods shift repeatedly, derives from the succession of acts presented in the kinds of American entertainment he greatly admired. The mixed program of such shows would typically include among other things animal acts, theatrical pieces, ventriloquists, minstrel performers, comedians, singers and dancers, perhaps a pornographic display, magicians, wrestlers, and acrobats, and contortionists. Appropriately a freakish version of the latter pops up unexpectedly in "Into the Night Life . . . " the seventh selection in *Black Spring*. Possessed of "a furry little head with frank doglike eyes," this female performer, "nude as a berry," "commences her trapezoid flights," rolling "herself into a ball, her head tucked between her breasts, her arms pinned to her crotch."[26] "Into the Night Life" is preceded by the wildly manic "Jabberwhorl Cronstadt," Miller's recollection of an absurd visit to a friend, a kind of dadaist poet who passes out dead drunk immediately after composing a poetic tribute to his kitchen sink and its two faucets, "Chaud" and "Froid." If the verbal silliness and extravagantly humorous behavior in this piece resemble a staged, comic routine, the hallucinatory, phantasmagoric dream imagery in what comes next ("Into the Night Life . . . ") parallels the effect of a magic lantern show, the projection of which was not uncommon in early twentieth-century variety shows.

Black Spring is profitably understood, then, as an attempt to reproduce in literature the arousing type of spectacle such shows constituted. Its aesthetic aim is to generate sensory excess, to assault the reader – thus positioned as the patron of a theatrical extravaganza – with a ceaseless barrage of astonishing acts. Rather than tell a story, Miller's priorities are non-narrative. He wants to surprise by showing his audience a diverting and dizzying array of performances. He does not seek to sustain the illusion of a self-contained fictional world that solicits spectator identification; instead he keeps the reader off-balance, disoriented. In sum, Miller adopts the variety show emphasis on exhibition, on confrontational self-display, publicly exposing himself in a decidedly indecent, albeit titillating manner. What good taste would require be disclosed only in private, Miller staged in the hope of being amusingly offensive. The therapeutic aspects of such an endeavor derive from its confrontational repudiation of the increasingly regimented mode of existence that the subjects of urban-industrial modernity must endure. Recreationally generated shocks were to function as a cure for the traumatized victims of life in the machine age.

In that it pays a great deal of explicit attention to an array of American amusements, *Black Spring* marks a turning point in his Depression-era enterprise, for it is in this text that the cultural determinations of his project first become evident. Paving the way for *Tropic of Capricorn*, where the vision of life depicted is profoundly refracted through a vaudeville lens, the transitional text in effect brings to the surface what the preceding work, *Tropic of Cancer*, had kept buried: the artist's profound dependence on non-textual modes of collective play. In other words, it is by reading *Black Spring* that the degree to which Miller's radical enterprise was mediated by his fascination with popular amusement becomes fully apparent.[27]

In "The Fourteenth Ward," the autobiographical reminiscence that opens *Black Spring*, Miller connects the awe and wonder he felt as a child to his existence in a recreational space. Mourning the loss of the community into which he was born, the speaker in this elegy remembers his old Brooklyn neighborhood as a sheltered, self-enclosed environment where individuals were licensed to indulge in unruly, delightful behavior without external interference. In the "post-mechanical open street where the most beautiful and hallucinating iron vegetation" grew, he and his comrades "were free, wild, murderous" (3–4). Whatever was occurring elsewhere in the United States, those dwelling inside the fourteenth ward at the turn of the century had been allotted "peace and contentment." For their daily pleasures there "was the saloon, the race track, bicycles, fast women and trot horses. Life was still moving leisurely" (5). Everyone congregated at the Bum – a local burlesque house, just "a stone's throw away" – to "watch the goings-on over the saloon across the street," where no one bothered to pull down the shades in the bedroom. In this room men could be seen pulling their pants down and women yanking off their corsets, while "down below they were scuttling the suds and biting each other's ears off," "such a wild, shrill laughter bottled up inside there, like dynamite evaporating." Though very young, Miller was securely ensconced in this informal world of festive excess, even performing as a piano player before his feet could reach the pedals at a saloon across the river where everything "was sheer lunacy" (8).

Lamenting a forced exile from his "native soil," when at the age of ten he and his family moved out of the neighborhood, Miller imagines the past as an emotionally fulfilling stage in which the self was fully integrated into society. The severing of ties thus threw him into an emotional disarray that continued through the "great fragmentation of maturity" (10), his progressive loss of psychic wholeness figured as usual in imagery of physical collapse whereby all his "parts" end up "separated by thinnest membrane" (12). His impression of wholeness as a youth was due to his happy immersion in a collective unit. Surrounded by "gorgeous unknown bodies," the jubilant child felt invulnerable, the world penetrating him "through and through" without doing permanent damage to his identity. However, once this social body is "buried" in the historical past, external reality tears the fragile individual to pieces: the "light devouring the innards, the sides of flesh bursting, the spears pressing in against the cartilage, the very armature of the body floating off into nothingness" (13). Due to temporal change, the spiritually expatriated speaker is left only with the memory of a communal existence. The exclusive survival of such pleasurable experiences "in the plasm of the dream" marks "the pain of separation" (12). Dreams in this sense are identical to memories of early experiences, which may in turn be called up as a form of judgment on a disenchanted, rationalized society that denies the shattered individual the opportunity to enjoy a vibrantly carefree, recreational life. Yet "Fourteenth Ward" is also modeled on the dream in the more psychoanalytic sense of the term. This is to say the piece contains a good deal of confusing imagery the implications of which require interpretive deciphering.

Though the speaker suggests the neighborhood as an area protected from economic and political concerns, the contents of his recollection contradict this impression. Ominous signs of war are visible on the horizon in the form of "steel-gray battleships in the Navy Yard," images that come back to Miller whenever he returns to the days of his youth "as a paranoiac returns to his obsessions" (5). The full significance of the "luxurious weight" these "sea monsters" place on Miller as he grows up will not be made apparent until much later in *Black Spring* when the First World War surges up as one of the devastating, traumatic events of his life. Only then will the fate of Rob Ramsay, who came back from the war heavily decorated and promptly committed suicide by walking off a pier, resonate as a social calamity. But the effect of the stylized visual details is already to register the early twentieth-century transformation of the United States into an imperialist force. Nor is evidence of labor lacking in the recollection. Though the tone of the reminiscence continues to be lyrical, after remarking for the first time on the battleships, Miller admits that he remembers, "with a vividness as if it were etched in acid," hellish scenes of work. He recalls "the grim, soot-covered walls and chimneys of the tin factory opposite us and the bright circular pieces of tin that were strewn in the street . . . the ironworks where the red furnace glowed and men walked toward the glowing pit with huge shovels in their hands, while outside were the shallow wooden forms like coffins with rods through them on which you scraped your shins or broke your neck . . . the black hands of the ironmolders, the grit that had sunk so deep into the skin that nothing could remove it." These men walked "into the furnace like devils with black hands" (5).

   This image of work is seemingly cancelled by the conclusion of "Fourteenth Ward," where Miller conflates his awe-struck exposure to Jonathan Swift with the boarding of a scenic railway at a local amusement park. This distorted composite image is preceded by his first encounter with Dostoevski, an overwhelming experience that Miller figures in typically grotesque manner as the tearing off of flesh and melting of "the very skeleton of the body," as if it were "wax" (14). This scene anticipates the next one in that the sound of the Russian writer's name generates "a chewing and grinding noise," which oddly brings to mind the ideas of wire mannikins "chewing each other alive" (15). The subsequent fusion of Swift with a Coney Island ride develops this imagery provocatively. The condensation of the writer with a mechanized amusement establishes Miller's aesthetic fascination with preceding forms of American entertainment as well as to surrealist (using the term loosely) art.[28] However, the connection also evokes the danger he detects in mechanized fairground attractions as surreptitious components of a totalized system of modern rationalization. Standing at the Dragon's Gorge (a ride at Luna Park) Miller simultaneously arrives at "the land of the Houyhnhnms." Beckoned toward this foreign realm by a man standing overhead "with a rattan stick," the boy is mentally overwhelmed, his psyche torn open to his surroundings. Miller materializes the experience in the form of a sexualized and internalized trope of corporeal destruction: "as if my brain were a uterus, the walls of the world gave way" (15).

The hallucinatory condensation of Swift and the Dragon's Gorge is logically intelligible as a result of their shared ability to evoke travel to exotic lands as a delightfully magical experience. Here initiation into the mysterious world of the other appears as a delightful devouring:

Overhead the green fire-eater, his delicate intestines wrapped in tarpaulin; two enormous milk-white teeth champing down over a belt of black-greased cogs connecting with the shooting gallery and the Turkish Baths; the belt of cogs slipping over a frame of bleached bones. The green dragon of Swift moves over the cogs with an endless pissing sound, grinding down fine and foreshortened the human-sized midgets that are sucked in like macaroni. In and out of the esophagus, up and down and around the scapular bones and the mastoid delta, falling through the bottomless pit of the viscera, gurgitating and exgurgitating, the crotch spreading and slipping, the cogs moving on relentlessly, chewing alive all the fine foreshortened macaroni hanging by the whiskers from the dragon's red gulch. I look into the milk-white smile of the barker, that fanatical Arabian smile which came out of the Dreamland fire, and then I step quietly into the open belly of the dragon. (15–16)[29]

The placement of the scene at the end of the collection's opening piece allows it to resonate reflexively as a call to the reader to enter further into the deliriously phantasmagoric text, which promises to be a Dreamland. Metaphorically equated with a scenic railway, avant-garde autobiography is to serve as a viable substitute for or prolongation of the intensities of mass fun. We are encouraged to submit ourselves to being torn apart, dismembered and consumed by the artwork conceived of as a grotesquely monstrous amusement. The masochistic appeal of the attraction is that when released one will find oneself transformed. Entry into the mouth of the mechanized dragon will lead by way of the multitude of visual stimuli the literary fairground furnishes to a marvelous change in existence. Being ground to pieces by an engulfing technological apparatus is the precondition for an emotional rebirth. The painful yet wondrous experience of riding the scenic railway is a metaphor for the joys Miller associates with the experience of reading.

Yet the valorization of the intense pleasures and pains of what I call the technocarnivalesque is belied by the possibility of reading this scene as a displaced reflection on the spread of the effects of industrialization from the realm of labor to the sphere of leisure. A desirable alternative to a mundane present, mechanized entertainment may also function as an instrument of subordination. This more ominous interpretive perspective indicates Miller's uncertainty as to whether American amusements were truly as spiritually liberating as he recalls.

The resemblance of the dragon's mouth to the tin factory furnace the ironmolders walk into prompts this latter point of view. Interest in the parallels between unskilled work and play in industrialized settings goes back in critical theory to Benjamin's work on Baudelaire in the thirties. More recent developments in this area of inquiry have continued to explore the ways in which the rhythms of technological play, the thrills it provides notwithstanding, replicate the rhythms of monotonously routine forms of work, investigating the atomizing effect both processes have on the individual's physical movements and sensory apparatus. Just as he is subordinated in the factory to the repetitive jolts of the assembly line, the constrained worker is rendered a passive appendage to the pleasure machine during what it thus becomes inappropriate to call his or her free time. The predicament of the worker in the age of mechanized entertainment is that the amusements he enjoys drill his body and mind, facilitating his synchronization to the devices he operates on the job. Under the aegis of recreation he continues to train to become an efficient and obedient part of a rationalized industrialized system, the segmented excitements in one preparing him for the numbingly chopped-up movements required for him to perform his duty in the other.

Miller's variation on this theme in the above passage is to imply that the pleasure industry reproduces persons as inanimate things. In that the riders move along "a belt of black-greased cogs" they resemble objects in the serial process of being constructed: they appear like commodities in the making. Consumed, ground down by the mechanical dragon, they are subsequently transformed into something different, into made artifacts. In the process of passing from the shooting gallery to the Turkish Baths and then into and through the digestive tract of the monster they become the manufactured product of a technological marvel. The function of recreation is in a sense to work on laborers. Most intriguingly, literature does not escape this (implicit) critique since the child about to ride the attractions is also the child about to become a reader of the grotesque imagery of the author of *Gulliver's Travels*.

One might say that exposure to new technologies of entertainment sparked Miller (and a few of his contemporaries) to rethink literature as itself a mechanized activity. But for Miller, the mechanization of literature did not necessarily entail that it would be assimilated to the disciplinary construction of individuals within machine culture. On the contrary, his turn toward technologically mediated forms of entertainment furnished him with a basis to develop an aesthetic practice that would resist the systematic manufacturing of docile persons. Thus, the energy his auto-biographical writing derived from the kind of attractions one might have enjoyed at Coney Island around the turn of the century supported a cultural endeavor designed to alter the functioning of the thoroughly mechanized subjects of urban-industrial modernity. This subject, the man of today as expertly built automaton whose behavior may be schematically planned, is characterized in "Megalopolitan Maniac," the finale of *Black Spring.* "The gymnasiums are open and one can see the new men made of stovepipes and cylinders moving according to chart and diagram. The new men will never wear out because the parts can always be replaced. New men without eyes, nose, ears or mouth, men with ball bearings in their joints and skates on their feet. Men immune to riots and revolutions" (239). The bodily organs and limbs of man in the twentieth century had been removed. "Look, there he is rolling along on his little sledge, his legs amputated, his eyes blown out" (239). In compensation for his lost natural parts, he has been hooked into society via new business and entertainment technologies. The spine of the "lonely man of the city surrounded by his inventions" rattles "with death telegraphs the song of love through all the neurones and from every shop on Broadway the radio answers with megaphone and pick-up, with amplifiers and hook-ups" (238). America is a "perpetual séance with megaphones and ticker tape, men with no arms dictating to wax cylinders" (239). The mechanized modes of collective play he recalled from his childhood held, for Miller, the potential to invigorate aesthetically an autobiographical literary practice which might in turn revive or regenerate technological man, emancipating him from the coercive rattle of the "death telegraphs."

Miller's ambivalence toward American amusement, his uncertainty of its redemptive power, again becomes evident as the speaker agonizes over the lingering, psychic residues of Coney Island. Whereas in the earlier piece the emphasis is on the capacity of the amusement park to provide great excitement, to be astonishing, "Into the Night Life . . . ," a surreal experiment in dream imitation (and to my mind a not entirely successful one), expresses a disgust with the locale. The internalization of the fairground repulses the subject. Within this "Coney Island of the mind . . . [e]verything is sordid, shoddy, thin as pasteboard." Artifice, the inauthentic, cheap materials and tools, rules in this "nuts and bolts" horrifying world "erected by a gang of carpenters during the night. Everything is a lie, a fake . . . The monarch of the mind is a monkey wrench. Sovereign pasteboard power" (160). Modernized public amusement now marks the disorientation and confusion of the henceforth densely populated, inauthentic mind. The pleasure industry's unhygienic colonization of the psyche fills it with disease ("catarrh, diabetes, whooping cough, meningitis"), knocks it dizzyingly off kilter (everything "slides, rolls, tumbles, spins, shoots, teeters, sways"), and brings it into distressful contact with other ethnic groups ("Greasy Japs," "Armenians," "Macedonians," and "Jews").

Yet his mixed feelings in regard to modern recreations notwithstanding, Miller still relied heavily on these throughout the Depression era. Nowhere is this reliance more revealingly disclosed than in the penultimate piece of the book: "Burlesk." At the same historical moment that burlesque was being stamped out in New York, Miller was assimilating elements of it into his prose endeavors.[30] Specifically, the strip show emerges as an analogy that, in retrospect, has governed in its entirety this psychoanalytically inflected installment of his autobiographical enterprise. Engaging in a kind of cultural transvestitism, Miller relocates the strip show inside the psyche, staging his humorous writing as a sequence of defiantly crude gestures of self-exposure, as a form of uninhibited mental exhibitionism. What is put on display are his uncensored thoughts and feelings, private ideas and emotions made public in what may be considered acts of cross-undressing. What holds the literary and the theatrical practice together is that both may be considered comic actions whereby individuals brazenly display what respectable society insists be kept concealed. It is then from the point of view of American burlesque, a form of entertainment initially dominated by assertive, unruly women, that light can be shed on the extent to which Miller's writing puts in question the line conventionally drawn between male and female artists.

As Robert Allen has pointed out, runway stripping did not become a central feature of burlesque until the 1920s. From its inception in this country in the late 1860s to the 1930s, American burlesque was a carnivalized cultural practice that, like vaudeville, incorporated theatrical farces, musical comedy, monologues, and numerous specialty acts and erotically seductive dances into its show.[31] Burlesque also stands as one of the country's most feminized forms of entertainment, consistently raising the issue of how femininity is to be represented on stage and in society.

Burlesque's treatment of this issue initially took shape as a comic rejection of characterizations of women as demure and retiring. Verbally abrasive, addressing challenges to the male spectator in the form of wisecracks and insults, and physically confrontational, winking, and blatantly flaunting their bodies, the original burlesque performers were

sexually charismatic women who resisted objectification. Though furnishing scopic pleasure to men, they made the specular relationship
between (male) audience member and (female) performer a volatile exchange in which there was no telling who would gain the upper hand.
However, in the latter decades of the nineteenth century a division of
cultural labor began to set in. Male comics take over the joking and
witty repartee and women ceased to be an unruly presence in the show.
The exclusive function of the muted female performer was to arouse and
entice male patrons. So rare had it become by the twentieth century for
a woman to speak on stage during a burlesque show that a phrase, the
"talking woman," had to be coined for a singular exception to the rule
of female silence (Allen, *Horrible Prettiness*, 236–42).

Insofar as it occurs at the expense of the actual female performers,
Miller's appropriation of elements of burlesque participates in their displacement from the cultural arena. By adopting both the exhibitionism
and the humor of the female burlesque performer, his prose helps remove her from a comic tradition inaugurated in this country by women.
Whereas Lydia Thompson and her troupe combined bodily display and
clownish theatrics in a female-centered cultural practice, Miller resitu-
ates such aspects of burlesque performance in the literary domain of male
artistry. With this in mind his odd predilection for grotesque inversions
whereby he locates the voice in the vagina amounts to an admittedly
bizarre return of the repressed. I am thinking in particular of the "Land
of Fuck" interlude in *Capricorn*. After commenting on a "deaf-mute"
(*Capricorn*, 183) whom he manipulates for his own sexual pleasure, Miller
takes up Evelyn's "laughing cunt," and here "the phallic" Miller seems
to have met his match. With her vagina "she put on a ventriloqual act"
that "could break down the most 'personal' hard-on in the world. Break
it down with laughter" (189). Claiming to be less humiliated by the experience than one would anticipate, Miller goes on in typically hyperbolic
fashion to invest this portion of the female anatomy with the subversive
force of a carnivalized destruction of religious and philosophical seri-
ousness. It generates "a bright, dewy, vaginal laughter such as Jesus H.
Christ and Immanuel Pussyfoot Kant never dreamed of, because if they
had the world would not be what it is today and besides there would
have been no Kant and no Christ Almighty. The female seldom laughs,
but when she does it's volcanic" (189).

Although such a presentation of the unruly female performer reduces
her to a mere body part and constrains her to an appearance on the page
as opposed to the American stage, it is also a trace of Miller's debt

to entertainment. Secreted within Miller's obscene portrait is a faint allusion to the tradition of the female carnival-grotesque in this country. His interest in the burlesque may fail to register explicitly the socially-determined elimination of women as the driving force behind an obstreperously humorous theatrical practice that challenged prevailing gender codes. Yet this interest complicates conventional characterizations of him as the most masculinist of American writers. For in a sense the clownish persona he constructs in his autobiographies in order to make a socially offensive spectacle of himself was originally female. Undoubtedly he was only partially aware of the transgressive implications of his aesthetic dependence on the grotesque performances of female comics. Still his declaration of hermaphroditism at the end of *Capricorn* – "Henceforth I take on two sexes," he shall be "double-sexed" (347–48) – is ludicrously apt, suggesting the historical debt his cultural undertaking owes to the female performer.[32] (The assertion also evinces his willingness to occupy the cultural position marked out for the human oddity or freak.)

At any rate, Miller's engagement with burlesque goes back at least to his initial attempts to become a published writer. In the mid twenties he informed friends that the *Menorah Journal* had assigned him to do an article on "Houston St. Burlesque" and a follow-up on the "Night Life of Second Avenue." Neither piece ever appeared in print. A 1934 letter to his friend Emil Schnellock identifies the form of entertainment as a valuable resource to him as an artist. A return to New York would help him and his then current book-project (*Capricorn*) if he could take just "a peek at Wilson's joint, at the Palace, at the Roseland, at Minsky's." However brief, a visit to a show would revitalize him, renewing "all those old nerve centers which are withering slowly."[33]

As Jay Martin has pointed out, Miller's fascination with dreams peaked in the early thirties. Encouraged by Anaïs Nin, who had recently undergone analysis with Otto Rank, Miller began to record his own dreams, eventually typing these up and binding them together to form his "Dream Book," a copy of which he gave to Nin in late 1933. Like the articles on burlesque, the "Dream Book" was never published, but it "was to cast its glow over his writing until the end of the thirties."[34] These two interests come together most visibly in "Burlesk," the form of entertainment and the psychic phenomenon combined here as potentially equivalent vehicles of relief for the distressed individual. Though often vilified as tasteless, coarse, and even criminally deviant, burlesque was from Miller's point of view invaluable due to its potential to release inhibitions. Possessed of the capacity to eradicate socially imposed repression, burlesque functioned as a means of personal and collective salvation.

Although the discontinuous piece opens in the present at a Parisian bar, the setting quickly shifts to the past and to New York. Recalling an evening out on the town after work, Miller's first, random stop this night is a storefront church, where he observes the energetic performance of the preacher in front of his congregation with a mixture of admiration and amusement. He then takes a taxi to the National Winter Garden, where the acts that pass before his eyes include the Oberammergau Players, chow dogs, bathing beauties, and Cleo (one of his favorite dancers). Here he is in heaven, his "soul is at peace" (*Black Spring*, 220). The juxtaposition obviously attributes to the burlesque show an effect analogous to that of the religious performance, both ways of easing the mind of the troubled individual living in a fallen world. Yet at the end of the piece, as Miller returns to one of his principal themes throughout the thirties, the book he plans to compose, burlesque unexpectedly emerges as a reflexive metaphor for the comic autobiography we have been reading and that is nearing completion. One detail of his outlandish description of the frontispiece of this book, which he intends to title *A Prolegomenon to the Unconscious*, is especially pertinent, closing the gap between psychoanalysis (and perhaps surrealist art) and burlesque. Miller declares that on this page there will be an illustration of the miniaturized writer as a dancer on the stage of his grotesquely large brain; it will be "a self-portrait called 'Praxus' showing the author standing on the frontier of the middle brain in a pair of tights." Dressed in the same outfit as the stripper mentioned earlier in *Black Spring* ("Margie Pennetti is standing on the runway in a pair of dirty white *tights*" [122]), the writer appears to be comparing himself to a female performer in a burlesque show. In the subsequent explanation of the method he will employ in this at the time hypothetical book, Miller's peculiar, intrauterine imagery implies further that disrobing on stage and self-analysis through dream interpretation have much in common. "By means of the dream technique he [the author] peels off the outer layers of his geologic mortality and comes to grips with his true mantic self, a non-stratified area of semi-liquid character. Only the amorphous side of his nature now possesses validity. By submerging the visible I he dives below the threshold of his schizophrenic habit patterns. He swims joyously, ad lib., in the amniotic fluid, one with his amoebic self" (230–31). The apparently achieved goal of the autobiographical discourse in this instance would thus be to facilitate a return to the womb, to get back to an embryonic state before the traumas of birth. The appeal of this regressive process is to a condition of biological dependency in which the organism is absolutely free of all social constraints.

Next, Miller takes the stripping metaphor to a grotesquely anatomical extreme, troping the presentation of the submerged, unconscious contents of his mind as the shedding of light on one's internal organs. After the book he anticipates composing is done, the "body will shed its skins and the organs of man will hold themselves proudly in the light." And as the dawn breaks "over the viscera" there "will be a new heaven and a new earth" (233).[35] Such acts of corporeal disfiguration, of self-mutilation, are a somatically intensified version of the reflexive use of burlesque as a figure for literary acts of self-display: writing remains the making visible of what the embodied subject usually keeps under wraps. It is in keeping with this logic that throughout *Black Spring* Miller continually discloses embarrassing personal and family secrets. The shameful incidents he recounts include the time his father took his best (male) friend to bed in a drunken haze (120) as well as the events surrounding the incarceration of Miller's aunt in an insane asylum. And he even confesses that he was too lazy to deposit at the cemetery the stillbirths entrusted to him by a local mortician; instead Miller tossed some overboard while riding the ferry and others down the sewer (227).

Notably, in this piece too, despite its point of departure in the natural female body, Miller again confronts the mechanization of the human within urban-industrial modernity. Playing out across the terrain of American entertainment anxieties pertinent to other areas of daily life in the machine age, Miller continues his interrogation of the vexing intimacy of the natural and the technological in one of the most thoroughly embodied forms of American amusement.

Initially, he conjoins the natural bodies and technological instruments by repeatedly associating burlesque with a modernized form of state execution: Cleo (a burlesque dancer)[36] is said to be the "queen of the electric chair" (222). The bizarre figure (Cleo as instrument of destruction) suggests the degree to which the feminine and the technological provoke both fear and desire. The power of these two "others" to cause excruciating pain, to punish, is as frightening as it is delightful.[37] The excessive charge of intensely exciting, sped-up attractions has a potentially damaging impact on the body. The accelerated onslaught of sensory stimulation may prove exhausting and difficult to assimilate. Consequently one may begin to lose all corporeal feeling. Miller registers this numbing effect by punning repeatedly on contemporaneous amusement as an "anesthetic." A necessary compensation for the dull monotony of rationalized forms of labor, a way to inject some vitality back into the worn-out, fatigued body of the worker, the thrilling assaults and intense shocks of contemporaneous recreation can do as much harm as good. Attending an upbeat and ongoing performance may be invigorating and may help alleviate alienation. Yet it can have the opposite effect on the patron, furthering perceptual loss and emotional detachment, leaving the forlorn city dweller in a state of "heartbreaking loneliness," confronted by "the void" in which there is a "lack of color," and "the absence of music." Consequently, American daily life as such can be conceived along burlesque lines as a "continuous performance from morn till midnight. The fastest, cleanest show on earth. So fast, so clean, it makes you desperate and lonely" (224). Despite the ardent intensity of his devotion to American amusement, Miller remains aware that on some levels it is as much the mirror image as it is an alternative to the hectic arduousness of American labor. In this country, "One is always falling to sleep with the fast pace" of mechanized work and mechanized play (225).

The ambiguous effects of modernized entertainment aside, "Burlesk" in particular and *Black Spring* in general clarify that the cultural impetus behind Miller's autobiographical endeavor was his impassioned memories of turn-of-the-century American amusement. He ambitiously struggled in the thirties to invent a radicalized writing practice that would match the sensory force of such amusements (which in turn rooted his intervention in communities existing on the fringes of mainstream society, the unorthodox behavior and eccentric attitudes of marginal people serving as his [a]moral point of reference). Moreover, the presentation of *Black Spring* as if it were the transcription of a dream suggests that Miller had to excavate his cultural heritage from his unconscious. The text is in other words structured as if it were an involuntary act of recovery, as if it were itself enacting the retrieval of buried psychic contents. From this point of view, the following scene, placed near the end of "Walking Up and Down in China," itself a late installment in the text, has the (reflexive) status of an inscribed, miniature version of the textual process as a whole.

Sitting in a bistro, Miller hears the stock report coming from a radio in the railway station across the street. Listening to this invisible machine in which the voice of a man "is hidden," he suddenly experiences a flood of memories, many of which refer back to the forms of entertainment he adored in his youth. What we may call, following Brown, the contents of the author's "material unconscious" finally come flowing back into consciousness. "Like a geyser spurting forth from the bare earth the whole American scene gushes up" (*Black Spring*, 203–05). Miller mentions, among many other things and persons, comic strip characters (Krazy Kat, the Yellow Kid, Little Nemo, the Katzenjammer Kids, the Hallroom Boys, Gloomy Gus, Foxy Grandpa), early film stars (Theda Bara, Sid Olcott, Nell Brinkley, Fatty Arbuckle, Lillian Russell), vaudeville performers (Pat Rooney, Elsie Janis, George M. Cohan), entertainment entrepreneurs (P.T. Barnum, George C. Tilyou), a dime museum (Hubert's Museum [sic]), Coney Island amusement parks (Luna Park, Dreamland) and an early tabloid newspaper (the *Police Gazette*). It is as if the buried source of the aesthetic energies driving *Tropic of Cancer* has at last become fully apparent.

The additional significance of Miller's explicit marking of his deep investment in cultural artifacts and institutions is that it in effect opens up psychoanalytically oriented inquiries into the forces behind literary enterprises to social and cultural matters that strict reliance on oedipal paradigms foreclose. Rather than affirm the reduction of unconscious desires to the structures of a family romance, Miller's technique demonstrates the complex entanglement of these desires with historically specific modes of recreation.

The opening up of the possibility of a materialist psychiatry (defined as the introduction of desire into the mechanism and the introduction of production into desire) goes back to Gilles Deleuze and Felix Guattari's *Anti-Oedipus: Capitalism and Schizophrenia*.[38] And it is therefore entirely appropriate that in their inquiry they repeatedly identify Miller as one of their crucial precursors in this regard. Most notably, just before citing a lengthy passage from his *Hamlet* (1939), a passage in which they claim "everything is said," they praise Miller's (and D.H. Lawrence's) resistance to the capture of sexuality by representational forms. "Why were expressive forms and a whole *theater* installed there where there were fields, workshops, factories, units of production? The psychoanalyst parks his circus in the dumbfounded unconscious, a real P.T. Barnum in the fields and in the factory."[39] For them, according interpretive primacy to mythic and tragic representations obscures the productive force of desiring machines and therefore veils libidinal investments in the social field, and the tendency toward such masking is precisely what they claim Miller has "to say against psychoanalysis."

Nevertheless, it is perhaps beginning to be evident – and this is the virtue of *Black Spring* – that there is some myopia in the point of view Deleuze and Guattari adopt. For their critical focus on labor, on industrialized production, as the core of an existence in which the primary agents are desiring machines prevents them from registering the *recreational* use Miller made of American amusements. His enthusiasm for a performance-based entertainment like burlesque and for Coney Island attractions enabled him to generate a carnivalized aesthetic capable of functioning as an anarchic mode of social protest. Technologically mediated play thus emerges in his writing as the basis of a grotesque literary practice that has the potential to facilitate the rewarding release of unconscious forces. Autobiography in turn becomes less a representational endeavor that diminishes the force of radical desire than a conduit through which comically charged energies are transferred from alternative sources of power to shocked readers.

The story that he tells in *Capricorn* is the story of how he eventually came to realize his aims in life, of how he came to conceive of himself as "a monster who belongs to a new reality which does not exist yet" (225).

A VAUDEVILLE MONSTROSITY

I began to feel a genuine attachment toward the machine [a typewriter], and loved it. (William Saroyan, "Myself Upon the Earth")

All the fierceness [of my body] has become transformed into *laughter*. It still looks like a visi-goth fighting machine, but it is in reality a *laughing* machine. (Wyndham Lewis, "The Soldier of Humor," *The Wild Body*)

Early in the opening chapter of *Cancer*, and thus at the beginning of his Depression-era output, Miller draws a bizarre portrait of one of his friends, whom he refers to here as Moldorf. The image this individual first presents is of a "caricature of a man." He has "thyroid eyes," "michelin lips," a "voice like pea soup," "carries a little pear" under his vest, and "fermented so long now that he is amorphous" (*Cancer*, 8). "His dilemma is that of the dwarf." He envisions himself as a roaring giant while others find him to be tiny and quiet. "With his pineal eye he sees his silhouette projected on a screen of incommensurable size, His voice, synchronized to the shadow of a pinhead, intoxicates him. He hears a roar where others hear only a squeak." In regard to his subjectivity, he is ceaselessly reinventing himself; in regard to his appearance, he is constantly metamorphosing. Possessed of a repertoire of different identities, he wounds the numbed persons who observe his explosive and expansive performances.

There is his mind. It is an amphitheater in which the actor gives a protean performance. Moldorf, multiform and unerring, goes through his roles – clown, juggler, contortionist, priest, lecher, mountebank. The amphitheater is too small. He puts dynamite to it. The audience is drugged. He scotches it. (8)

There is something oddly divine about the gruesome entity Miller is attempting in vain to evoke. "It is like trying to approach God, for Moldorf *is* God." Yet this sacred being is also a subversive rebel in relation to conventional society. When he speaks, it is the name of a utopian faith in freedom from the current order of the world: "The word in your mouth is anarchy. Say it" (10).

Though Miller mocks and disparages his friend, he also establishes him as a viable model for the subversively oriented artist – for Miller himself. Moldorf is thus to some extent Miller's double: "We have so many points in common that it is like looking at myself in a cracked mirror" (9). More precisely, he provides a persona that Miller may adopt in order to express his own radicalism. "You [Moldorf] are the sieve through which my anarchy strains, resolves itself into words. Behind the word is chaos" (11).

Whereas in *Cancer* Miller alludes to the origins of this figure in the distant past and gives the impression that he is an eternal type, *Capricorn* connects him to a modern entertainment. In evoking the tradition to which Moldorf belongs as extending at least as far back as the Renaissance, the earlier text is vague as to where Miller came into contact with this strain of grotesque humor.[40] In contrast, by identifying the presence of this strain in American vaudeville, the later text helps bring the genealogy of comic radicalism up to date. The traits Miller's writing makes visible were passed on to him through a popular amusement. If *Black Spring* struggles to retrieve a sense of what *Cancer* represses, *Capricorn* makes Miller's fascination and aesthetic dependence on an array of recreational practices part of the thematic substance of its narrative. In a sense, the latter text gives us access to the material conscious of Depression-era American writing.

The relation of autobiography to vaudeville is not as straightforward in Miller's case as was his use of burlesque. Though carnivalized to a moderate degree, vaudeville was actively shaped by its promoters to conform to prevailing, mainstream tastes. In appropriating this entertainment for radical purposes, Miller found it necessary to alter as well as incorporate its elements into his prose. To achieve this end he (re)combined vaudeville with a much more thoroughly grotesque American amusement: the dime museum freak show.

In the latter instance a change of sorts was also required. Miller had to avoid the social function of these exhibits. Rather than frame human anomalies as objects of cognition, he aims in *Capricorn* to unsettle the self/other dichotomies the dime museums often served to reinforce. Rather than furnish the middle classes with spectacles of the strange against which these classes might define themselves as normal, Miller now strives to deploy the monstrous to shatter conventional understandings of difference. (This had not always been the case. In *Cancer* Miller shows himself willing to adopt the position of the delighted and distanced observer of proletarian degradation. Walking through Paris on a day when "the proletariat possesses the street in a kind of dumb torpor," "certain thoroughfares," he claims, "remind one of nothing less than a big chancrous cock laid open longitudinally." And this sight in turn recalls the aesthetic desires inspired by a turn-of-the-century amusement. These "highways" "attract one irresistibly, much as in the old days, around Union Square or the upper reaches of the Bowery, one was drawn to the dime museums where in the show windows there were displayed wax reproductions of various organs of the body eaten away by syphilis and other venereal diseases. The city sprouts out like a huge organism diseased in every part, the beautiful thoroughfares only a little less repulsive because they have been drained of their pus" [*Cancer*, 40].[41]) In *Capricorn* the intent is to use the unpredictable excesses of the loathsome and the vulgar to undermine the self-certainties of dominant society. What is laughable has here, as it does elsewhere for Georges Bataille, the force of "the unknowable."[42]

The carnivalized depiction at the beginning of *Capricorn* of his escapades as personnel manager at the Cosmodemonic or Cosmococcic Telegraph Company sets the tone for the book as a whole.[43] Affirming the spontaneity, exuberance, and irreverence characteristic of recreational activities as infinitely preferable to the restraint and sobriety that most jobs require, Miller represents his presumably serious occupation "as if it were a vaudeville performance" (*Capricorn*, 72). Surrounding him at his place of business is a cast of lunatics and human oddities seemingly drawn straight from a carnival sideshow. In addition to the messengers, most of whom are characterized as refugees from the mental asylum, there is, for example, the circus midget Miller refuses to hire on the grounds that "he was a she," but whom his mulatto secretary, Valeska, takes under her wing and promptly seduces. Valeska is later incensed when Curley, "the pet of the office," an immoral "lad" whose parents "worked 'the griffs and grinds,'" beds the "little Lesbian" (112–13). The setting of sexual abandon, petty larceny, and maniacal fun, the workplace emerges here as the festive locus of intoxicating joy, erotic transgression and psychological deviance. Discussion of the long passage that brings this wildly chaotic opening section of Miller's autobiographical text to a close will help isolate precisely the historical specificity of his intervention into the tradition of carnivalized writing.

Summarizing his condition during the years that he conformed to social expectations by working as personnel director for the Cosmodemonic Telegraph Company while maintaining a family, he compares himself to a towering structure firmly fixed in place.

I was like the lighthouse itself – secure in the midst of the turbulent sea. Beneath me was solid rock, the same shelf of rock on which the towering skyscrapers were reared. My foundations went deep into the earth and the armature of my body was made of steel riveted with hot bolts. Above all I was an eye, a huge searchlight which scoured far and wide, which revolved ceaselessly, pitilessly. This eye so wide-awake seemed to have made all my other faculties dormant: all my powers were used up in the effort to see, to take in the drama of the world.

If I longed for destruction it was merely that this eye might be extinguished . . . I wanted the earth to open up, to swallow everything in one engulfing yawn. I wanted to see the city buried fathoms deep in the bosom of the sea. I wanted to sit in a cave and read by candlelight. I wanted that eye extinguished so that I might have a chance to know my own body, my own desires.

Miller wants as well "to shake the stone and the light out of my system. I wanted the dark fecundity of nature, the deep well of the womb, silence, or else the lapping of the black waters of death." His wish is "to be englobed and encompassed and to encompass and englobe at the same time," to "be decomposed, divested of light and stone, variable as the molecule, durable as the atom, heartless as the earth itself" (76–77).

The symbolic oppositions structuring the passage are familiar ones. On the top or high end is the phallic skyscraper or panoptic lighthouse. Imaged as an immense, rigid, stable singularity, solidly rooted in the ground, this steel body "riveted with hot bolts" protects the fragile ego from external forces of flux and fragmentation. The sequestered self is safely defended against the dangerously jagged edges and fluid nature of its surroundings: "I was like a man sitting in a lighthouse: below me the wild waves, the rocks, the reefs, the debris of shipwrecked fleets" (74). In this obviously masculine realm, the "I" is further defended by the visual omniscience granted to the eye. Comfortably situated in a well-lit chamber high above the chaotic scene, the individual may gaze down on the wild, untamed realm of catastrophe beneath the room (the "continent itself perpetually wracked by cyclones, tornadoes, tidal waves, floods..." [74]), surveying the disorienting whirlpool with no risk of being drawn into it. In contrast, the darkened, bottom end of the scale is without question gendered female. For the low is characterized as a soft and receptive, womb-like site, a place of caves and deep wells, of globular embodiment and liquid movement, where one can feel "the blood running" through one's veins. Division and disintegration lurk at the base of the lighthouse, where the solidity of stone gives way to "the dark fecundity of nature," the "bosom of the sea."

The structure and imagery of this passage resemble closely the male fantasies Klaus Theweleit has catalogued and analyzed in his study of the post-First World War novels and autobiographies of German fascist soldiers (the officers of the Freikorps).[44] Yet Miller's ambition is to reverse the value judgments and emotional affect frequently attached to such figurations. His wish is not to ward off the threatening floods of the "feminine" (which is in truth both outside and inside) by maintaining a position towering above the streaming, mobile wetness beneath him. Rather he yearns to plunge downward and immerse himself in all that flows in the hope of experiencing a release from bodily and psychic constraints. Perhaps in this case the desire to escape social inscription simply amounts to an exchange of an anti-oedipal fantasy for an oedipal one, and in so doing protects the subject from a potentially traumatic encounter with the real. Still, the inversion is worth underscoring, since Miller's relatively uncommon aspiration is to be shattered, to descend to the level of the crumbling earth, to plunge into the rhythmically undulating waters of the unconscious, to get in touch with his own bodily processes and even to accept female sexuality.

The fact that Miller articulates this desire while employed as personnel director at a telegraph company suggests that his phallic status is part and parcel of his position as a member of the mechanized labor force. It follows that play is an unmentioned component of the non-lighthouse condition. And it is therefore appropriate that toward the end of the text vaudeville emerges as the spark that ignites his artistic career. The excitements of modern entertainment facilitate the destruction of socially prescribed identities. The capacity to reinvent the self, to adopt a new persona, comes from the modeling of autobiography on public amusement. One can become a "real schizerino" and abandon the "so-called whole self" (*Capricorn*, 206) by plugging oneself in to mass recreations.

Miller's allusions to vaudeville in *Capricorn* may seem superfluous; yet they are in truth key points of access to his conception of his cultural endeavor. It is by way of this form of entertainment that he articulates alternative values to the sober, constraining world of work *without* taking recourse (as he does in the above passage) to the terrestrial. Whereas the fully ambivalent system of imagery operative at the beginning of the text fits into the Bakhtinian concept of grotesque realism, with nature posited as the source of regenerative energies, elsewhere the mechanical will rise up as a similarly redemptive force. In short, Miller opens up inside the category of technology a difference with political significance. Rather than remain caught in the traditional polarity between the natural and the technological, he locates within the latter a tension between conservative and radical functions. Machine culture emerges as the site of conflict between death and life drives, and this conflict corresponds in Miller's system of thought to the distinction between modernized labor and leisure. The lineaments of this system can be set forth most efficiently by attending to the places in *Capricorn* where he reflects back on past experiences connected to American vaudeville. In the first, he posits the comedic stage performer as a grotesque ideal, as the monster the writer aims to become. In the second, he announces his rebirth as a writing machine that flows in the context of a visit to a vaudeville show. But first a bit on the intertwined histories of vaudeville and the dime museum.

If the specificity of *Capricorn* is that in it Miller combines the practice of displaying human oddities with the comic energy of a vaudeville performance, the fusion of these two forms of entertainment has historical precedent in the United States. One of the seedier venues of the variety show, the coarser, disreputable precursor to vaudeville, was the dime museum, the "sordid institution"[45] that staged for its principally male patrons both human curiosities and a raw, comically robust concatenation of animal acts, blackface routines, burlesque theatrical farces, circus gymnasts, singing and dancing. At the end of the 1870s, B.F. Keith, a kind of latter day P.T. Barnum, became a staff member at Bunnel's Museum. The cultural entrepreneur, who had begun his career working with the circus, then moved to Boston and set himself up as the proprietor of his own dime museum with a modest number of attractions including "Little Alice, the Baby Queen," a prematurely born infant. Finding it difficult to survive amid stiff competition, Keith soon started to supplement his small collection of freakish exhibits with variety and dramatic performances, his innovation in this area to run them continuously, all day long, which turned out to be the key to drawing large crowds.

His next goal was to aim for a more socially respectable audience by manufacturing a form of vaudeville entertainment suitable for the entire family while censoring lewd acts and prohibiting profanity. Keith thus helped shape a form of entertainment with mass appeal, one that "assumed the centrality of bourgeois values and norms of appropriate discourse, bearing, subject matter, and behavior both onstage and in the audience."[46] With female shoppers and children as his target patrons, in 1886 he bought the Bijou Theatre, a venue capable of seating close to a thousand, consigning the lingering traces of the dime museum to the "art gallery" in the lobby. By 1894 the success of his project of creating a refined public amusement offering wholesome, clean fun was apparent upon the opening of B.F. Keith's New Theatre, this magnificent palace establishing vaudeville as a legitimate commercial counterpart to the mainstream stage. A forerunner to the grandiose movie theatres of the 1910s and twenties, its appearance sealed the fate of its cultural precursors. Vaudeville had successfully assimilated the elements of the variety show and subsumed the dime museum, in the process cleaning them both up and making them palatable to a much wider audience.

Thus Miller's aim in appropriating the form of entertainment as a model for his own literary practice hardly coincided with Keith's commercially motivated ambitions. Moreover, if, for the writer, vaudeville had the potential to supply the basis for an anarchic cultural politics, it could do so only in conjunction with the dime museum freak show, which itself had to be similarly radicalized. This combination resulted in the literary production of a vaudeville monstrosity.

Recalling with great affection the Monday nights he spent one summer while still in his early twenties congregating with a group of exclusively male friends, Miller returns in his memoir to this recreational experience "because it was typical of something I have never encountered elsewhere in the world" (*Capricorn*, 302). A time when he needed not work but leisure, "a life more abundant," he was delighted to be greeted at a friend's house not as an intellectual but "as a clown," discovering there an intoxicating party atmosphere where everything was free of charge. "It was entertainment from the word go – and the sandwiches and the drinks were on the house." And when things got going, "it was better than any show I've ever seen put on and it didn't cost a cent" (302). This joyous period of his life came to an end "not," Miller claims, because of the war, but because even a joint like this one was not immune to the "poison" of professionalism "seeping in from the periphery." Hired by "the radio or the movies," where the bulk of their talent was wasted, musicians who would formerly have remained amateurs ceased to play "just for the fun of it" (303). The communal, subcultural gatherings were curtailed when the artistic skills the participants possessed became marketable commodities, the pleasures of male camaraderie giving way to the temptations of financial gain. The opportunity to indulge in collective rowdiness disappeared as the comic performers vanished into the entertainment industry. "Any man in America who had an ounce of humor in him was saving it up to put himself across" (303).

Miller, having retained his memory of some of these "wonderful nuts," the "best we produced," is nevertheless able to draw on them to prescribe a home remedy for the spiritual and physical ills of contemporary society. Switching abruptly to a vaudeville comic he used to see occasionally, "an anonymous performer on the Keith circuit," Miller reflects on the significance of the spellbinding show this recreational creature, "probably the craziest man in America," put on three times a day, "every day in the week." Possessed of boundless energy, his act pure improvisation, neither his jokes nor stunts ever repeated, this man's act provided "more therapy than the whole arsenal of modern science." Dazzled by the memory of these spontaneous, inventive performances, Miller hyperbolically asserts that this man "could cure any disease on the calendar." Such a clown deserves to run the country. "They ought to sack the President of the United States and the whole Supreme court and set up a man like this as ruler" (304). The "type of man which empties insane asylums" by making "everybody crazy," he offers perhaps the best solution to the "perpetual state of war, which is civilization," to the "stabbing horror" of everyday existence. And the only way beyond the awful conditions of the present, Miller claims, is to become a being "with six faces and eight eyes," with a head that is "a revolving lighthouse" and a hole "which ventilates what few brains there are" at the top. If such a monstrous being, one whom Miller eventually designates as God, is the only type of man to be placed above the comedian, it is the task of the latter to make this being, who is in truth inside of us, speak up. "When the whole human race is rocking with laughter, laughing so hard that it hurts, I mean, everybody then has his foot on the path" and in "that moment you have the annihilation of dual, triple, quadruple and multiple consciousness" (304–05). Upon achieving this state of absolute freedom we will no longer wish to do violence to others and will cease to care about abstract philosophical systems. "Nobody can persuade you at that moment to take a gun and kill your enemy; neither can anybody persuade you to open a fat tome containing the metaphysical truths of the world and read it" (305). The vaudeville comic has the power to make us all into divinely pacifist, happy monsters. The spirit of play he reproduces will serve as a means of resisting the impulse to murder.

The point is that this performer (who directly recalls the figure of Moldorf in *Cancer*), is an ideal model for Miller the writer. The recollection functions as a reflexive portrait of the type of entertainer Miller is bent on becoming, of the cultural figure he is in the process of constructing himself into as he composes the text. The thoroughly carnivalized outlook on social existence that the performer expresses is in perfect harmony with Bakhtin's characterization of the fearless, utopian spirit coursing through traditional folk humor practices. Life appears as an endless performance. To sharpen our understanding of the technological specificity of Miller's enterprise it is necessary to take a step backward to an earlier, equally revealing moment in the text. Shortly before, Miller has imaged his rebirth or refashioning as an artist as the successful setting in motion of a mechanized apparatus he has constructed. This achievement satisfies a requirement articulated at the beginning of the text: "What was needed was a mechanic, but according to the logic of the higher-ups there was nothing wrong with the mechanism."

Having installed a gigantic desk in his parlor as part of a "scheme to consolidate his anchorage" (283), Miller's initial efforts to gain "contact with reality" were failures. Though he wrote millions of words, which were "well ordered, well connected," what he produced remained "museum stuff," nothing that might "catch fire" and "inflame the world" (284). Even his dreams, he reports, "were not authentic." What he lacked was "the lever which would shut off the juice," that would shut down the machine of the world whose "current was running through" him without his control. At last a dramatic reversal takes place under the auspices of a theatrical entertainment:

I lacked something much more important [than "thoughts," "words," and "power of expression]: the lever which would shut off the juice. The bloody machine wouldn't stop, that was the difficulty. I was not only in the middle of the current but the current was running through me and I had no control over it whatever.

I remember the day I brought the machine to a dead stop and how the other mechanism, the one that was signed with my own initials and which I had made with my own hands and my own blood slowly began to function. I had gone to the theater to see a vaudeville show. . . . Standing on line in the lobby, I already experienced a strange feeling of consistency. It was as though I were coagulating, becoming a recognizable mass of jelly. It was like the ultimate stage in the healing of a wound. (284)

It is as if Miller, in this autogenetic fantasy (or is it more than a mere fantasy?), gives birth to himself simply by purchasing a ticket for a matinee show. Certainly, his mode of existence alters drastically. "I was experiencing for the first time in my life the meaning of the miraculous. I was so amazed when I heard my own cogs meshing" (285). Rather than stay and watch the performance, Miller bids farewell to his old "sleepwalking" self, who appears here in the form of a "man slowly mounting the steps" to the balcony. Rushing home, he feverishly sets to work "in order to keep the world alive." There is no need to stay and watch the performance, because he now understands how to make his writing serve as a viable substitute for the thrilling intensities of the recreation. The metonymical, contiguous link between the visit to the vaudeville house and his reinvention of himself as an artist is thus in truth the manifestation of a latently metaphorical relationship. The vaudeville performer (as the burlesque dancer had done in *Black Spring*), supplies Miller with the analogical basis of his identity as an artist. And the energy he derives from the amusement furnishes the basis for an alternative existence, one in which he will no longer be a subordinate "part of a monstrous death machine, such as America" (289). "Listen, they had me on the run, these crazy horsepower fiends; in order to break their insane rhythm, their death rhythm, I had to resort to a wave length which, until I found the proper sustenance in my bowels, would at least nullify the rhythm they had set up" (289). The writer as desiring machine is now free to engage in an ecstatically productive recreational activity. And what is produced? States of extreme emotional intensity. "Delirium and hallucination are secondary in relation to the really primary emotion, which in the beginning experiences intensities, becomings, transitions." More precisely, this is a description of the functioning of the "celibate machine" which, for Deleuze and Guattari, is forged through an alliance of desiring machines and the body without organs. Here "A genuine consummation is achieved by the new machine, a pleasure that can rightly be called autoerotic, or rather automatic: the nuptial celebration of a new alliance, a new birth, a radiant ecstasy, as though the eroticism of the machine had liberated other unlimited forces" (*Anti-Oedipus*, 18).

On what basis does the glorious amalgamation of the body and the machine take place?[47] A quick return to the opening pages of *Cancer* provides an answer. As I mentioned above, early in this book he asserts with delight that he is "a writing machine. The last screw has been added. The thing flows. Between me and the machine there is no estrangement. I am the machine." The scene in *Capricorn* not only closes the autobiographical circle, taking us to the threshold of his initial Depression-era achievement; it also deepens our understanding of the preceding one. The dependence of Miller's mechanized practice of writing on American amusements now becomes legible. Conversely, the earlier scene illuminates its repetition, suggesting that the actual machine Miller joins himself to is the typewriter that he mentions on occasion at the outset of *Cancer*. And it is at this point that the various elements that together constitute the carnivalized mode of technologically mediated play he generated throughout the 1930s visibly coalesce. The radical writer comes into existence by reassembling himself as a typewriter man plugged in to electrifying forms of entertainment.

The prosthetically endowed authorial figure who comes together here should not be confused with the body imagery that corresponds to a technophilic, (proto)fascist subjectivity. Miller does not strive to imagine himself as a perfectly complete, ostensibly invulnerable individual protected against corporeal intrusion and psychic dispersal by a mechanical shell. Elsewhere in *Capricorn*, however, Miller does comment on precisely this kind of "reconfiguration of body and psyche as weapon," which Hal Foster, following Theweleit's lead, has commented on as a distinguishing feature of fascist ideology in its cultural and political forms.[48] Soon after describing his reinvention as a writing machine, Miller reflects back on his mode of existence before his glorious transformation. What people who observed Miller at this time saw "was the periscope of the soul searching for its target. Everything that came within range had to be destroyed, if I were ever to rise again and ride the waves. This monster which rose now and then to fix its target with deadly aim, ... dove again and roved and plundered ceaselessly" (321). To survive he found himself compelled to do violence to others, to become, in the hyperbolic figuration of the passage, a murderous instrument of mass destruction, a kind of metallic phallus or submarine man. It is against this (proto)fascist subject, desperately striving to hold itself together by devivifying what exists in the objective world, that the non-unified, imperfect, multiply constituted writing machine described above triumphantly *plays*. If the protective armoring of the fascist subject "allows for desiring production to be both suppressed and expressed as 'murdering production.'"[49] Miller, as anarchic writing machine, pursues, in contrast, the liberating, humorous discharge of unconscious emotional flows. The mechanized comic monstrosity's release of its partial drives occurs with a life-affirming burst of laughter aimed at eliminating the need for working persons to become lethal submarine men in order to protect themselves from falling apart.

By the same token the chaotic, uncontrolled creations of the writing machine exceed the logic of a machine aesthetic modeled on the instrumental and rational, on socioeconomic processes governed by functional or narrowly productivist imperatives. Against the disciplinary, rational thrust of machine culture and its modes of mass production and reproduction, Miller calls for and generates a mode of writing that remains open to chance and the irrational. The anti-fascist aesthetic generated by the technocarnivalesque consists of a series of hazardous operations; it is an unpredictably comic process that generates alternating currents of pleasure and pain in the hope of improving the collective state of mind.

Instead of appealing to the natural body and untarnished soul, as he does earlier in the text during his fragmenting "Bloomingdale's experience," Miller rebuilds or reinvents himself at the book's end as a heterogeneous assemblage. The radicalized autobiographer now takes the stage as a comically monstrous machine.[50] That he does so while alluding directly to vaudeville and indirectly to dime museum freak shows clarifies the debt his grotesque aesthetics and his radical politics owed to carnivalized American amusements. Still writing "museum stuff," but in a much different sense than before, native forms of recreation proved indispensable in his effort to make literature the location at which "in technology body and image space so interpenetrate that all revolutionary tension becomes bodily collective innervation." The phrase, taken from the final paragraph of a Walter Benjamin essay ("Surrealism") is a difficult one, and has been helpfully glossed by Miriam Hansen as referring to the process whereby images are converted into "somatic and collective reality." As psychic energy is transmitted to the nerves through figuration, technology becomes "an organ" through which human beings may decisively alter their relation to their external surroundings.[51] This is the utopian edge of the confrontation with technology, the guiding aspiration being that, if mastered, technology has the capacity to generate revolutionary upheavals. As the site of violent intersections of the natural body and inorganic matter, radical writing thus becomes one forceful technological procedure among others, a mechanized activity with the potential to bring about sexual, social, and political transformations. Enabling the subject to adapt to and change modernity, carnivalized literature manages to avoid being complicit with the murderous violence of everyday life. Registering in brutally shocking fashion the emotional and physical pain that are conditions of contemporary existence, grotesquely humorous writing performs a decidedly therapeutic task, achieving a redemptive balance between bodies, persons, and machines.

Another way of putting this is to argue that Miller's Depression-era autobiographical prose constitutes, as Haraway puts it in "The Promises of Monsters," a "chiasmatic borderlands, liminal areas where new shapes, new kinds of action and responsibility, are gestating in the world."[52] Moreover, though his project is not without its contradictions and regressive swerves backwards, and is partly constrained by its appeal to the individual (as opposed to a collective group) as the agent of social regeneration, he successfully complicates traditional understandings of writing as a mechanized or *machinic* activity.[53] In his articulation of the relation of the human, textual, and technological, these categories no longer make their customary sort of sense. And the same goes for the distinction between male and female within his autobiographical enterprise. Decisively pushing beyond representation to a more active, performative approach, he labors toward the construction of a heterogeneous entity that joyfully assembles together feminine and masculine traits as well as elements of the organic and inorganic and even joins the mythic to the actual. As the authorial self ceases to be the distanced object of expressive literary recollection, writing turns into the instrument whereby the author reinvents himself as a grotesque monstrosity whose radical energies derive from carnivalesque sources of power. Yet if such a multiply constituted creature diffracts the dominant economic rationalism of his social formation, urban-industrial modernity has produced other more ominously functioning monsters. These are the more legitimate "offspring of militarism and patriarchal capitalism"[54] whose malignant disposition and violent tendencies were also elements of Miller's experience.

METROPOLITAN MANIACS

Ever since the invention of the radio tube and the photo-electric cell . . . the search for bigger and better Frankensteins has gone forward. (*Newsweek*, April 24, 1939)[55]

The distinction Miller articulates late in *Capricorn* (inside the category of the monstrous) between comedic performers and horrifyingly pathological murderers merits comment. For it is apparent that a fine line separates the aggressive workaholic and the liberating comic insofar as both develop out of a historically determined conjunction of bodies and machines. Whereas he conceives of one as a revolutionary force (albeit of a pacifist sort), he depicts the other as a reactionary threat. Clowns on stage (or in literary texts) are thus designed to provide a humorous outlet for mounting pressures that might otherwise find release in the slaughter of other persons. If industrialized modes of capitalist production tend to bring automatized killers into existence, recreationally derived laughter has the therapeutic potential to alleviate psychic and physical tensions before they lead to violent attacks on living beings. It is the utopian affirmation of technologically mediated humor as the precondition for future states of social happiness that marks Miller's autobiographical enterprise as a profoundly politicized cultural intervention. Yet the radical promise he perceives in the possibility that bodies and machines can come together in play is inseparable from his nightmarish fears of the potentially disastrous outcome of the thorough mechanization of existence.

Near the end of *Tropic of Capricorn* Henry Miller attempts to defend and explain his preceding inability to hold a job. Admitting that he could not get himself "to believe in this business of work," not even to save his life, he looks back in horror, realizing that he had become in essence a ruthlessly violent criminal due to his efforts to conform to social expectations. "If I shudder now and then, when I think of my active life, if I have nightmares, possibly it is because I think of all the men I robbed and murdered in my day sleep." Though he uses the term nature to identify the external cause urging him on, it is clear that the determinations of his abominably cruel behavior were social. "Nature is eternally whispering in one's ear – 'if you would survive you must kill!' Being human, you kill not like the animal but automatically" (321). Programmed to destroy, he habitually and unnecessarily brutalized those around him ("you kill without even thinking about it, you kill without need"). This villainously "automatic process" has little to do with innate, biological instinct; it is, on the contrary, primarily a direct consequence of existing within a rationalized system that transforms the individual into "a puppet" and then places in his hands "a Gatling gun" (322). As "personnel director of a telegraph company" (320), in charge of hiring and firing messengers, Miller was fully complicit with this system, joining in the managerial reduction of persons and bodies to mathematical abstractions, converting living beings into quantifiable and substitutable entities. "I was like an equals sign through which the algebraic swarm of humanity was passing. I was a rather important equals sign, like a general in time of war," and our "whole life was built up on this principle of equation. The integers had become symbols which were shuffled about in the interests of death." While involved in this "endless juggling" of persons, Miller's internal emotions, his subjective feelings became nothing more than effects of adopting a particular point of view on the objects he was manipulating.

"Pity, despair, passion, hope, courage – these were the temporal refractions caused by looking at equations from varying angles" (322). In sum, to return to Seltzer, we might say that Miller is remarking upon his previous capitulation to the disciplinary logic of machine culture, upon his past willingness to conflate the life process and the machine process and participate in the production of individuals as "statistical persons."

In recalling this troubling predicament, Miller does not posit writing and the creation of works of art as desirable alternatives to the situation. Rather, for him, literary production closely resembles the highly formalized, meaninglessly repetitive and thoroughly unfulfilling aspects of capitalist labor; writing like working is a compulsive, instrumentalized, serial activity born of frustration and devoid of identifiable purpose, a means to no specific end. "The dissatisfaction which drives one on from one word to another, one creation to another, is simply a protest against the futility of postponement" (320). He does propose that the attainment of complete satisfaction and absolute lucidity is something a genuine artist can hope to accomplish. Yet insofar as he defines the latter as an individual who has successfully overcome the impulse to write and therefore to make actual texts, this proposal is of minimal interest for my purposes. Oddly enough, the impulse to write is here inversely proportional to the ability to achieve the status of an artist: "The more awake one becomes, as an artistic microbe, the less desire one has to do anything" (320). Anyone who falls short of the transcendent state of the artist, anyone who still feels the need to produce material artifacts, appears to be caught up in the oppressive routinized procedures of urban-industrial modernity. If "action, as expressed in creating a work of art, is a concession to the automatic principle of death" (320), then writers and workers alike have yielded to a proliferating death drive. Such spiritless automatons, rationalized and nearly inanimate entities, lack agency, having been set in motion by historically determinable forces.

Miller then characterizes such typical persons as gruesome abominations by alluding to a recent horror movie. Addressing the reader, Miller asks "Did you ever see a synthetic monster on the screen, a Frankenstein realized in flesh and blood? Can you imagine how he might be trained to pull a trigger?" (322). Such a figure "is not a myth"; on the contrary, it "is a very real creation born of the personal experience of a sensitive human being" (322–23). The point seems to be that the individual responsible for rendering such a freakish entity in cinematic form has correctly perceived the hideousness of modern life. But even this visibly shocking creature fails to do representational justice to the unbearable aspects of the historical reality in question. "The monster of the screen is nothing compared to the monster of the imagination" (323). Nor are the mentally deranged abnormalities one might encounter in the actual world, those "pathologic monsters who find their way into the police station," adequate to the frightening conceptualizations that the attentive individual has generated in his mind. The criminal deviants are "but feeble demonstrations of the monstrous reality which the pathologist lives with" (323).

Next, Miller articulates the relatively unique, mixed category to which he presumably belongs: he is both the patient and the doctor. And it is at this stage of his slightly mad argument that he affirms a vague yet to my mind intriguing difference between industrialized workers and mechanized writers (the authentic artist remaining a blissful ideal out of reach for both).

To be the monster and the pathologist at the same time – that is reserved for certain species of men who *disguised* as artists, are supremely aware that sleep is an even greater danger than insomnia. In order not to fall asleep, in order not to become victims of that insomnia which is called "living," they resort to the drug of putting words together endlessly. This is *not* an automatic process, they say, because there is always present the illusion that they can stop it at will. But they cannot stop; they have only succeeded in creating an illusion, which is perhaps a feeble something, but is far from being wide awake and neither active nor inactive. (323)

I take the burden of this confusing and perhaps not entirely coherent taxonomy to be the isolation of the difficult to measure value of writing as a form of resistance to an intolerable dilemma. Though it is an intoxicating activity that the obsessed author ultimately does not control, writing enables one to escape absolute submission to the status quo. Writing no doubt involves a considerable degree of self-delusion, writers fooling themselves into thinking they are not addicted to what they are doing and that they are not to a large extent automatons engaging in a prescribed set of operations. And writing neither offers full enlightenment (writers are "far from being wide awake") nor allows one to transcend the dichotomy between passivity and aggression. Still, those who merely masquerade as artists do evade complete victimization by virtue of their admittedly compulsive behavior. In the process they generate "a feeble something," an admittedly illusory construction that nevertheless is not completely inconsequential as a vehicle of social protest.

Miller's Depression-era autobiographical output, I have been arguing, amounts to a powerful attempt to short-circuit the currents of violence running through machine culture. Crucially, his comic literary performances repeatedly refer back to city-based recreations, modernized forms of play, as the basis for his cultural intervention. Instead of taking the discourses of industrialized labor as the historical prototypes for his machinic writing practice, Miller looked to carnivalized, exhibitionist attractions for rhetorical inspiration. American vaudeville and burlesque as well as the kind of amusements one could find around the turn of the century at Coney Island or the Bowery furnished him with the repertoire of symbolic images and thematic motifs he endeavored to put to radical use. The grotesque aesthetic he fabricated was intended to function as a challenge to the disciplinary imperatives of urban-industrial modernity. Radical play was to serve as a means of contesting serious work. Correlatively, the undeniably peculiar, manic persona he invented for himself constitutes a politicized alternative to the malignant and dangerous type of person he found to be a disturbing product of the machine age. The possible construction of such an alternative is an essential part of the promise driving the mechanized mode of recreational writing I have called the technocarnivalesque.

Intermission: Vulgar Marxism

> In the penchant of modern art for the nauseating and physically
> revolting ... the critical material motif shows through.
>> Theodor Adorno, *Aesthetic Theory*

Late in Meyer Levin's *The Old Bunch*, two characters articulate their
disparate responses to Chicago at the time of the 1933–34 Century-of-
Progress Exposition:

> Both men looked up, simultaneously. From where they stood, the buildings on
> the other side were like a single, flung-out construction, splash-colored.
> "It's like a bright scarf," Joe remarked appreciatively.
> "Yah. Around the neck of a consumptive," Sam added.
> There below stretched the rotting lungs and the rotten guts of Chicago. Close
> against the bludgeon stone-head, the Loop, lay the decay of the body.[1]

Joe is a liberal sculptor while Sam is a left-wing lawyer, and the referential
object of their conversation serves as the backdrop to the final portion
of the mammoth narrative fiction. From the sculptor's admiring point
of view, the World's Fair has made the city more attractive. Implicitly
figuring the city as a gigantic body, he is impressed with the makeover
it has received. The lawyer counters his interlocutor's aesthetic delight
by redirecting his trope away from the body's decorative accessories to
its actual physiological condition. For Sam, the artificial beautification
project functions to screen out the devastated nature of the environment
and by extension its suffering inhabitants. The narrator's perspective
clearly coincides with the lawyer's more critical standpoint, for the figure
of the city as a sickened individual is then elaborated in an increasingly
grotesque manner. The anthropomorphic characterization of Chicago as
a gravely ill entity stretched out horizontally, as if on its deathbed, evokes
in turn the fact (represented in the book) that an epidemic of amoebic
dysentery has broken out during the fair. The local Health Department's
decision to suppress information pertaining to the spread of the disease

until the event has come to a close is a repressive gesture that conforms to the dressing up of the landscape in a misleading manner. The "fantastic illumination" of the city, with "threads of neon zigzagging through the phosphorous haze,"[2] may strike the eye as wonderful; yet such pleasing appearances tend to deflect attention away from the miserable truth that people are dying.

The conversation also discredits the compositional ambitions of the sculptor, which tend toward the classical, judging by the artistic aspirations he will articulate in a later scene. Gazing down from a "skyride car" on the dazzling spectacle that the exposition constitutes ("the lake of color, the red and yellow lightnings, the field of white, the firework parabolas"), Joe comes up with an "an idea." Someday he will create "a striding man of power." He intends "to leave a monument in Chicago," to be done "in large masses, carved with an honest, native simplicity." What is needed is a "body electric. A colossus," one "out of Whitman" and "out of electricity and Boulder Dam, a striding man of power."[3] The body of the (male) worker must be represented as an enormous yet attractively proportioned entity. Rather than depict in a more or less accurate fashion what material conditions have caused laboring bodies actually to look like, the sculptor hopes to produce an idealized image in which massive strength is combined with corporeal elegance. "None of your squeezed, flatted men wrapped around cogwheels. And none of your bunchy muscled proletarians swinging the pickax."[4]

For Levin, the aesthetic distinction between grotesque and classical figurations of the (gigantic) body has epistemological and political ramifications in relation to social reality. Images of corporeal anguish and corruption disclose the traumatic conditions of present existence more reliably than do pleasant and reassuring but cognitively misleading images of physical vitality and organic wholeness. Dominant society's defensive disguise (in the form of the World's Fair) of the degraded, torturous nature of everyday existence in Depression-era America is countered by the radicalized intellectual's determination to register perceptually the fact of widespread anguish. To achieve his aim he finds it necessary to forgo referential accuracy in favor of figurative excess, his hope that the shocking intensity of his disgusting trope will dislodge the reassuring beliefs the commercial spectacle encourages. An imagery of corporeal violation stands or (better) stretches out horizontally in opposition to the projections of public well-being produced by towering constructions of colossal individuals.

Here we arrive at an interpretive frame for understanding the ambitions underlying Nelson Algren's *Somebody in Boots* (1935), for this is a novel that puts a vast number of grievously wounded physiques and distressingly marred faces on display. The book, an example of what might be called grotesque naturalism, presents an array of severely debilitated and filthy bodies of the sort that eventually triggered a fit of critical hysteria in Edward Dahlberg ("We are, finally, so defiled unto ourselves that we have to shriek at the Uncleanness of man's organs and functions out of the ugly cloaca of the naturalistic novel."[5]) What we are to learn from the "brains and bones" of the "fetal things" Algren sets before us is that life amid the disenfranchised is excruciatingly awful.

In his notorious address at the First American Writers' Congress (1935), Kenneth Burke proposed that proletarian novelists shift from the "negative symbol" of the proletariat to the "positive symbol" of the people to broaden the appeal of revolutionary discourse in the country. To combat the skillful coalition-building efforts of protofascists like Huey Long and Father Coughlin, left-wing writers, Burke advised, should incorporate the ideals of the middle classes. The new political strategy should be *"propaganda by inclusion."*[6] In this same year, Algren sought to narrow the focus of radical fiction by taking as his subject matter the heterogeneous social elements that constituted a kind of counterbody politic, albeit a formless and perennially decomposing one: the lumpenproletariat. It was the anguished state of mind and debased physical condition of the least assimilable, most downtrodden members of American society that Algren aimed to make legible. Such an undertaking may be understood in context as an effort to register the existence of those persons whom grandiose, homogenizing public amusements like the Century-of-Progress World's Fair refused to recognize. Openly "conceived of as festivals of American corporate power" and putting "breathtaking amounts of surplus capital to work in the field of cultural production and ideological representation,"[7] Depression-era expositions hid as much as they revealed. To cultivate through massive spectacle the impression that full recovery from economic catastrophe was imminent, the gaze of the nation had to be deflected away from the devastating sight of those situated at the lowest stratum of American society.

TOWARD THE AMERICAN LUMPENPROLETARIAT

> Lumpenproletariat, me
> Trespassed private property
> Wondering always how it comes
> There's just no rest for such poor bums.
>   Nelson Algren[8]

The vexed status of the lumpenproletariat within political theory closely resembles the odd rank of the grotesque in aesthetic theory. Much as the aesthetic category disrupts generic distinctions and classifications in the cultural arena, the political category exceeds the opposition between social classes, drifting across the spaces dividing labor from capital. Both terms seek to encompass hybrid entities that do not respect conceptual barriers; that interfere with stable definitions and upset fixed taxonomies. This is perhaps the reason that we often find politicized theoreticians of grotesque art taking up problems associated with the lumpenproletariat.

Thus Peter Stallybrass' "Marx and Heterogeneity: Thinking the Lumpenproletariat" is a logical corollary to *The Politics and Poetics of Transgression.*[9] More important, the article, with help from Georges Bataille's "The Psychological Structure of Fascism" (1933–34),[10] argues that the lumpenproletariat is one of the keys to understanding the political process as an ongoing quest to *articulate* heterogeneous social masses into homogeneous collective agents.[11] Stallybrass stresses that the unpredictable behavior of the lumpenproletariat at times of social upheaval and crisis is what makes it an essential topic for political thinkers. Commonly designating the scattered collection of disaffiliated individuals "who are most open to historical transformation" (88), the term directs attention to such persons as the malleable material which either reactionary or revolutionary parties might mold and thus incorporate into a movement. Because the inner world of those who fall into the category of the lumpenproletariat is an inchoate mix of ardent feeling and poorly formulated opinion, they are especially vulnerable to forces of *concentration*, to being *bound, united,* or *wrapped* around a compelling social idea or charismatic personality.[12] By no means antithetical to political unification, members of the lumpenproletariat, because they lack a secure identity, are extremely likely to come together with others on the basis of what they feel, correctly or incorrectly, they have in common with them. Rather than resist totalizing procedures, the lumpenproletariat is in fact a condition of possibility of such operations, always ready to convert difference into similarity, to make the transition from heterogeneity to homogeneity.

A related insight – albeit one communicated in negative form – into the linguistic dimensions of forging political identities can be read out of a late scene in Edward Dahlberg's *From Flushing to Calvary*. A comic reflection on the politics of reading in relation to left-wing organizing in the very early thirties, the scene suggests that the conceptual dynamics required to build political agents are entangled with metaphorical procedures. Taking up the problem from the point of view of the lumpenproletariat, Dahlberg's parody illustrates the importance of figuration in efforts to transform marginal individuals into militant revolutionaries.

As he went along, he remembered how hard it was for him to understand the word *consciousness*. Lorry had taken up William James with much hopefulness. He borrowed books from the public library. When he discovered that James took some stock in the mystic which he called a leaky conscience, he expected considerable help from him. Still it took him a long while to understand what *stream of consciousness* meant. Thinking of this, he recalled a book he had picked up at a secondhand bookstore. The author, whom he had never heard of before, was a man named Trotsky. Lorry had never paid much attention to politics. He had never been able to see where it let him in. However, he thought he'd try the book to see how it read. The words interested him. This time he came across *consciousness* used in a different sense. The writer called it *class consciousness*. There were other words in the book that puzzled him. Although he wrote them down in his notebook, and after each word jotted down the definition when he had looked it up in the dictionary, they were still hazy in his mind. Words like *proletariat* and *class consciousness* were new to him. Emerson, he had read somewhere, had eight to ten thousand words in his vocabulary. For the past year he had been attempting to work up a list of words that long. Lorry had an unabridged *Webster's* in his Y room. Time and again until he felt groggy and as if his nerves were being sawed he went back to it to see if he could make out the definition. But he tried to keep cool and to reason it out for himself. *Proletarian*, the dictionary said, and his fingers went from word to word *of or pertaining to the proletaries; belonging to the commonality; hence, mean; vile; vulgar.*

Consciousness, he repeated out loud while he added the copulative verb *to be* to make it clearer, is *the state of being conscious*. His mind went back to the *stream of consciousness* for help. Then it sort of sprang like a big-ben alarm clock completely run down.[13]

Lorry's mechanical, clock-like mind gives out on him as he finds himself circling back to his verbal point of departure. Caught in a definitional tautology, he can make no further headway beyond the non-insight that consciousness "is the state of being conscious." Ironically, were he able to understand the meaning of the words, separately and then together, Lorry would be able to grasp better his objective social position and in so doing enhance his political awareness. Lorry lacks "class-consciousness," does not realize that he fits into a specific social category, the proletariat, because he cannot grasp the meaning of the term. Radical self-consciousness eludes the individual who is unable to formulate knowingly the proposition "I am a member of the proletariat." Failing to perform a specifically verbal act of conceptualization, Lorry remains ideologically isolated from those with whom he has a great deal in common, those situated at the bottom of the social formation. Encountering for the first time a word (proletariat) that in fact signifies or refers to others like him, Lorry is unable to use the term to convert difference into sameness and in the process establish a relationship between himself and others on the basis of their comparable social positions. Whether or not Lorry has perceived in his everyday life the ways in which his experience is *not* unique is irrelevant if the conceptual terminology that would transform such a perception into a stable cognition remains incomprehensible. Baffled by the significance of two key terms within Marxist discourse, Lorry is unable to complete the metaphorical procedure that would enable him to identify himself with other marginal persons. The successful completion of a figural operation is the precondition of the passage from heterogeneity to homogeneity, to use Stallybrass' terms, and thus from political passivity to political action.

Dahlberg reiterates Lorry's predicament in the last scene of the novel by showing him being trampled by the participants in a Communist Party demonstration. Catching sight around Union Square of the procession of singing marchers, the ignorant character initially believes that he is watching a funeral. Unaware of the significance of the banner he sees out of the corner of his eyes, believing it to be "an auctioneer's red flag," Lorry, apparently famished, bends down to pick up a peanut he has spied lying on the ground. Before he can straighten out, the police arrive, wielding blackjacks and arresting people. Caught in the middle of what has become a riot, Lorry gets to his feet and runs to safety, bending "his back way forward like a football player making an end run" (*Flushing*, 291). Bruised and bloodied yet delighted to find that he still has the peanut in hand, the character saunters off, blissfully singing a religious victory hymn, the political meaning of the break-up of the parade inaccessible to him. (There are scenes in Chaplin's *Modern Times* [1936] that resemble this one.[14])

As the decade wore on Dahlberg began to address the topic of the lumpenproletariat in an increasingly explicit manner, both as a political reporter and as a critical defender of the political significance of his own fictional undertakings. In regard to the latter incarnation, one may cite his brief defense of the novel. Exasperated with the accusation that his work is defeatist, Dahlberg counters that the reason "the gelatinous mass of floating population" which appears in his novels, "don't take their hunger and social abasement singing the 'Internationale' is that they have never heard of it. Never heard of communism. Words like

Bolshevism either do not exist in their vocabulary at all, or are at best a kind of obscenity to be included in the national lavatory esoterica. And it is this phenomenon which the *New Masses* and other intransigent organs of the left wing do not appear to be sensible of in their manifestos on 'proletarian' literature."[15]

That this same sociopolitical phenomenon was at the center of Richard Wright's literary thought and practice throughout the Depression era is made evident in "How 'Bigger' Was Born" (1940), his retrospective account of the genesis of the protagonist of his most famous novel, *Native Son*, published earlier that same year. The stimulus to invent Bigger Thomas was the novelist's concern to anticipate the future of the volatile, unstable type of actual individual the fictional character represents. His passions frustrated by an oppressive environment and lacking a lucid understanding of his historically determined situation, the tendency of such a "dispossessed and disinherited man" will be to affiliate himself with the most persuasive force in the political arena. An "American product, a native son of this land," he carries "within him the potentialities of either Communism or Fascism." Whether he ends up following some "gaudy, hysterical leader who'll promise rashly to fill the void in him" or reaches "an understanding with the millions of his kindred fellow workers under trade-union or revolutionary guidance depends upon the future drift of events" in his country.[16] What is certain, however, is that this "free agent" is a reservoir of energy, roaming "the streets of our cities, a hot and whirling vortex of undisciplined and unchannelized impulses."[17] (Wright also perhaps alludes to the dime museum's pseudo-scientific display of anatomical oddities in his tropological characterization of the social phenomenon, the "distinct type," that fascinates him. "Just as one sees when one walks into a medical research laboratory jars of alcohol containing abnormally large or distorted portions of the human body, just so did I see and feel that the conditions of life under which Negroes are forced to live in America contain the embryonic emotional prefigurations of how a large part of the body politic would react under stress."[18])

The concern with the hard-to-predict fate of members of the American lumpenproletariat also links Wright's work to that of his friend and political associate (the two met at the Chicago John Reed Club) Nelson Algren. And it is therefore not surprising that in his introduction to Algren's 1941 novel, *Never Come Morning*, Wright defended the author's decision to make the agitated state of mind of the most debased stratum of American society his primary narrative topic. Undaunted by the fact that many novelists "would have condemned this subject matter, no doubt, as being sordid and loathsome," Algren plunges into the sphere of the filthy and the repulsive in search of insight into the obstacles (and promises) of radical political practice.

> [Algren] has long brooded upon the possibility of changing the social world in which we live, has long dreamed of the world's being different, and this pre-occupation has, paradoxically, riveted and directed microscopic attention upon that stratum of our society that is historically footloose, unformed, malleable, restless, devoid of inner stability, unidentified by class allegiances, yet full of hot, honest, blind striving. Algren's centering of his observation upon the lowly and brutal strivings of a Bruno Bicek is the product of his sound instinct and reasoning, for, strangely enough, the Bruno Biceks of America represent those depths of life – the realm of the irrational and the non-historical – that peri-odically push their way into the arena of history in times of crisis, war, and revolution.[19]

The statement articulates explicitly what Algren had conveyed im-plicitly in his previous novel, *Somebody in Boots*, by using specific passages from *The Communist Manifesto* as epigraphs to the book's third and fourth parts.[20] By echoing the pseudo-scientific analogy that Émile Zola had previously established as the ground of naturalist literary undertakings, Algren frames *Boots* as a textual experiment designed to examine the validity of Marx's political theory. The novel is set up as a test aimed at determining whether his hypothesis was applicable to conditions in the United States in the 1930s. By taking Marx's well-known pamphlet as one of his intertexts, Algren reveals that, like Wright, one of his primary inter-ests as a novelist in the 1930s was in the mode of existence and ideological swerves of the American lumpenproletariat.[21] And while there is much to be gained by interrogating the better-known writer's Depression-era output from this point of view, it strikes me that the less appreciated novelist's first work has a great deal to offer us as well. For one might claim that the significance of Algren's novel, originally titled "A Native Son,"[22] is that it helps bring forth what more conventional proletar-ian novels neglected: that the lumpenproletariat was an element in the unconscious of Depression-era left-wing subjectivity in this country. It was from this repulsive, unsettling substance that most ordinary radicals sought to maintain their distance. In reading closely the text that pro-vided Wright with the title to his groundbreaking commercial success we may reach a more profound understanding of what was at stake at the time in the radicalized novelist's encounter with a politically grotesque phenomenon.[23]

THE RHETORIC OF FLOWERS; OR, REVULSION
AND REVOLUTION

Roots, in fact, represent the perfect counterpart to the visible parts of a plant. While the visible parts are nobly elevated, the ignoble and sticky roots wallow in the ground, loving rottenness just as leaves love light. (Georges Bataille, "The Language of Flowers")

> What
> if lilacs last in *this* dooryard bloomd?
> Robert Duncan, "A Poem Beginning
> With a Line by Pindar"

Like *Bottom Dogs* and *From Flushing to Calvary*, Algren's *Somebody in Boots* is an episodic representation of the experiences of a member of the American lumpenproletariat in the early decades of the twentieth century. Although both Dahlberg and Algren treat this social phenomenon from a post-romantic or post-transcendentalist perspective, the comic tones evident in Dahlberg's autobiographical fictions are muted in his successor's work. Correlatively, in terms of compositional method, *Boots* may be categorized as an example of a grotesque naturalism.[24] This rhetorical strategy is best understood in relation to ideological celebrations of modernization as an inherently progressive social process and wholly positive historical force. In response to current attempts to ground utopian visions of the future on evolutionary models of scientific and technological growth, Algren turned to corporeal images of decay and sickness. His concerns are most apparent at the end of the novel when, in denouncing the Chicago World's Fair, he offensively and obscenely figures the urban landscape as a diseased and dying prostitute. The critical aggression behind the trope stands out vividly in relation to the monumental fountain set up outside the Exposition's Hall or Temple of Science. Upon arriving at this shrine to invention, presented as the redemptive solution to the nation's economic ills, visitors encountered at the entrance a giant sculpture, *Science Advancing Mankind*, which showed an immense robot bent over a tentative man and woman, gently guiding them into the future.[25] But Algren's hostility toward industrialization is made evident earlier in his novel through a series of brutally gruesome representations of bodily mutilation, for most of these are the result of a human being's contact with the railroad, an obvious (and traditional) figure for modern capitalism as a brutally destructive force. In both cases the radical novelist registers the violent underside of technological improvement and economic expansion on the body of the nation's most victimized and abject inhabitants.

In the numerous literal depictions of corporeal injury that *Boots* contains, the main character, Cass McKay, is either the witness or victim. Algren's purpose is clearly to show the devastating impact his protagonist's environment has on him as he grows up, the sensitive youth numbed by the bloody violence he either observes or experiences. For instance, early on Cass is horrified when, on two separate occasions, he is confronted by the corpse of another of the youthful inhabitants of the Texas border town where he lives. In both cases, a passing train has killed a child. The first victim is a boy whose "left arm was spewed off slantwise at the shoulder, the jaw hung limp. This Cass saw first. One eye hung out of its socket by one long thin wet thread, the filament rising and falling a little straight up and down as it hung" (*Boots*, 24). The second is a Mexican girl who, too eagerly grasping for coal from a moving car, is decapitated. Like the "carnival kewpie doll that had no head" which she had been pushing in a buggy, the human child, her long black shawl drenched scarlet, now "lay on her back, and her head had been severed from her body" (27–29). Between these two events, Cass stands by in agony as his brother Bryan, an alcoholic veteran whose health was destroyed when he was gassed in the First World War, cruelly wrenches off the head of the family cat and then flings it at Cass. Shortly thereafter, Cass sees his father, Stub McKay, repeatedly kick Bryan in the groin with such severity during a fight that the "flesh ripped and tore" (36). Overwhelmed, Cass runs away from home, eventually finding his way to a New Orleans brothel, where, due to his naivete, he sleeps with a prostitute without having the money to pay his bill afterwards. Beaten senseless by the house bouncer, Cass is left in an empty lot. He wakes up to find his chin caked with dried blood, "a deep furrow into the flesh" below his mouth where they "had tried to cut his throat," the head of a bodiless dog, "ants in both eyes," smiling up at him (50–51). Later, while standing in line for a free meal, Cass observes a bum's ravaged face. "Disaster or disease had torn or eaten the nose away until only the nostrils now remained" (105). Even more grisly is an event depicted shortly thereafter. Chased by the police across the top of a moving train, Cass leaps blindly down into a "reefer pit," unfortunately landing on the stomach of a pregnant woman. She then begins labor prematurely, giving birth to a stillborn child that Cass wraps in a wet newspaper and places in the corner. Dazed and too weak to move, the woman, forced to lie on the floor, "a cess-pen running with blood, stinking of urine and strewn with rags," vomits "down her own breast," pieces "of stuff" dribbling out "the corners of her mouth" (114–15).

The obvious intent of these ghastly yet by no means gratuitous descriptions is to shock the reader into an awareness of the miseries those living on the fringes of society suffer – before and during the Depression. The primary agent of destruction, the railroad, is a familiar symbol for the brutal economic forces whose invasive presence has shattered any semblance of rural paradise in the country. In post-industrial America the machine, and by extension the economy as a whole, terrorizes more than the flesh of the individual. The fragile, lyric consciousness is also severely damaged by its exposure to such harsh surroundings, the external world brutalizing bodies and poetic minds. Consequently, the attempt to establish a harmonious balance between the self and the environment is anachronistic and subject to ridicule. Offering a more politicized explanation than Dahlberg does in "Ariel in Caliban" for why "no one would now write a pastoral,"[26] Algren's parody of faith in nature as a source of redemption nevertheless runs parallel to Dahlberg's more elaborate critique in *Mimes* of this aesthetic ideology. Both mock (and mourn) the notion that the exchange between the self and its milieu can today be anything but an unequal battle between the mechanized world and its vulnerable inhabitants.

The narrator's repeated, negative allusions to Whitman's "When Lilacs Last in the Dooryard Bloom'd" convey this changed perspective. An early scene in the novel serves on the one hand to establish a point of reference for Cass's fall and to mark out the novel's distance from romantic transcendentalism. At fifteen, the still innocent, untarnished protagonist is on the verge of developing a genuinely poetic consciousness, an internal radiance flashing in his brain at times such that "a common bush becomes a glory, a careless sparrow on a swinging bough a wonder to behold" (*Boots*, 20–21). At this stage of his mental growth he establishes a narcissistic relationship with "a blooming lilac." He tenderly cares for the flower as if it were a mirror image of himself, brushing the soot off it that passing trains have left, watching it religiously as it raises itself "out of the dust" and yearns "toward sky." One night, awakened by the rain, Cass is compelled by the smell of the flower to leave his bed:

Then the velvet smell made a purple image in his brain; his throat seemed to swell with the wild-dark odor . . . And the smell from the dooryard's corner drew him as powerfully as though a woman waited for him there: he traced the texture of the lilac leaves as though touching a young girl's breasts for the first time. He closed his eyes; his fingers wandered wantonly, to stroke that delicate blooming. (21)

Cass then buries "his face deep in lilac-leaf," which leaves "his heart pained, first trembling a little, then swelling slow" (22). The comic representation of a boy caressing an anthropormorphized flower disfigures Whitman's serious use of the lilac trope in his elegy to an assassinated president. The erotic charge emanating from the somnambulist's ludicrous mix up of female person and leafy plant degrades the poet's strategy of using the natural entity as a model (cyclical) for social regeneration. When lust replaces mourning as the dominant passion of the figure, it ceases to convey the reassuring sense that the country will soon recover from its civil war and the death of its leader. If the trope is partly aimed at marking the final moment in the protagonist's life when his mental development can be thought of as a natural developmental process, as a blooming, it has the additional effect of humorously reducing idealist or transcendentalist appeals to "spiritual elevation." By placing Cass in the grip of "urges that draw him to what is low," Algren keeps the gaze of the text on "matter, vile and base reality."[27]

Algren's negative modification of grotesque systems of imagery dovetails with his dismal assessment of the incorporation of festive motifs into acts of brutality intended to sustain racial hierarchies. This critique is most apparent in a sequence of scenes designed to illustrate the internal tensions that at the time divided one segment of the American lumpenproletariat against another. The sequence begins with Cass's arrest, in part for having befriended an obstreperous black man. Sentenced to ninety days in an El Paso jail, Cass is taught never to "treat a black or a brown man as he would a white" (*Boots*, 140). A carnivalesque practice plays a formative role in his initiation into the necessities of being a racist. Cass's cellmate turns out to be the one-handed Nubby O'Neill, whose "highly-feigned hatred of everything not American and white was the high-point of his honor" (125). Known within the prison community as "the Judge" who presides over all sessions of the prisoners' "kangaroo court," O'Neill is the agent of Cass's education. If this mock court brings the official and serious down to the level of the unofficial and comic, it does not do so in order to pervert or disregard standard principles of law. Reproducing the penal system, complete with its prohibitions, rules of conduct, codes of behavior, and regulations, imitative mimicry in this case serves to establish further gradations of power or to reinforce existing hierarchies within the realm of the oppressed. "The play-pretend of the underdogs aping the wolves on top, the man-child game at once so terrible and so ludicrous" (137) creates a behind-bars version of the power relationships between the incarcerated and their jailers. The prisoners have learned from experience that one of the most efficient techniques for establishing or maintaining order is to produce a spectacle of corporal punishment. Playfully conducted yet viciously brutal in its effects, the preferred mode of inflicting pain is to force the victim to submit to a public thrashing. Thus when a helpless Mexican boy joins the prison community, the inmates, guided by Nubby, form a gauntlet and cruelly flog the boy with their leather belts. All the men must participate in this sporting activity "each waiting his turn" in line like "sand-lot semi-pros at batting practice" (139). When Cass, out of sympathy for the sobbing victim, fails to strike the already black and blue buttocks with the appropriate force, Nubby declares that Cass must be subjected to the same abuse he was supposed to mete out. His training consists then of the lesson that in "tank ten" full participation in festive rituals, in symbolic thrashings that double as acts of racist aggression, is mandatory if one wishes to remain a part of the sovereign group.

Stallybrass and White have termed this process whereby the low exert real and symbolic power over the even lower *displaced abjection.*[28] The function of carnivalesque motifs in such cases is to erect and preserve boundaries, one marginal social group maintaining its integrity through the ritual humiliation of more defenseless, disorganized persons. And it is therefore hardly surprising that the laughter generated in such an atmosphere does not resound as a rejection of all authority and as a call for freedom from intimidation. In an earlier prison scene, Cass listens in horror as Nubby mocks his "punk," Creepy Edelbaum, a seemingly retarded prisoner whom the Judge repeatedly molests. Though "sick with pity for the bending boy," and "cringing with fear," Cass "laughed, loud as any. He was afraid not to laugh" (133). That Creepy, his face "angelic and girlish," must also perform domestic tasks for O'Neill, in effect serving as his wife, suggests the gendered nature of the power relationships inside the prison. Throughout the book, feminine traits are attributed to the perennially downtrodden, those who lie beneath the boots of the strong. For example Cass's brother Bryan, mentally as well as physically damaged by the war, infuriates their father (Stubby) by giggling in a "womanish" manner and tittering "slyly, girlishly" (14). Moreover, the implication of the names Algren gives to several of his male characters is that they lack masculine or phallic power. In the economy of gender in the novel, Nubby (who is missing a hand), Stub, and Cass (who has a scar running down the side of his face as a result of his visit to a brothel) have been socially castrated. (In addition to evoking castration, the name Cass also evokes his status as a social outcast and, perhaps, more ironically, the character's lack of class-consciousness.)

The logical result of the use of gender to characterize social inequities is that Algren eventually selects the figure of a female prostitute to epitomize the condition of the socially abject. The site at which class and sexual structures of oppression overlap, "the whore" is, for Algren, a summary trope for the plight of the American lumpenproletariat.[29] (At the beginning of part three Algren weaves into the text another narrative thread, one that focuses on Norah Eagan, who eventually becomes a "harlot" after losing her job. Had Norah remained a mulatto, as she was in the original manuscript, she would have been the point of convergence of three [race, class, and sex] structures of oppression. James Farrell, the reader for Vanguard, felt it was not believable that a person like Cass would become involved in an interracial love affair. Algren therefore had to rewrite the character as a white woman.) Yet the prostitute is also the figure in the novel around which the tensions inscribed in the author's relationship to socially marginal persons gather. On the one hand, the female prostitute supplies the writer with the vulgarly grotesque bodily imagery through which he expresses his revolutionary fury, the lumpen thus tapped by the radicalized novelist as a source of critical energy. But his compassion notwithstanding, the writer also fashions himself as a politically aware commentator on social injustice by differentiating himself from lumpen political ignorance. For my purposes it is revealing that such tensions manifest themselves most strongly in the midst of the writer's aggressive denunciation of an international festival trumpeting worldwide economic growth, in the midst of his hostile reaction to an extreme example of the capitalist appropriation of popular carnival: the World's Fair.

Perceptually more attentive than usual due to a ten-month incarceration (his second), Cass is, upon his release, shocked into an awareness of the extent to which preparations for the 1933 Century-of-Progress Exposition have transformed South State Street into a carnivalesque marketplace. "On either side hawkers sold patent medicines, World's Fair flags and World's Fair flowers, World's Fair souvenirs and World's Fair balloons" (219). In the midst of such commercial excess, Cass also observes the difficulties the socially marginal have as they try to cash in on the event as well. Pimping, selling contraceptives, or begging, they must also keep an eye out at all times for the police. The startling sight provokes a recollection of the emotional desperation such a sordid existence produces. Whereas the visual spectacle is designed to prevent the out-of-town visitors to the fair from realizing the social conditions of the surrounding environment, such distractions only work on tourists. The spectacle's contrary effect on those who know the city is to intensify their awareness of widespread suffering. Misleading appearances, when grasped as such, heighten an awareness of the truth. Most strikingly the duplicitous actions of the fair sponsors and participants are characterized as in sum a coercive act of figuration.

> Cass had forgotten something of the suffering in this city, and what he had forgotten came back to him with redoubled force now. Almost it was like seeing South State for the first time; his eyes were opened by unfamiliarity; a street of misery unspeakable.
>
> He had known long of hungering thousands here, of Chicago's maze of graft and rackets, of its gangster politicians and its crooked mayors. But never before had Cass seen its hunger-ridden streets decorated with flags, nor its whores selling tin souvenirs. He had known long that the price of common bread here, was, for thousands, degradation. That here, just in order to eat, thousands lived in fear, furtively, with lust, shamefully.
>
> And now the city itself seemed a whore, selling a tin souvenir.
>
> Now the city had been made to wear a painted grin and a World's Fair smile, in order that business (which had been ailing somewhat) be made whole once more. (219)

The "misery unspeakable" may nevertheless be figured visually, an image used to express an experience of extreme violation. The grotesque trope of Chicago as a whore is a reaction to what the text describes as the prosopopoeiac imposition of a part of a face, a smile, onto the surface of an inanimate entity, a city. Aiming to restore the health and integrity of the business community, the fair's promoters and civic leaders have (the passage argues) personified the city to try and heal its economically fragmented condition. The figure of the city as a whore thus disfigures the figuration of the city as a cosmetically enhanced, gigantic grin. Struck by the literal sight of a prostitute selling tin souvenirs on the street, the character adopts this as a suitable metaphor for the urban situation in its entirety. The similarity the prostitute trope isolates, however, has to do with a discrepancy between looks and feelings, outside and inside, surface and depth. What the glittering urban landscape in its World's Fair attire has in common with a prostitute on the job is that each employs seductive tactics to entice customers, putting on flashy apparel and facial expressions as a prerequisite to doing good business. The city in the context of the exposition is, like an exploited whore, a commodity packaged for consumption. The meaning of the critically deployed figure of speech then is that Chicago has become part of a system of signification in which visible signs are manipulated to produce misleading meanings. The prostitute is the tropological embodiment of an otherwise abstract linguistic structure, and what it registers is the artifice involved in the way signifiers and signifieds are attached. The flags, flowers, and balloons (and later "purple totem poles" [239]) are certainly signifiers that connote pleasure; but these are inaccurate expressions of the actual situation of the city, or, by extension, of the social body its degraded inhabitants constitute. The semiology of the fair, like the semiology of prostitution, is a form of false advertising designed to trick gullible customers into believing that the body they see is the body they will get.

To grasp the commercial imperatives behind visible appearances one must therefore go beyond aestheticized surfaces; but does the character really possess the intellectual and rhetorical skills to disclose how beautiful appearances mask factual corruption? On the contrary, one of the main burdens of the narrative undertaking has been to show why he lacks such skills, to account historically for his ignorance. It is thus Algren's outrage at the incongruous juxtaposition of economic euphoria and mass penury that finds expression in this section of the novel. The urgency of his need to denounce the event causes the writer to push beyond the limits of his representational project. Though he continues to insist on the epistemological authority of his figurations, it is evident that the force of the imagery has become crucial. Knowledge and truth yield the stage to the grotesque, whose disruptive power is needed to do battle against the ideological seductions of aesthetic displays.

That Cass is not capable of the insights that are attributed to him here is evident later when the narrator comments upon the blunting effects of the character's previous experiences. "He [Cass] was an ignorant man. The real world he never saw. Daily he saw suffering and want, but he saw through a veil of familiarity. What he saw he took for granted. He could not trouble himself, one way or another, about any better or happier world. He had become too hardened to pain and to suffering. His heart had become calloused." "All those faculties which might have enabled Cass to see farther than the end of his nose had been dulled; they had been dulled into atrophy by hunger and cold and frequent humiliation. So Cass had not only gone hungry and cold, but he had been blinded to that which had robbed him" (230). Algren attempts to obscure this inconsistency by proposing that the text's tropes come from Cass's actual perception of a literal whore, that a random sight is the origin of the figurations. Yet the purportedly metonymical origin of the metaphor fails to persuade us that we are still within the consciousness of the character. (The novel makes extensive use of free indirect discourse to keep us lodged in the emotionally devastated mind of a member of the American lumpenproletariat.) As the critical discourse becomes increasingly aggressive and more explicit, Algren continues with minimal success to struggle to hide the obvious split opening up here by containing the extension of the trope in parentheses. Yet despite the growing distance between the narrative point of view and the main character, the lumpenproletariat still provides the offensive imagery with which the writer attacks their common enemy.

(The divide will increase as Algren introduces a model of leftist integrity into the novel in the form of Dill Doak, a black performer at the burlesque house where Cass works. Impressed by the intelligence and pride of Doak, Cass accompanies his new friend to a political rally, a "gathering of white and Negro workers in Washington Park" [242]. Though bored by the speeches, most of which point to the need to articulate radical unity across racial lines, and unable to grasp the speaker's calls for revolution, Cass's political fate still seems to be hanging in the balance. Then O'Neill arrives back in town and chastises Cass for associating with the racial other: "How come you forget how I slap hell out o' you once fer messin' with them ugly black sons-abitches?" [247]. The political education of a member of the "dangerous class" ends here, his future no doubt to play the "part of a bribed tool of reactionary [and racist] intrigue.")

Sliding from the face down to the lower parts of the gigantic female body, Algren's (or the narrator's) Marxist critique of the collusion between the news media and the business classes becomes exceptionally vulgar and offensive. The grotesque body in the form of a physically ailing woman becomes the truth beneath the city newspaper's duplicitously sanitized *coverage* of the commotion at the World's Fair. The social meaning that the continuation of the gendered figure continues to express is that the wretched, miserable inhabitants of the city have been traumatized, castrated in the logic of the figuration. Like the artificially decorated landscape, the reportage deflects attention away from the wounded and sickened condition of the lowest of the low, the abject. The vulgar use of a grotesque image of a woman makes a Marxist point: the disenfranchised lumpen masses lack power.

(Just as in the final stages of syphilis a dying prostitute is given an urethral smear, so did a World's Fair now seek to conceal the decadence of a city sick to death. This city was trying with noise and flags to hide the corruption that private ownership had brought it. The *Tribune* was its smear. The *Tribune* gave glamor to its World's Fair reportage, but said nothing of homeless thousands living in shelters; not a word about women being forced into prostitution under its very nose. The *Tribune* printed pictures of Buckingham fountain, of merry-go-rounds and royal weddings, but had no space for warning its readers of an epidemic begun at the Fair. Publication of such a warning would have saved many lives, but it might also have hurt World's Fair receipts. The *Tribune* was the World's Fair's pimp. Its concern was for the money-bags of Lake Shore Drive, of Winnetka and Wilmette; it had no concern for the truth. Systematically it fought, as always, any change in an order of society so beautifully calculated to permit the plundering of the millions by the few, so ideally suited to enhance private interest at the cost of the masses: The system which requires of each generation that millions be slain in wars for world-markets. The *Tribune* calls such killings: "A war to end war," or "A war for democracy." Its editors spew "patriotism," "love," "kindness," "brotherhood of man," – the while piously resigning themselves to the approach of another war whose sole purpose will be that of profits for just such men as the *Tribune*'s editors and owners. The *Tribune* prints false news, doctors its news, distorts its news, shouts "America First!" ...) (219–20)[30]

The verbal attack eventually flattens out into a compellingly literal, ethically driven critique of the epistemological fraudulence of mainstream journalism. The newspaper's complicity with the interests of corporate capital leads either to lying or to a refusal to report important facts. The *Tribune* occludes the economic determinations of military conflicts and ignores the unhealthy conditions at the exposition to ensure that money will continue to be made by those in power. Choosing to attend only to the carnivalesque atmosphere of the civic event, reinforcing the fair's trumpeting of scientific achievement and technological invention as the means of improving the quality of everyday life, the newspaper's social function was to abet the fair in making people sick.

The figural point of departure of the critique, however, is for my purposes of greater interest. The unpleasant aspects of the equation of the festive atmosphere outside the exposition with a preparation applied to the genital region of a syphilitic woman are apparent. Since the smear is less of a cure than a way to mask the effects of a sexually transmitted disease, the visibly ailing sex organs have the status here of a trope for the scandalous condition of Chicago in the 1930s, for the naked truth of Depression-era existence.[31] Almost two decades earlier, Carl Sandburg had figured the city in a comparably gigantic yet much less grotesquely obscene style.[32] In "Chicago" (1916) the poet too remarks upon the "painted women, criminals, the starving poor" who inhabit the location. But his response is to characterize the city as a huge and healthy (Whitmanesque) masculine body. Drawing his images from the "high" portions of the body, he refers to Chicago as the "husky, brawling/ City of the Big Shoulders," one that sings proudly with "lifted head" of its indomitable strength. A "tall bold slugger set vivid against the little soft cities," he laughs with certainty that victory will ultimately be his.[33] While Sandburg's praise of the working class joins male vigor to spiritual fortitude in a sublime image of vertical elevation, Algren's base imagery, his grotesque naturalism, stresses the physically corrupt material body of a woman on the threshold of death. Here we have a rhetorical figure that, intentionally or coincidentally, disfigures a pre-existing one, that performs a critical task. (Does Algren's trope disfigure the Statue of Liberty as well? Lauren Berlant refers to the icon as "our national prostitute" and reads the monument as an "object of collective fantasy" that gives "formal expression to the utopian promise of the United States." Perhaps Algren means Miss Lumpen [my phrase] to take Miss Liberty's place in the "National Symbolic," thus giving formal expression to the pessimistic facts of material decay in this country.[34]) In sum, Algren's vulgar method of intertwining repulsive imagery and Marxist dissent includes the use of the wounded, unhealthy body in literal representations of extra-texual reality and in inter-textual confrontations with competing figurations.

For Stallybrass, once the domain of politics was opened up "as something other than reflection," which I take to mean once the necessary link between class position and ideological commitment was broken, the problem of politics was clarified as the process of articulating classes. This was, as he sees it, the problem that Marx figured "under the name of the lumpenproletariat" and that may be understood as "a play (an often violent play) between heterogeneity and homogeneity" (*Marx*, 90). My addition to this assertion is to claim that engaging in the play (an often *critical* play) between figuration and disfiguration is one of the ways in which literary texts can and have participated in the political process. And this was the problem that Algren among others addressed in the 1930s in relation to the grotesque body.

In the first half of part four of *Boots*, set in 1934, the narrator temporarily displaces the character in order to construct a montage of social evils. As the fair reopens in the spring, Cass is pushed to the side so that the radical novelist as grotesque naturalist may directly protest the pernicious effects of the collusive news media. The writer now steps forth to depict the loathsome facts of social existence and to account for them as a direct result of economic inequities. The reader's attention is drawn to the prostitutes, compared to flies buzzing around "the dungheap," who have traveled across the country to ply their trade at the fair; to the backed up sewers of Tenement Town; to the "welter of diseased slum-streets" filled with "half-sick kids"; and to the "old men, like unclaimed curs with tentative claws, pawing in garbage barrels or ash cans" for food (236–38). Brief reports of domestic violence; of police brutality (the unprovoked shooting of a black man recently arrived from the South); of gang fights between different ethnic groups; and the suicide of an out-of-work electrician follow (238–39). Though there is a "jungle in the depths of Chicago's rumbling gut, a charnel-dump next to Donnybrook fair" (238), ensuring that "the star-spangled banners decorating the city will end up as "a soft wipe-rag," one would not know it by reading the papers. Run by, as Algren sees it, the hypocritically respectable owners of the city's major newspaper, they have no interest in acknowledging the nauseating truths of everyday life outside the fair gates.

The *Tribune* had nothing to say of this, for the *Tribune* was owned by the pure-in-heart, and the pure-in-heart averted their eyes. They were good Christian editors proud of their paper, of the greed-inspired lies and the sweet christfablings and the starspangled spew that they termed "editorials." They were proud of their souls, for their souls were clean; and proud of their churches, for their churches were large; and proud of their schools, for their schools taught conformity. (237)

To clarify further the purpose of the fair the narrator picks up the grotesque figuration previously attributed to the character's imagination. To protest the *"colossal event"* (237) by emphasizing its principal aim – to boost sales by stimulating desires for new products – Algren again tropes the urban landscape at the time of the fair as a gigantic female prostitute. An embodiment of the city's miserable inhabitants, she is this time lying submissively on her back. The fair is a "great Century-of-Progress slut stretched out on a six-mile bed along the lake with Buicks for breasts and a mayor standing up to his neck in her navel making a squib-like noise" (237–38). That the preceding paragraph refers to the mayor as "a pimp for Big Business" ("Even a mayor has to pimp a little now and then to make ends meet: for the Chrysler outfit, or Standard Oil") makes him the intermediary, the middleman who arranges for capital to fuck the city. In short, the exposition is conceptualized as an exploitative, commodified sexual practice. The grotesque body facilitates a rhetorical exchange between the economic and the erotic across the urban landscape for the purpose of articulating a political critique of corporate capital. The image of the tiny mayor engulfed by the personified event suggests, however, the eruptive force contained within subordinate social groups. Were they to come together and form an organized political entity, a collective body, they would, the trope implies, have the ability to overwhelm or absorb those that exploit them.

Fittingly, in a parenthetical aside that is undoubtedly a reflection of the energies generated by the strike wave that broke across the country in the year preceding the novel's publication, Algren forecasts a political insurrection, one to be undertaken by those whom mainstream society has deemed filthy and vile. "(Be pure in your hearts, be proud yet a little while, wave your flags, sing your hymns, close your eyes, save your souls, go on grabbing. Get all you can while yet you may. For the red day will come for your kind, be assured)." The prediction counters the historical vision promulgated by the fair's promoters. As Rydell puts it: "America's depression-era fairs represented a drive to modernize America by making it an ever more perfect realization of an imperial dream world of abundance, consumption, and social hierarchy based on the reproduction of existing power relations premised on categories of race and gender."[35] Confronted with an ersatz utopia of this sort, one in which class antagonisms seem to vanish into the sensory swirl of a commercial phantasmagoria, Algren promises a future revolution of the revolting classes.

He then goes on to contest the theme of the fair – announced on a neon sign at the fairgrounds: "A Century of Progress. Bigger and Better than Ever" – vigorously in a late scene utilizing Cass, who has become a barker at the Little Rialto (a burlesque house). By juxtaposing the character's spiel and the mayor's affirmation of the capitalist spectacle as a sign of future prosperity, the novelist degrades the notion that scientific innovation and industrial growth are sufficient to ameliorate social problems.[36] As Cass shouts to passersby to "come in an see the *hottest woman-show off the grounds,*" "*All she wears is sleeves an' two beads of perspiration*" (*Boots*, 235), a "street-radio" overhead amplifies the mayor's remarks on the exposition. "*This is an event to be remembered as the climax of man's ideals. There is not a business which will not profit by this epochal event. The bettering of economic conditions will increase our attendance. An historic milestone on our national journey toward greater and finer and better things for our people*" (234). Whereas Cass refers to the pleasures of watching jiggling flesh in motion – "*she shakes like jello,*" "*Stella the little dawncin' girrul!*" "*Yo' can put ever'thin she wears on a letter behind a two-cent stamp*" – the mayor praises the exposition as an indication of social change for the better. Incorporating into the collage fragments of

Roosevelt's clichéd comments on the fair as a sure indication the economic crisis is over, that "*the national emergency*" has passed, Algren mocks the idealist faith in manifest destiny that the President articulates. For the nation's leader the event, by creating "*a demand for the latest products of science and industry*," will improve the collective spirit of the country. The fair indicates "*the strengthening of national morale*," and is "*an inspiring demonstration of courage and confidence*" (235). Those who visit the glorious exposition "*will see signs pointing the way along that upward path upon which we as a nation have set our feet*" (235).

These rival discourses obviously register an antithetical set of values. As the prosthetically enhanced voice of the disembodied (and crippled) leader is challenged by the lumpen as burlesque barker, the presidential ("high") vision of collective transcendence through historical progress is sullied by the "low" image of the gyrating female body. Affiliating himself with the social sphere of the grotesquely exposed dancer, the novelist strips away the aura of political idealism, mocking a hypocritically constructed fantasy discourse by bringing it into contact with the debasing description of a corporeal-based form of popular entertainment.

Algren's *Somebody in Boots* thus helps make it possible to grasp the way in which images of the grotesque body were inscribed in the thirties in sociopolitical and cultural conflicts. It is not just that he marshals the aesthetics of the ugly – of somatic disease and physical injury – against more traditionally pleasing, classical systems of bodily representation. His rhetorical tactics are the means whereby he aligns himself with excluded and severely impoverished persons *and* affiliates his literary undertaking with a particular amusement. The radical (male) novelist stands alongside the lumpenproletariat and burlesque in their common opposition to the dominant classes and to world expositions. Following the path of the grotesque body – one gendered female in this case – not only leads back to a recreational practice in which women played a prominent role as performers. Focusing on this body also leads us toward the ideological and real battles being played out in the period between opposing social forces. The literature and amusement relay turns out to be one of the more illuminating routes toward a better understanding of the politics of the novel in the Depression era.

Somebody in Boots also alerts us to the interpretive challenge the concept of the carnivalesque poses to critical commentary on this aspect of the decade. By registering the degree to which the World's Fair stands as a conservative appropriation of a carnivalesque repertoire for purposes antithetical to the interests of oppressed persons, Algren reminds us that the context of their use tends to overdetermine the impact festive forms can have in a given historical situation.[37] It is for this reason that the narrator condemns the excessive spectacle that the fair's multiple attractions constitute as "a zigzag riot of fakery." The function of among other things "nude dancers, wind-tunnels," "alligator wrestlers," "flame-divers" and "five-legged cow[s]" (235) contained inside the fairgrounds is to help facilitate the marketing of new goods outside the entertainment zone. Modes of collective fun retain hardly any subversive energy in such a milieu, and when confronted with the capitalist incorporation of public revelry on a grand scale, the radicalized writer may well be pushed to violently grotesque extremes. Hence Algren's deployment throughout the novel of exceptionally offensive and obscene images of physical decay and death – a vulgar Marxism in which revolution "begins in the bowels of the earth, as in the materialist bowels of proletarians."[38]

3

Fascism and fragmentation in Nathanael West

Will America laugh or step up to shake hands with Colonel Cooper?
Carey McWilliams, "Hollywood Plays with Fascism"

Si was stripped to the waist with two cartridge belts crossed over his chest and a canvas legionnaire's kepi on his head . . . "My dear Si," he [Sam Margolies, a movie director] was saying, "you must make them feel it. Every ripple of your muscles must make them feel passion . . . They all feel they are you, you are loving her for them, the millions who want love and beauty and excitement."
John Dos Passos, *The Big Money*

"Hollywood has suddenly become a fascist recruiting station." So begins Carey McWilliams' 1935 article on the rise of a "flamboyant militarism" inside the film industry around mid decade. Operating under the banner of such slogans as "Strictly disciplined! Smartly drilled! Colorfully uniformed!" several fascist units emerged in the Depression era, seemingly as a conservative reaction to fears about a burgeoning radicalism in Hollywood. But these units were also intended to serve another, more promotional function. They were "designed to advertise the charms of fascist organization to the American public. Through the publicity medium of the industry, the most powerful propaganda machine in America, these gaudy units sponsored by popular and well-known stars can be advertised to millions of Americans as the latest and snappiest fascist models." Of the actors who had lent their names to such organizations, McWilliams attends in particular to Gary Cooper, ostensible founder of the Hollywood Hussars – a regimental entity whose ambition was to inspire "other communities to organize similar bodies of trained Americans throughout the nation."[1]

No doubt the long-forgotten fact that fascism was briefly in vogue in Hollywood in the thirties strikes us as little more than a bit of historical trivia. A kind of politicized fashion statement, the trend has little meaning today. Nevertheless, it retains a certain hermeneutic suggestiveness when we recall that in the famous riot scene depicted at the end of Nathanael West's *The Day of the Locust* (1939), a member of the over-excited crowd outside Kahn's Persian Palace Theatre hollers, "Here comes Gary Cooper." Is there some hidden significance embedded in this seemingly innocuous reference? Certainly the scene itself has frequently been read as a manifestation of authorial anxiety concerning the possibility that "It Could Happen Here,"[2] that the enraged lower-middle-classes, were they to become enamored of a charismatic leader, might provide a social base for the creation of a domestic fascism. Here I would like to take this reference as the point of departure for a reconsideration of the extent to which West's last two novels constitute critical responses to what he perceived to be the threatening possibility that the political movement might take hold in this country.

Aided by some of the preceding critical scholarship on the nature of fascist and protofascist subjectivity, I seek to trace West's (psycho)analytical encounter with this phenomenon through his final two novels, *A Cool Million: The Dismantling of Lemuel Pitkin* (1934) and *The Day of the Locust* (1939). Both works seek to discover and disclose the degree to which the identifications mass-produced bodies solicit are responsible for the reproduction of potential agents of violent aggression. His aim was to contest the proliferation of idealized images of powerful, organically whole bodies as a means of fabricating group identities. To ironize the politically coercive force of attractive corporeal models, he constructed grotesque images of somatic mutilation and dismemberment. Comic fragmentation became a constitutive element in critically motivated acts of literary radicalism directed against the reactionary use of spectacularly built bodies to facilitate libidinal investments on a mass scale.

To situate West's rhetorical strategies more precisely it will be helpful to mention a few of the decade's more fascinating corporeal figurations. The epigraph above, taken from the third volume of Dos Passos' *U.S.A.* trilogy, takes us behind the scenes of the construction of a run-of-the-mill militarized physique. Here the body image that will soon be projected on the screen is intended to make the spectator "feel" powerful while also directing his desire toward a specific object: the female lead (played by Margo Dowling).[3] Si lacks, however, the genuinely amazing qualities of the enduring heroic character who, in 1938, burst onto the national scene in the pages of Action Comics: Superman. Perfectly shaped and virtually invulnerable, the "Man of Steel" needed to fear only the red or green colored fragments of his exploded birth planet, Krypton. (Lead would protect him from the debilitating effects of this planetary matter.)

Five years earlier, his pulp fiction prototype had made his first cultural appearance. Having developed a taste for adventure "back in the War" ("'We all liked the big scrap'"), Clark "Doc" Savage, the statuesque "Man of Bronze," was so admirably and solidly shaped that upon first glance he could be mistaken for a figure "sculptured in hard bronze," a "bronze bust." His straight hair "lay down tightly as a metal skullcap." The tendons of his hands "were like cables." Despite his immense size, the man was "so well put together that the impression" is one of immense strength. "The bulk of his great body was forgotten in the smooth symmetry of a build incredibly powerful." And through a rigorously ritualized form of self-punishment, he had trained his hand muscles to the point where "they were like cushioned steel, capable of withstanding the most violent shock." In fact, his masochistic daily exercise routine had enabled Doc to make his body nearly impervious to threatening external forces. He had repeatedly subjected "all parts of his great body to terrific blows in order that he might be able always to steel himself against them."[4]

In Theweleit's analysis of a comparable experience in the form of an actual historical practice, the outcome of such a disciplinary assault on bodily peripheries is to cancel out desires for sexual contact with others. The effect of the regular beatings German youth received at military academies was to estrange them from the pleasure principle; they were drilled to the point where they became beings for whom the only legitimate bodily feelings were painful ones.[5] To further dam up and maintain control over internal drives, such soldier males fantasized the metallization of their bodies. "The new man is a man whose physique has been machinized, his psyche eliminated – or in part displaced into his body armor."[6] The figuratively reinforced ego is in this manner protected from the terrifying possibility of dissolving amid the flow of the individual's libido. The man of steel is a defensive construct designed to suppress the productive force of unconscious desire. (To the degree that passion may cause uncomfortable sensations of overheating, it is not surprising that Doc Savage and Superman built their respective "Fortresses of Solitude" in arctic regions.) Correlatively, this desire manifested itself in the external world through images of frighteningly oceanic or sickeningly infectious forces. For the Freikorps officers, this danger from the outside took shape as the Red Flood of communist insurgency. For Doc Savage and his men in their first adventure, it was contamination from the Red Death they had to combat. (This "weird malady," the symptoms of which include the breaking out of gruesome red spots on the flesh, was responsible for the death of Doc's father, who contracted it in the course of his financial dealings with a Central American republic.)

Such fascist or protofascist fantasies of the armored body provide a politicized frame for investigating West's grotesque technique of depicting persons in dadaist fashion as dysfunctional automatons. His pathetically mechanized characters, whose actions and desires are clearly determined by forces outside the self, generate a corrosive laughter aimed at reactionary motifs. Radical parody takes place here at the level of body imagery. (Of course I'm not suggesting that Superman was an expression of ideological support for European fascism. In fact, in 1942 he went to war against the Nazis. Still, the figure does resemble the contents of the fascist imaginary. In other words, put another S on his chest and things begin to look a bit disturbing.) In that West's comically debilitated machine-men are intended to serve an anti-fascist function, they take their place alongside Miller's reinvention of himself as a comic writing machine. Both devices are meant to generate radical effects. They are, however, distinct constructs. Miller envisioned the alignment of the natural body with a technological apparatus as a subversively recreational enterprise, as a means of releasing the productive forces of unconscious drives. West, in contrast, viewed the increasing intimacy of human beings and machines less as a vehicle of radical emancipation than as a condition demanding intense scrutiny. Rather than seek to regenerate his readers physiologically and emotionally by joyfully positing their future transformation into desiring machines, West's radicalism took shape as a critical inquiry into the troubling aspects of the mechanization of desire. It was this condition or pathology that his use of grotesque motifs sought to make legible.[7]

Similar differences between the two writers' methods are evident in regard to their relationship to American amusement. For Miller, carnivalized entertainment supplied the aesthetic energies driving his literary practice; grotesque autobiography took its cues straight from early twentieth-century recreations. West's approach toward a wide array of amusements was a much more cautious one. Though perpetually intrigued by vaudeville, burlesque, the dime museum, the dime novel and Hollywood film, and willing to incorporate elements of these practices into his writing thematically and at the level of composition, he did not, however, embrace fully these forms of entertainment. Rather, his grotesque prose emerged as the place where modernized fun was subjected to intense scrutiny as a social force. As the novel mutated into a critically reflective practice, the effects of American amusement became the writer's primary topic. Literature and amusement were, for West, interdependent in that he turned the ideological impact of one into the object of critical analysis of the other.[8] To attempt to separate them would rob the politicized writer of one of his most valuable sources of insight into the nature of the anxieties and aggressions circulating through contemporary society.

If the face is a politics, dismantling the face is a politics. (Gilles Deleuze and Felix Guattari, *A Thousand Plateaus*)

If you don't want to suffer you should tear yourself apart . . . Saved by separation (Djuna Barnes, *Nightwood*)

In "The State Kettle," the final section of "Superstition and Images," the last chapter of *Do These Bones Live,* Dahlberg derisively conjoins the American public's fascination with famous movie actors to the collective devotion to political rulers in Russian and German society. If the dictator "heals the collective consciousness," so too are screen stars "immediate and practical as purification." Stalin, Hitler, and film icons are "fetiches" [sic] the overvaluation of which is the means whereby a deluded populace assents to its own destruction. In the political arena a misguided equation of a collective self with the government results in the mutilations of the worker: the "mystical identity between state and proletariat always makes the latter the sacrificial flesh and blood of the former." Specular exchanges between an admired leader and his victimized followers have the unfortunate consequence of furthering the corporeal suffering of those who assent to the "hoax," who misrecognize themselves in the figure of the "Fatherland": the worker's "own life and limbs are dismembered. Unwittingly complicit in their own torture, the oppressed embrace their own exploitation. Betraying the possibility of present change in the vain expectation of future improvement, they willfully assent to the tearing of themselves apart: "humanity [is] forever rending its own limbs and drinking its own blood so that it can resurrect itself."

A whole people can be taught to swaddle its tenderest expectancies in its own cerements and to yearn for its own eclipse and dissolution in the mistaken belief that its sacrifice will heal and ennoble men who have not yet been born. National self-sacrifice is so rooted that men and women die more loftily for the race than they live for it. Suicide squads are the undeniable signs of the death cult that is abroad today and not the tokens of a deep moral fervor. Death is the magnetical mountain, and each man, saturated with the death-ethics that political partisanship demands, asks not how he is going to live, but how he is going to die so that another generation may live.[9]

If the relief from a painful existence, which technologically-based entertainments and authoritarian politics provide, requires masochistic acts of submission that result in physical damage, the complement to this violently integrative process is the sadistic outlet that mechanized forms of humor offer. The function of these, according to Dahlberg, is to allow for the release of pent-up energies while maintaining present hierarchies, the social order held firmly in place by the discharge of resentment in ways that do not alter the material conditions of existence. The contemporary filmgoer's perniciously vicarious, ritualized participation in comic orgies of destruction leaves existing class relations unchanged.

> The cave rites today are performed in the rotting apocalyptic darkness of the movie-grotto: the American goes into this hidden pit to purge his fatigued and galvanic lusts. His nerves are appeased by mechanical motion-picture deities. He takes his revenge against the fates, misery, unemployment, sexual starvation, through the sadic furies of Popeye the Sailor: the little mechanized underdog demolishes walls, furniture, hurtles pianos, chairs, dishes, and makes the whole world propertyless. Comics, automobile accidents, tabloid sex crimes take the place of sacrifice. The Little American *breaks out* into laughter over the abstract tombstone cartoons of Walt Disney. Small wonder American Humor is so fulsomely reverenced and advertised: our bulk humor is as insidious an inculcator of obedience as kneeling and prayer. (*Bones*, 152)

Dahlberg's analogical recourse to the "primitive" is less important than is his likening of various forms of mass amusement to political spectacles. What sustains the comparison is a similarity at the level of ideological effect. The collective consumption across political and entertainment spectrums of transfixing images achieves and reinforces an impression of unity or solidarity which in turn maintains the capacity of those in power to maintain control over those they wish to dominate: "Oh, how the gods that rule know how to use man." Dahlberg's radical solution is that we must "throw away idols" and as Moses did, destroy "all graven images" (155). Only in this manner can the untenable substitutions that function as the cornerstone of systemic oppression be obliterated.

Since Dahlberg's hostility (which I have suggested is a reversal of the position he adopted as a practicing novelist) has superficial affinities with West's attitude toward commercial entertainment, it is essential to underscore the differences between the two in regard to the literature/amusement/radicalism nexus.[10] For Dahlberg (at the end of the

Depression era), the redemptive antidote to collective diversions would be an authentically erotic literature in which men and women mingle in a sexually procreative fashion. Modern industrialism, mass politics, and technologically mediated entertainment stand in the way of achieving aesthetic redemption. Rather than retreat to such an anachronistic position, West proposes that an incisive contribution to radical thought and practice requires the writer to pay close critical attention to an array of modern amusements – especially to the use these make of grotesque images of the fragmented body.

His parodic treatment of the dime museum renders the politics of such cultural institutions, at least in their Depression-era incarnations, indeterminate. The "Chamber of American Horrors, Animate and Inanimate" is in truth, we are told, "a bureau for disseminating propaganda of the most subversive nature" (*Novels, Cool*, 222). Yet the fact that its operations are overseen by "the fat man," who is a double agent, serving the interests of international capitalism (Jewish bankers) and communism, empties the claim to subversion of all its force. That the museum's manager, Sylvanus Snodgrasse, is characterized as a resentful poet whose "desire for revolution" is really "a desire for revenge" (due to his lack of commercial success) further undermines the idea that such an amusement might make a contribution to progressive causes.[11]

West's critical treatment of American entertainment is more penetrating, however, when he addresses the topic from the perspective of its effects on its patrons rather than when – as is the case with the museum – he raises suspicions as to the motivations of its proprietors. The episode in which Lemuel Pitkin, *A Cool Million*'s hapless protagonist, finds work as a "stooge" in Riley and Robbins' burlesque act, "Fifteen Minutes of Furious Fun with Belly Laffs Galore," is a hyperbolic illustration of the way violent amusements work to fix individual and collective identities in place.[12]

By this time, Lemuel Pitkin, "ragged" and "emaciated" in appearance, has been thoroughly "dismantled" and has dropped socially into the abyss of the American lumpenproletariat. His teeth removed by a prison dentist, an injured eye removed, his leg amputated at the knee, his scalp torn from his head, he is now fully submerged "in the great army of unemployed" (*Novels, Cool*, 230). As a comically exaggerated depiction of the physically damaged and emotionally devastated (ex)worker in an industrialized system of labor, Lem is well suited for his role in the burlesque show. All he has to do is submit to further beating. The two comics bring him out and pound him mercilessly with newspapers rolled up into clubs until his artificial parts, "his false hair, teeth and eyes," fall from his body. The performance comes to a close only after the comic duo has brought out an "enormous wooden mallet labeled 'The Works' " and proceed to pulverize the prosthetically reconstructed protagonist (233).[13] Clearly, we are far from the positive endorsement of burlesque aesthetics that Miller's *Black Spring* makes available.

Lemuel provides the spectators, who are "convulsed with joy" at the spectacle of his disintegration, with a striking image of the cruelties of social castration. He is put on stage and made to embody a "feminine" lack so that the presumably male audience may defensively reassure themselves of their own "masculine" integrity. Rather than induce anxiety in the spectator, the corporeal shattering Lemuel suffers enables the members of the audience to distance themselves from the distressingly passive condition he displays. Aligning themselves with the active agents rather than the humiliated victim of somatic pain, the "heartily" laughing spectators are briefly relieved of whatever unconscious fears they may harbor in regard to their own vulnerability.

The apparel of Riley and Robbins indicates that within the show they are representatives of the financially well off (their suits are "of the latest cut" while Lemuel wears an ill-fitting outfit indicative of impoverishment). Thus for the more economically stable members of the audience, Lemuel's awful fate allows them to reinforce with sadistic satisfaction their sense of being different than the socially misfortunate. The spectators whose situation more closely approximates Lemuel's end up, however, applauding their own corporeal mutilation. Such persons are unwitting masochists who in effect assent to their own punishment. Without becoming conscious of the fact, these individuals are encouraged to take pleasure in the symbolic recapitulation of their own mistreatment. In the process they unknowingly accede to the corporeal barbarism enacted within capitalist social relations. Rather than inspire subordinated persons to mount a challenge against their oppressors, burlesque inserts the abused into a spectacle in which they observe the physical rending they experience in the world as a source of great fun. Offering a fantasy of dominance, the show encourages the delighted spectator to misrecognize himself as the powerful agent of acts of aggression directed at an other who is in truth a substitute for the self insofar as he shares the latter's lack of economic power.

For West, then, the sadomasochistic dynamics of the entertainment help secure audience assent to an otherwise intolerable status quo. By encouraging them to overlook their actual position in society, American burlesque enables the disenfranchised to repress any awareness of the pummeling they perennially receive in their daily life. Recreational pleasure derives from the illusory and perhaps fleeting sensation that one is the master as opposed to the slave. Amid the vicarious participation in a violent assault the ambition to alter the material conditions of society bleeds away. Laughing at the hardships of economically determined devastation as if they belonged to someone else dispels the passion required to engage in social protest. As Miriam Hansen puts it in the context of a gloss on Adorno: "Humor provides the glue that prevents the subject from recognizing him/herself as the object of mutilation."[14]

This outlook helps mark the difference between West's and Bakhtin's respective assessments of the radicalism latent in carnivalized practices. The scene in *A Cool Million* coincidentally resembles the episode in Rabelais's work in which Pantagruel travels to the island of the Catchpoles, who, like Lemuel, earn "their living by letting themselves be thrashed."[15] As Bakhtin interprets them, such comically symbolic actions display a powerfully optimistic faith in social and political becoming. In traditional, folk-based systems of violent imagery, the Catchpoles stand as substitutes for the King, and the festive beating the clowns absorb augurs the inevitable uncrowning of any current ruler in the future. Carnivalized brutality expresses and reinforces collective belief in historical change as a force of becoming, one that will eventually result in the death of the governing classes and rebirth of the people. Rabelais's grotesque realism borrows from and extends such utopian aspirations. In *A Cool Million* the situation is quite different: here the literary text is a critical instrument that discloses the horrifyingly regressive aspects of modern laughter. The task of the writer is to convey the ways in which violence on the stage sanctions and perpetuates violence in the streets against the downtrodden.

The political importance of attending to the acts of identification contemporary amusements facilitate becomes apparent at the end of the novel when West takes aim at the political rally as a communal phenomenon. That the novel moves from the dime museum through burlesque to such an event suggests that, for West, the latter spectacle has affinities with the others as a pernicious form of public entertainment. The finale of *A Cool Million* demonstrates that one of West's primary concerns as a writer is to ironize the libidinal binding of frustrated persons on which political movements hinge. In the course of satirically evoking the rise of Lemuel to the status of the heroic martyr of a fascist revolution in the United States, West clarifies further the way in which the fragmented body may be utilized to fabricate a collective ego.[16]

West's critical aim in *A Cool Million*, then, is to negate the coercive force of reactionary political oratory. For example, in chapter 29, Shagpoke Whipple, ex-President of the United States, provokes a mass riot in the South while stumping for his new National Revolutionary Party. Tapping into the patriotic spirit of his audience, Whipple asserts that " 'the only struggle worthy of Americans is the idealistic one of their country against its enemies . . . class war is civil war, and will destroy us' " (*Novels, Cool*, 226). His nativist appeal and correlative denunciation of the foreign "enemy in our midst" galvanizes his Southern listeners. A "foul conspirator," he informs them, has made his way into "the bosom of the body politic" (228). They become a frenzied mob and go on a violent rampage against women as well as racial and religious minorities. "The heads of negroes were paraded on poles. A Jewish drummer was nailed to the door of his hotel room. The housekeeper of the local Catholic priest was raped"(229). The impetus behind this hysterical assault on the disenfranchised, a case of displaced abjection whereby the weak discharge their socially determined frustrations on the weaker, comes from the "projection device" the speaker deploys. These others are substitutes or scapegoats. Whipple has handed over his listeners' "infirmities to a vessel, or 'cause,' outside the self," so that they "can battle an external enemy instead of battling an enemy within." Rather than "consider internal political conflicts on the basis of conflicting interests," Whipple offers "a noneconomic interpretation of a phenomenon economically engendered."[17] The point would be that West's comic ventriloquism conveys the same critical insights, if in a more indirect manner.

It is the duplicitous way in which fascist discourse maintains an ostensibly healthy "body politic" that West mocks in the final chapter of the novel. At the beginning of the chapter Lem has been convinced by one of Whipple's storm troopers, or "Leather Shirts," to interrupt Lem's performance in the burlesque act and come out in support of Whipple's fascist organization. The character agrees, but after a few preparatory words, Lem is assassinated. Evidently his death helps spur the reactionary movement to victory over its opponents, for the next time we see Whipple he is the triumphant dictator of the country. What follows in the text is a description of a post-revolutionary celebration, "Pitkin's Birthday," a national holiday set up in honor of the dead boy. Whipple appears here as a showman orchestrating the political festivities for the purpose of solidifying his hold over the nation's youth. To ensure that they remain inscribed in the new authoritarian social order, he need only secure their devotion to the hero who sacrificed himself for their cause: Lem. Irony

functions as the instrument of an oblique yet penetrating critical negation of the narrative and lyric procedures that subtend such ideological
operations. In essence, West seeks to answer critically Whipple's query:
"Why does the martyr move in triumph and the nation rise up at every
stage of his coming? Why are cities and states his pallbearers?" (238).

The verse of the "Lemuel Pitkin Song" as sung by the parading boys
draws attention to one of the key rhetorical devices deployed in such acts
of political persuasion. The use of prosopopoeia, the trope whereby absent, deceased persons are made to speak, invests Lemuel's death with a
significance that is at best hypothetical. " 'Who dares?' this was L. Pitkin's
cry, / As striding on the Bijou stage he came – / 'Surge out with me in
Shagpoke's name, / For him to live, for him to die!' " (237). The use of
the boy to mediate between the individual and the social formation presupposes a certainty as to his intentions while alive. The feeble-minded
state of the character before the assassination, however, makes it highly
unlikely that he possessed the internal commitment to the cause the
song attributes to him. Rather than a courageous crusader for justice,
the overly trustful and rather idiotic Lem was again the victim of his
passive acceptance of the advice of others. The glaring discrepancy between his perpetual lack of volition and the posthumous interpretation
of his actions as those of a fearlessly determined soldier clarifies the epistemological liberties that may be taken in the construction of what Kaja
Silverman has called "the dominant fiction." Such a fiction, a "libidinal
apparatus" that facilitates ideological investments, functions by isolating
"from the whole repertoire of a culture's images, sounds, and narrative
elaborations those through which a consensus is established," which per-
mits "a group identification and collective desires."[18] For West, it is the
rhetorically produced fiction of a voice speaking from beyond the grave
that supports the dominant fiction of a hypothetical fascist America. Indeed, despite its cognitively debatable status, the act of putting words in
the mouth of the dead is shown to be an effective organizing tactic in the
political arena. " 'Although dead, yet he speaks. Of what is it that
he speaks? Of the right of every American boy to go into the world and
there receive fair play and a chance to make his fortune by industry and
probity without being laughed at or conspired against by sophisticated
aliens" (*Novels, Cool*, 238). Such a gesture aligns and tightly binds heterogeneous persons together around a compelling idea, a purpose they may
all share in common. The false transmission of the wishes of the dead
manufactures a loyal fascist subjectivity *en masse*. "A million hands flung
up reply, / a million voices answered, 'I!' " (237).

The cornerstone of their belief is largely nonexistent, for Lem did not share their faith in the revolution; but once posited, the internal feeling, the emotional willingness to lay down one's life for one's country, effectively brings into existence the passionate enthusiasm it presupposes. The circularity of ideology is no obstacle to its coercive force. A fascist identity is fashioned as a relationship between a unique Other or Absolute Subject (Lem) and the million selves who have mistakenly seen their own reflections mirrored in the image of the dead pseudo-hero. The narrative construction of a native tradition of past warriors helps support the specular exchange whereby the individual is inserted into a pre-existing social order. In *A Cool Million* it is the audible register that sustains this imaginary transaction between self and Subject, though, as *The Day of the Locust* reveals, the visual also serves as the mainstay of processes of identification, inside and outside the political realm. Together, the seductions of the eye and the delusions of the ear constitute the perceptual, or, better, *facial* ground of *fascist* interpellation. For West, an anti-facist poetics corresponds to an anti-fascist politics.[19]

The ironic presentation of Whipple's oratorical machinations demonstrates the technique whereby concrete individuals are made into fascist subjects or citizens and inspired by utopian discourses to participate eagerly in political movements, to desire violent social upheaval. Millions of particular boys discover their proper place in society and in the nation as a whole through the hero's (fabricated) address. A unique and absolute Boy calls them to their position as American boys; the latter are so many mirror reflections of their idol, are made in his image. This relationship is organized around Lemuel as center, as the projected Subject whose apparent existence allows in turn for the interpellation of multiple subjects. He is the fixed figure in and through which males in the country come to believe they are (and always have been) inherently, essentially American. They become self-conscious of their necessary status as natives by identifying with an exemplary American. The ideological effect appears in their conviction that they have freely chosen a position in fact already marked out for them. The coercive force of the procedure stems from the degree to which the call seems obvious, to the extent that the subject recognizes himself in the address. "Lem must be talking to me, for that is indeed who I am." Greeted with such reassuring familiarity, the individual fails to understand that he is being set up as a subject; acted upon rather than acting, he is in effect being *patriated*. The subject willingly accepts his position and behaves with such obedience because he mistakenly believes that he has not been socially constructed but is naturally or essentially an American. Within ideology, or the imaginary, the mystified subject feels as if he has shaped himself, whereas external forces have put him together and impressed him by giving him his identity as a member of a collective whole. What comes from the outside is misperceived as being innate. The horror in this case derives from the willingness of individuals to kill and be killed in the name of such a misperception.

As West presents it, the mass rally or political spectacle performs the tasks of an ideological state apparatus. The dominant (though not exclusive) function of such an apparatus is to produce individuals as subjects in order to facilitate the reproduction of the existing relations of production. For Louis Althusser, another word for this operation whereby subjects are recruited into the system is hailing.[20] With this description in mind one can register the full force of the irony embedded in the novel's concluding lines. " 'Hail, the Martyrdom in the Bijou Theatre!' roar Shagpoke's youthful hearers when he is finished. 'Hail, Lemuel Pitkin!' 'All hail, the American Boy!' " (238). In this enthusiastic salute the subjects mistakenly believe that they intentionally choose to identify themselves with their divine hero, so to speak. In truth, West suggests, the process occurs in the opposite manner: these boys, selected by the State, are stamped out or branded as imitations of a prefabricated model.

West also demonstrates that biographical narration may be ideologically effective despite being cognitively unreliable and misleading. Whipple's condensed retrospective account of Lem's "pilgrimage" through the world inspires great "wonder" and deep "feeling" as a logically coherent story: Pitkin "was dismantled by the enemy. His teeth were pulled out. His eye was gouged from his head. His thumb was removed. His scalp was torn away. His leg was cut off. And, finally he was shot through the heart. But he did not live or die in vain. Through his martyrdom the National Revolutionary Party triumphed in this country," and it was by this means that the country was "purged of alien diseases and America became again American" (238). The boy has here the status of a grotesque exhibit, a dead freak. (Shagpoke's earlier scheme was to secure a tent and exhibit Lem "as the last man to have been scalped by the Indians and the sole survivor of the Yuba River massacre" [219].) The dictator's pedagogical lecture insists on making this spectacle an object of knowledge. The (recollected) sight of the fragmented body must be made meaningful; a coherent story must be told explaining why Lem ended up in such a state of disarray. Yet the actual narrative of *A Cool Million* has presented his life as a series of unrelated incidents. The discrepancy between the dictator's neat recapitulation of Lem's past as a fully comprehensible tale and the novel's depiction of his adventures as a haphazard, contingent set of chance accidents illustrates the process whereby random experiences may be converted into didactic lessons. The text's repetitious, seemingly unmotivated plot can thus be retroactively grasped as a challenge to facile accounts of the impact of society on persons. The interpretive claim Whipple makes on the basis of his version of Lem's history is that his wounding showed that justice and equal opportunity for all had ceased to be distinguishing features of the nation. The character's failure to make his fortune was the direct result of the insidious penetration into the domestic arena of "Marxism" and "International Capitalism." The physical maiming of the boy is understood as the effect of a particular cause. The boy's numerous injuries are symptomatic evidence that something was dreadfully wrong inside the body politic. Somatic damage and emotional indignity were not the result of bad luck; they were the logical manifestations of an unhealthy condition. To profit politically from Lem's wrecked body, Whipple must leave out of his concise narrative any details that do not fit the framing of the character's life as a social tragedy. There is room for epistemological uncertainty and interpretive ambiguity when erecting a persuasive political icon like "The American Boy."

What then is the significance of West's figurative use of images of the grotesquely fragmented body and how does this process relate to the Algerian myth that supplies West with his inter-textual point of departure? For it should be apparent that the ludicrous protagonist of the novel hardly has the status of a literal representation of the physical and mental agonies endured by the subject of urban-industrial modernity.

From a psychoanalytical perspective, the imagery reactivates an unconscious anxiety: the fear of coming apart physically and mentally – a fear that fascist political ideologies work to alleviate. The shattering of the subject exhibits the horrifying condition of dissolution against which the vulnerable ego seeks to defend itself (often by seeking to eradicate violently what is perceived as a threatening fluidity coming from outside the self).

From a sociological perspective, the figure, one of West's many dysfunctional automatons, may be said to have been designed to make fun of anachronistic appeals to the aesthetically appealing, natural body. In the age of industrialized labor, such images are compensatory. West's decision to subtitle the novel the "dismantling" as opposed to the dismembering of Lemuel Pitkin supports the notion that the historical referent of the mutilated character is the mechanized worker. Admittedly, his fragmentation is not tied directly to workplace injuries, much less to Taylorist or Fordist (though Whipple does invoke the latter as being an admirable kind of American capitalist [236]) methods of organizing the labor process. Still, the boy's disintegration does suggest the somatic and psychic effects of economic rationalism. The dismantling of Lem illustrates, or is an emblem of, what happens to bodies when their minutest movements are subject to analysis, when physical actions are segmented and made the object of precise measurement. The corporeal dispersal and reconstitution the character suffers thus gestures toward the manipulative breaking apart of the human being and consequent taking of control over all his parts in modernized modes of production.

Alger's fictional heroes obscure this historically specific experience by retaining their physical and mental integrity during their travails.[21] Similarly, in making a singular, unique body impervious to all external forces available to his fans for imaginary inhabitation, Superman deflects attention away from the effects of the system of commodity production that give birth to him. Moreover, in addition to offering "his tremendous physique," his "magnificent frame," which comes complete with hands like "steel talons" and "pistoning bronze legs"[22] to his readers, Doc Savage's medical and technical know-how enables him to invent a "health ray apparatus." This device has the "remarkable properties for healing tissue burned out by the ravages of the Red Death."[23]

West's caricature of a heroic protagonist discredits the appeal of such charismatic cultural figures. Rather than an attractively embodied role model, the radical writer gives us a boy who has, like Poe's "Man," been used up. The reconstruction of his brutalized body provides no solution to his condition. Artificial attachments can be lost just like the parts they replace. The technologically enhanced body is as fragile as its organic original. In the end, the prosthetic image[24] fabricated to mask and alleviate the feeling and fact of possessing a grievously wounded body is torn to shreds. (The connection between the automaton motif and mechanized labor will be made more explicit in *The Day of the Locust* in regard to Homer Simpson's uncanny hands. There we are told that as "a bookkeeper, he had worked mechanically, totaling figures and making entries with the same impersonal detachment that he now opened cans of soup." West then shows the character accidentally cutting his thumb nastily while opening a can of food. The nearly severed digit, part of a "wounded hand," is an emblem of the physical dislocations the modernized worker suffers, which culminate in a loss of volition, a lack of control over one's assorted body parts, and sensory deprivation. "Someone watching him go about his little cottage might have thought him sleep-walking or partially blind. His hands seemed to have a life and a will of their own. It was they who pulled the sheets tight and shaped the pillows" [275]. Motive power derives from the machine of production; the worker is simply one part among others consumed in the economic process.)

From a rhetorical perspective, Lem's disassembly is a constitutive feature in a critical endeavor: the taking apart of a metaphorical construction. This is a linguistically reflexive or allegorical procedure in which the grotesque body has the textual status of a trope of a trope. Corporeal fragmentation functions as an image that makes perceptible an otherwise abstract critical process: the taking apart of a figure of speech. The disfigured body becomes a key element in an act of rhetorical disfiguration. The erection of the symbolic figure of "The American Boy" as model citizen at the end of *A Cool Million* makes such an interpretation feasible in retrospect. Yet the fact that this figure is merely a politicized version of the Alger "type" from which the book set out clarifies that such an interpretation was implicitly feasible throughout.[25] (I will pursue in greater depth the tropological dynamics of the reconciliation of the particular and the general at the end of the following chapter by way of Dos Passos' treatment of the Unknown Soldier.) West's irony negates the assumptions on which such reassuring tropes depend. The claim that the individual and the body politic are homologous entities is grounded in the notion that the same spiritual substance, the same revolutionary conviction or patriotic fervor, flows through both. Without the guaranteed presence of this widespread substance, rhetorical constructs like The American Boy tend to collapse. The gouging, puncturing, rending, and sundering of the body in *A Cool Million* is an image of this destructive process.

All the interpretive options listed above strike me as legitimate (even though the sociological one has some affinities with Whipple's cynical conclusions), and it is the multiplicity of possible understandings that may take us to the center of West's grotesque tactics. What he does in this text is make the figure mean too much. The production of semantic excess prevents the fragmented body from being incorporated into an ideological endeavor as a cautionary display. The variety of meanings attached in the course of the novel to Lemuel's ruined physique interfere with the effort to inscribe it into a single, univocal system of representation and signification. Whipple seeks to control the discursive flow by putting the shocking sight of Lem on display as an educational warning to those who refuse to join the Party: what happened to him will happen to you too if you don't become a good fascist. Pitkin as penis gets chopped up so the dictator can have his phallus. In sharp contrast, West makes the fragmented body available for so many possible interpretations that the whole thing ends up seeming like comic nonsense.

ARMORICAN FASCISM

In the case of the migratory locust, the transition within a generation from the solitary to the gregarious form can be obtained by exposing the individual, at a certain stage, to the exclusively visual action of a similar image, provided it is animated by movements of a style sufficiently close to that characteristic of the species. Such facts are inscribed in an order of homeomorphic identification that would itself fall within the larger question of the meaning of beauty as both formative and erogenic. (Jacques Lacan, "The Mirror Stage as Formative of the Function of the I as Revealed in Psychoanalytic Experience")

Like an entomologist [he] has studied what we call love in order to expose beneath the ideology, the mythology, the platitudes and phraseologies the complete and bloody machinery of sex. (Henry Miller [on Luis Buñuel], "The Golden Age")

The conclusion of *A Cool Million* suggests that the iconography of virile, seemingly indestructible male bodies is not in fact essential to fascist discourse (though such figures were certainly one of its main attractions). Lem remains useful to Whipple even though all that is (said to be) left of the boy are audible traces. He survives merely as a disembodied voice encouraging subsequent generations to support the cause. In *The Day of the Locust*, West does, however, touch on a couple of occasions on the way leaders deploy charismatic bodies to help them organize coherent movements.

In a religious vein, for instance, the image of the divine appears as the site of an act of identification by means of which a frail and weakened congregation may anticipate future redemption alongside an enhanced corporeal prowess. At the "Church of the Christ, Physical," those with "drained out, feeble bodies" are taught that "holiness" is "attained through the constant use of chest-weights and spring grips" (*Novels, Day* 337). Similarly, at the "Temple Moderne," "Brain Breathing, the Secret of the Aztecs" is taught. A visit by one of the novel's main characters, Tod Hackett, to the "Tabernacle of the Third Coming" suggests that the problem such rhetorical maneuvers pose is that they make it possible to channel mass aggression toward violent ends. The message the fanatical speaker delivers at this meeting does have to do with "dietary rules" and "economics and Biblical threats"; but it is the "emotional response of his hearers" to his "messianic rage" that strikes the observer as especially ominous. As Tod sees it, the fury of those possessed of "wild, disordered minds" has the potential to generate an "awful, anarchic power" suffi- cient "to destroy civilization" (337). Shortly before this, a woman who identifies herself as a "raw-foodist" asks Tod "Who do you follow?" (334). She lives, she claims, according to the strict doctrines of Dr. Pierce. This figure is never represented in the novel; yet he is alluded to again at the end of the narrative. The context is a narrative reflection (via free indirect discourse) on an aspect of Tod's work-in-progress – a painting titled "The Burning of Los Angeles." He plans to depict in this artwork "the cultists of all sorts, economic as well as religious, the wave, air- plane, funeral and preview watchers" as "marching behind his [a "super 'Dr. Know-All-Pierce All' "] banner in a great united front of screwballs and screwboxes to purify the land" (387–88).

The use of the term "united front" should give us pause, for since 1935 this had increasingly become a slogan associated with the communist Left (toward which West was by no means hostile in the latter half of the decade) in the United States.[26] Is it fascism (as traditional commentary on the novel would have it) or communism that is the object of fear here? This may be the wrong question to ask. Perhaps West's critical focus in the novel is less on the disturbing potential of the lower-middle- classes to rise up as a force of civil unrest than on the anxiety this social group induces *in the subject.* Clearly, Tod is simultaneously terrified and intrigued by the crowds. My claim is that it is precisely this affective ambivalence that, in *Day,* West takes as a point of access to the problem of fascism in the United States. The character's divided response to the sociopolitical phenomenon the dissatisfied and easily enraged masses constitute is inseparable from his equally complex attitude to internal drives, to the productive force of the unconscious. The seemingly wild and disorderly behavior of the film and disaster enthusiasts thus amounts to an eruption outside the observer of the swirling chaos inside him. Tod's speculative self-analysis is therefore right on target: "He began to wonder if he himself didn't suffer from the ingrained, morbid apathy he liked to draw in others. Maybe he could only be galvanized into sensibility and that was why he was chasing Faye" (336).

That Tod's fascinations extend to a particular woman complicate the diagnosis. It is the masses and the feminine that the male subject is alter- nately attracted to and repulsed by. Both are perceived in an analogous manner as the terrain upon or through which desires flow in a terrifying yet alluring fashion. The vicissitudes of identity formation are to be conceived along the lines of the individual's desire to obtain a hard body and to avoid being overwhelmed by a shapeless one. West's political inquiries have thus gained a degree of psychoanalytic nuance. The question of the possibility of American fascism has become inseparable from the question of the crisis of masculinity.[27]

That the movies are coded in the text as a feminine force (Faye as the embodiment of Hollywood) clarifies the place occupied in the system by technological amusement. From the character's perspective, modern spectacles, the crowd of spectators such entertainment gathers together, and women are strongly associated as threats to his physical and psychic integrity. There is something disturbingly carnivalesque about all these entities, and it is for this reason that the emotional affects one (Faye) gives rise to may be displaced onto the other (the crowd). In "an effort to put Faye out of his mind," Tod begins to "think about the series of cartoons he was making for his canvas of Los Angeles on fire." He "was going to show the city burning at high noon, so that the flames would have to compete with the desert sun and thereby appear less fearful, more like bright flags flying from roofs and windows than a terrible holocaust. He wanted the city to have a gala air as it burned, to appear almost gay. And the people who set it on fire would be a holiday crowd" (308).[28]

We may begin tracking West's examination of the anxiety-ridden subjects of Depression-era America by way of a peripheral character in *Day*. Adore Loomis, eight years old, a would-be child star whose agent has dubbed him "the biggest little attraction in Hollywood" (333), has been making faces at Homer Simpson. Apologizing for her son, Adore's abrasive mother explains that "He thinks he's the Frankenstein monster" (335) – this figure having appeared on American screens eight years earlier. The annoying child's talent clearly lies in his skillful ability to imitate external models. "Dressed like a man," he moves "like a soldier," and bows stiffly as if he were a cultured gentleman, his gestures corresponding to "the way they do it in Europe" (334), his mother explains. She then instructs Adore to perform a song. Uncannily mimicking a world-weary adult, the boy expertly sings a blues song while "his buttocks writhed and his voice carried a top-heavy load of sexual pain" (336). Aping the physical mannerisms and vocal styling of a black woman, the white child manages to inhabit the body of and in so doing virtually become the other.

In the "peculiar half world"[29] West depicts in *Day*, Adore's copying is hardly atypical. The child willingly does what most of those around him do unwillingly: assume the form of another human being and in so doing precipitate the first outlines of that form inside. Specular identification with an external body image inaugurates the process, subsequently lodged in the unconscious, whereby the individual's ego takes shape as a bounded entity. Adore's "talent" makes visible what others prefer to ignore: identity develops from the outside in. The disclosure of the narcissistic foundations of subjectivity puts gender and racial distinctions at risk; no longer presumed to be innate, they become available as roles anyone might choose to play. For someone like Homer, however, who feels the need to avoid fusion of any sort, such an insight is likely to prove intolerable rather than liberating. And it is therefore not surprising that at the end of the novel he goes into a trance state and viciously assaults the child actor by jumping up and down on the boy's prone body. For those with an ego prone to fragmentation, the solution may be violent assault on anyone who awakens them to their condition of instability.

Jacques Lacan first articulated his well-known concept of the "mirror-stage" in 1936 in a conference talk. For him, a primary identification with a "mirage" that appears to the infant "in a contrasting size" enables this child to anticipate a mastery of his own body he has yet to achieve. Here too the specular investment in a seemingly larger and more unified corporeal image in turn plays a formative role in the psychic existence of the individual. The by no means finished product of this mental process is the "I."[30] As a correlative, a more aggressive (self-directed) fantasy of the "body-in-pieces" develops, which may be taken as an expressive manifestation of the fear of psychic collapse. Recent commentators on this psychoanalytic model have convincingly argued that it has political significance. As Susan Buck-Morss bluntly puts it, "the mirror stage can be read as a theory of fascism."[31] The further enigma to be touched on below is whether an inquiry into the fascist imaginary can draw support from the Freudian notion of the death drive. Can this notion help us grasp the oddness of those who in *Day* are said to have "come to California to die" (*Novels, Day*, 242)? And does Tod (death in German), who is intent on learning more about such persons, fall inside or outside this category?

Lacanian motifs have in addition proved valuable as a way to comprehend spectatorial dynamics within mainstream cinema. The infant staring at images in a mirror has furnished a model for understanding the effect on film viewers of staring up longingly at the larger than life images projected onto the screen of a movie theatre.[32] What West's novel adds to the theoretical convergence of fascism and film around the topic of body imagery is the question of grotesque art. The traditional point of entry to this question in *Day* is Tod's painting style. A distinction drawn from one of Lacan's most assiduous readers – the French Marxist philosopher, Louis Althusser – will put us in position to approach this matter.[33]

In "Cremonini, Painter of the Abstract" (1966), Althusser distinguishes firmly between what he calls an "aesthetic of *deformity*" and a technique of *deformation*. The distinction corresponds neatly to the difference – which will prove useful for grasping the tensions in West's *Day* – between grotesque expressionism as an expressive *style* of representation and the grotesque as a feature in an analytical *technique* that undermines this style. Whereas deformity confirms the ideology of the centered and free subject, deformation undermines it. Althusser works out this opposition by commenting upon "what happens to human *faces*" in Cremonini's artworks. His "distorted and sometimes apparently monstrous, if not deformed faces" have led to his classification as an expressionist. This, for Althusser, mistaken interpretation convicts the painter of adhering to "an idealist ideology of *ugliness*," which in turn presupposes the existence of a "soul" within the subject, of individuals with unique feelings. The hideous features of the portrayed faces purport to reveal the emotional depth they in fact help to produce. The spiritual agony of the subject becomes visibly apparent in an aesthetic of deformity that thus makes physical ugliness expressive. The alternative approach, which Cremonini employs, is to employ the grotesque as a technique that withdraws expression from the face, that involves "a determinate absence of form," a depiction of anonymity that in effect subverts the category of the subject and the humanist assumptions it sustains. "If Cremonini's faces are *deformed*, it is because they do not have the *form* of *individuality*, i.e. of *subjectivity*, in which 'men' immediately recognize that man is the *subject*, the center, the author, the 'creator' of his objects and his world."[34] The lack of identifiable features discloses an internal emptiness. The absence Cremonini paints is negative in that he removes or refutes the "soul," but positive in that he draws the viewer's attention to the structural, real relations of which people are, their beliefs notwithstanding, merely effects. By virtue of his technique Cremonini is a materialist whose artistic practice makes us aware of the external forces outside consciousness that overdetermine our behavior and our sense of who we are (237–39).

Of the two approaches Althusser articulates – an aesthetic of ugliness in which contorted physiognomies disclose subjective passions and a critical practice that locates the soul as an illusory effect of mechanical procedures – it is the first that best accounts for the aesthetics of "The Burning of Los Angeles." The status of the set designer and aspiring artist's representational project has become an interpretive crux of the novel, and commentators remain divided on the extent to which the painting may be considered a miniature, inscribed version of the book itself. Not only does the decision one makes on this point guide interpretation of the novel as a whole but it also tends to govern interpretive understandings of West's attitude toward the high/low cultural dichotomy. Is the writer following the same painterly models as the character?[35] And does Tod's commitment to "authentic" art as a desirable alternative to mass entertainment parallel West's?[36] Both questions can be answered affirmatively and negatively: which is to say the concept of an aesthetic of deformity accounts for a considerable portion of the novel, yet one can locate a technique of deformation operative in the text as well.

The inside/outside correspondence on which the painter relies matches the author's use of distorted body shapes to exhibit mental states. In Tod's view the peculiar appearance of the dwarf Abe Kusich conforms to his perverse personality, and the "little man's grotesque depravity" excites Tod and convinces him that he must paint. A comparable perspective underlies West's portrayal (by way of Sherwood Anderson) of Homer Simpson's freakishly large hands. The exaggerated size of the disproportionate appendages provides a perceptual clue to the male hysteric's inner condition, his otherwise repressed passion announcing itself in their symptomatically swelling enormity.

The proliferation of analogies in the book comparing human beings to an assortment of animals, insects, reptiles, and fowl is also compatible with the painter's aesthetic of deformity. Whereas in one of Tod's lithographs Abe and other subjects "leap into the air with twisted backs like hooked trout" (*Novels, Day,* 245), West employs similar motifs throughout *Day,* often through an intricate reflexive cross-referencing of scenes. The initially literal description of the lizard Homer observes in his back yard as it earns "a hard living catching" flies (276) is a case in point. For the description turns out to be a trope for Faye's relation to her many suitors; the green color and darting "fine, forked tongue" of the creature is like her dangerously alluring manner of "running her tongue over her lips," "one of her most characteristic gestures and very effective" (355). The well-known representation of the cockfight has a comparable function. Narrated shortly before the men, excited by Faye's presence, savagely fight each other, the fierce battle of the two roosters anticipates the behavior of the humans. Abe's identification with the disabled bird (at one point he takes the bird's head in his mouth) solidifies the implicit simile. Moreover, during the fight the dwarf lowers his head "like a goat,"

"like a tiny ram," yet is dashed against the wall "like a man killing a rabbit against a tree" (363). Lastly, Faye, who in Tod's painting is in "wild
flight" like a panicked "game bird" (297), has an animal counterpart in
the "dirty black hen" that disgusts Homer. Though the narrative does
not represent her horrendous end, the condition of the bird anticipates
the human's future. "The roosters have torn all the feathers off its neck
and made its comb all bloody and it has scabby feet covered with warts
and it cackles so nasty" (343).

This last ghastly trope hints at the fragility in *Day* of the art/mass
culture, literature/Hollywoood film dichotomies. The figural reduction
of a glamorous, attractive woman to the level of a hideously brutalized,
filthy hen may well have been inspired by the frightening conclusion
to Tod Browning's MGM film *Freaks* (1932). Seven years before *Day* was
published (and two years before the Production Code began to be strictly
enforced) the nightmarish film comes to an end with the transformation
of a previously "normal" circus performer into a "human/barnyard
fowl hybrid."[37] As punishment for her arrogance and manipulation of
her midget husband, Hans, the other "freaks" band together and mys-
teriously change Cleopatra into a "HIGHLY UNUSUAL ATTRACTION,"
a Chicken Woman. (The novel's odd cast of characters would have
been even closer to the film's had West not eliminated a description
of Mrs. Schwartzen as a seven-foot woman in need of a daily shave, and
a weird portrait of a "sloppy old nude" cello player who drools and kisses
her instrument's neck.[38]) West might also have lifted elements from two
other pre-Code horror films: *Frankenstein* (Universal, 1931) and *The Island
of Lost Souls* (Universal, 1933), both of which end with scenes of collective
frenzy that anticipate the chaotic riot at the movie premiere that concludes the novel. The torch-bearing peasants who hunt down the monster
in the earlier movie may have supplied Tod with imagery for his painting
(320), and the enraged mass of beast-men's lifting of Dr. Moreau over
their heads resembles Homer's brief appearance atop the violent bestial
crowd in the book. Moreover, the political implications of the painting
and the movie seem roughly analogous. In both instances, explosive mob
violence discloses the potential of the socially oppressed, once enraged,
to wreak havoc on a social system that denies them satisfaction. From
this perspective the biologically reductive nature of West's tropes communicates the kind of vision of widespread "regression and de-evolution"
that has been posited as the "ur-theme" of pre-Code horror films.[39]

But how valuable is such a perspective with respect to an attempt to deepen our understanding of the aggressive tendencies of the

"Angelenos," whom Tod believes to be "the pick of America's madmen" (308)? Reducing anger to the level of animal lust or instinctive need by-passes the question of the mechanical determinations of subjectivity. To grasp wild behavior as the regression to biologically determined urges, as evidence of the beast within, evades the issue of whether violent impulses are conditioned by the increasing prominence of technology in everyday life, especially in the form of mass entertainment. Nor is the suggestion that as an artist Tod is able to overcome his destructive impulses through expressive representation a compelling solution to the social and political matters the book raises. The character himself acknowledges the limits of aesthetic sublimation when he mocks his attempt to stop chasing Faye by putting away his drawings of her in a trunk "as a childish trick, hardly worthy of a primitive witch doctor" (337).

The grotesque aesthetic of deformity is inscribed then in *Day* as a symptom of a mental condition deserving of critical analysis. As scopophilic as those he observes, Tod not only watches others watching with a good deal of paranoia ("When their stare was returned, their eyes filled with hatred" [242]) but relies on visible mannerisms – Harry Greener's "clownship," for example – for clues as to what motivates people (261). West's ironic deformations put at risk the conviction that appearances reveal psychic states, that by looking one penetrates inside to the essence, soul, or emotional core of persons.

That Tod, who is said to have numerous personalities ("one inside the other") and a "large, sprawling body," which makes him appear to be what he is not, "doltish," has inserted Faye into a narcissistic relationship is hinted at in an early scene in the novel. Dressing in front of "the bureau mirror," Tod tries to keep his eyes on his fingers as he fixes his collar and tie. The act has masturbatory undertones here, and it is therefore fitting that he cannot help staring at a photograph of Faye she has given him, "a still from a two-reel farce in which she worked as an extra" (250). Since he has pushed the picture into the frame of the upper corner of the mirror, Tod looks at Faye's face and his own simultaneously, and this juxtaposition suggests his predilection for mixing them up. Faye's status here (and throughout the novel) is that of a screen or reflecting surface onto which Tod projects his own image. She is an essential extra, a projected duplicate on which he (unsuccessfully) depends to procure an ego. It is perhaps for this reason, as William Carlos Williams has noted, that Faye "hasn't any face that amounts to anything."[40]

The scene as a whole discloses the interplay within the imaginary between narcissistic and aggressive impulses. The proximity of his mirror image and the movie still evokes the male character's tendency to confuse self and other; but this vision soon gives way to a fantasy, based on the picture, of what he feels it would be like to achieve sexual fusion with the actress. "If you threw yourself on her, it would be like throwing yourself from the parapet of a skyscraper. You would do it with a scream. You wouldn't expect to rise again. Your teeth would be driven into your skull like nails into a pine board and your back would be broken" (*Works, Day,* 251). The image of corporeal smashing belongs in the Lacanian category of the *"imagos of the fragmented body"* and may be understood as the registration of a psychic anxiety. The impaled body corresponds to a punctured identity.[41] The initially striking aspect of this anticipation of somatic shattering is that it is presented ambivalently as a terrifying yet thrilling and therefore hard to resist experience. More important, however, is the possibility of interpreting the pleasurably painful threat Faye is said to pose as in truth something arising from within Tod. There is a libidinal source for the masochistic longing to disintegrate. It is the character's unconscious impulse to crack his ego apart that is figured in the form of a leap – a death dive – over a fortification and subsequent plunge downward from the top of a tall building. What he perceives as a danger to his psychic status seems to exist on the outside in the form of the feminine; yet this is an urge toward destruction that comes from inside the subject. The self-aggression inside the male character has been displaced onto an apparent femme fatale.

In the course of the novel West will isolate several psychic defenses against such an internally generated urge to experience physical and per-haps psychic obliteration. Figuring the body-ego as an armored construct is one such tactic. Another is to contemplate assaulting the misperceived agent of potential injury. "If only he [Tod] had the courage to throw himself on her. Nothing less violent than rape would do. The sensation he felt was like that he got when holding an egg in his hand." "It was her completeness, her egglike self-sufficiency, that made him want to crush her" (295). The sadistic longing to hurt the other redirects an impulse originally aimed at oneself: the hidden referent of her apparently "egglike self-sufficiency" is his own ego, which he alternately wants to damage and preserve. Torn between competing impulses, he simultaneously wants to protect and destroy himself. Were the contemplated act to be carried out, it would no doubt fail to satisfy him, for the intended victim is as much inside as it is outside. (In a later scene, this aggressive urge recurs in a metonymic context that again evokes the metaphoric association of Faye and film. Sitting next to her in the dark at "the pictures" is an "ordeal" because her apparent "self-sufficiency," makes Tod want to strike her and "break its smooth surface with a blow," [336].) His destructive impulse can be aimed at either the screen or the woman because for him both are surfaces on which he unwittingly projects the image of his ego. What he thus wants and doesn't want is to tear himself apart. Which is not to say that the actual woman would not be the one to suffer physically as the male subject unconsciously struggles against himself.

For the most part Tod resists acknowledging that he has inserted Faye into his own imaginary fantasies. Yet toward the end of the narrative he manages to evoke the peculiar dynamics that have governed their relationship from his perspective. At this point he figures Faye as being "like a cork. No matter how rough the sea got, she would go dancing over the same waves that sank iron ships and tore away pieces of reinforced concrete. He pictured her riding a tremendous sea. Wave after wave reared its ton on ton of solid water and crashed down only to have her spin gaily away." "It was a very pretty cork, gilt with a glittering fragment of mirror set in its top" (375).[42] The association of Faye with oceanic forces links her to the potentially engulfing drives that the male subject seeks unsuccessfully to harbor within himself through the use of images of the body as an iron vessel or concrete structure. On the other hand, the reflective image she offers on this streaming mass of water performs a different task in that it furnishes the subject with the debatable impression of the capacity of his ego to survive amid the surging waves of unconscious desire. The comic dialogue Tod has with Claude Estee helps clarify this essential aspect of Tod's relationship with Faye.

Estee's surname and vocation (he is a screenwriter) suggest his status as a stand-in for the author, and the two writers also share a penchant for irony. It is therefore not surprising that Claude occupies a position of analytical insight in relation to his troubled friend.[43] Claude is in addition more at ease with the potential discrepancies between body surfaces and psychic depths, than those enthralled by imaginary fixations can afford to be. His semiological playfulness manifests itself, for example, in his rejection of any necessary link between visible appearance and identity. He enjoys impersonating a Civil War colonel, his dwelling is "an exact reproduction" of a Southern mansion, and he inaccurately refers to his Chinese servant as a "black rascal."(A later scene demonstrates, however, that Claude's awareness doesn't render him immune to the fascinations of aesthetic beauty. He is as visually transfixed by Faye's dancing body at the party at Homer's house as are the rest of the men.)

In any event, the content of the dialogue between the two men has to do with Tod's unwillingness to join Claude and some others who are heading to a brothel to see a pornographic movie. As Tod endeavors to justify his hesitation and Claude analyzes his friend's resistance, the comic scene takes on therapeutic overtones. Their verbal repartee consists mainly of a string of similes with commentary. "I don't care how much cellophane she [Mrs. Jennings, the owner of the brothel] wraps it in, he [Tod] said – nautch joints are depressing, like all places for deposit, banks, mail boxes, tombs, vending machines" (255). Initially, the simile is based on the shape these entities have in common. The series of hollow receptacles enables Tod to compare sex with a prostitute to the leaving behind of something, dropping off of a letter, dumping a corpse into the ground, or putting money "down." Estee seizes upon the final analogy, wittily reversing the process his interlocutor evokes. It is not what one gives but what one receives that is at issue in what may be taken as a critical thesis on machine-age erotics:

> "Love is like a vending machine, eh? Not bad. You insert a coin and press home the lever. There's some mechanical activity inside the bowels of the device. You receive a small sweet, frown at yourself in the dirty mirror, adjust your hat, take a firm grip on your umbrella and walk away, trying to look as though nothing had happened. It's good, but it's not for pictures." (256)

The use of love, a conceptual abstraction, as opposed to sexual intercourse, a concrete physical act, is appropriate because what is at stake in the discourse is a mental process. Claude's mocking allusion to mechanized modes of obtaining physical gratification nudges Tod toward a recognition of the decisive role visual dynamics play in efforts to fix one's ego in place. What Tod is unwilling to admit is that his desire for the female character is mixed up with his ongoing effort to solidify his ego by misperceiving the other as a self-reflection.

If the patron/vending machine interaction materializes the narcissistic dimensions of Tod's fascination with Faye, it simultaneously evokes the cinematic relays between spectator and filmic images of bodies and faces. In other words, the vending machine is a gendered figure for the "dirty mirror" of the cinematic apparatus, one of the functions of which is to allow persons to overlook differences in order to identify with the apparently same. The analogy is "not for pictures" because it is about the pictures. The impossible copulation for which he yearns is routed through a mechanical contrivance, which further guarantees that the fusion he wishes for is destined to remain beyond his grasp. The vending machine may therefore be classified, as the cinematic apparatus often has been, as a "bachelor machine." As West shows, the operator of such a machine, the bachelor machinist, is lodged, as Penley puts it, inside "a closed, self-sufficient system," is caught up in a "fantasy of closure, perfectibility and mastery."[44] In sum, the "vending machine" is a viewing machine, and love is a displaced name for watching movies, a practice that implements the psychic process of misrecognitions whereby the ego is borrowed from a surrogate body.

The reference to the erotic transaction as an economic one is in accord with the brothel allusion, where sex is of course a commodity. Yet it is feasible to detect in the passage a pun on the specular investments one makes to secure a sense of self. In the illusory exchanges the apparatus facilitates, the patron simultaneously loses and gains something, albeit without full satisfaction. What he secures for his money in "fooling with a nickel machine," the "small sweet," is less the pleasures of sexual orgasm than a sense of self. The reward for the spectator's "abysmal curiosity" to see himself "reflected in the magic mirror of the machine age," as Henry Miller put it in 1938,[45] is a manufactured soul suited for "the robots of this age."[46] The psychic prosthesis the technical medium enables one to purchase has, however, a paradoxical dimension. For the individual to acquire something he feels to be missing, he must first tear himself in two. The ego derives from an act of identification that entails the splitting apart of the looker.

Elsewhere, West connects the industrial reproduction of subjects with the numerous attractive bodies Hollywood ceaselessly puts into circulation. This time the source of insight is a conversation between Tod and Faye. Faye is proposing to her suitor that he write up and sell to the studios the series of story lines, the "swell ideas," she has little trouble manufacturing. Though she only smiles "at the mechanics," her critical awareness of the standardized, formulaic nature of the day-dreams the film industry generates leads toward an understanding of the repressive aspects of contemporary modes of modeling individuals. The first picture idea she comes up with derives from a Tarzan poster hanging on the wall of her room. It shows "a beautiful young man with magnificent muscles, wearing only a narrow loin cloth" and "ardently squeezing a slim girl in a torn riding habit" (294).[47] If we assume that the imaginary investments such idealized figures solicit are offered as a means of alleviating a sense of physical and psychic turbulence, then the reason the process must be repeated over and over again becomes evident. The completion of the eroticized act of identification the spectator hopes will provide him with a sense of wholeness presupposes a preceding act of separation. Furthermore, the stress on healthy, natural bodies masks the technological mediation of subjectivity, instanced here in the fact that the images are mechanically reproduced. To constitute a self in relation to such images amounts to a coupling of human beings and machines, and it is precisely this intimate relation between the organic and inorganic that Hollywood seeks to occlude while exacerbating.

Mainstream film is repressive not because it joins humans and machines together but because it tends (there are of course always exceptions) to organize desires so that these conform to pre-established representational molds. In Hollywood's implementation of the imaginary, whole bodies take precedence over drives of a more partial sort. Consequently, the productive force of the unconscious is constrained; desire ceases to couple "continuous flows and partial objects that are by nature fragmentary and fragmented."[48] The film industry thus contributes to the damming up of streams of pleasure that, for West, is a distinguishing condition of the type of subject prone to unexpected outbursts of violent rage. Tod remains the principal object of analysis in the case study or profile that *Day* constitutes in this regard; but the portrait of the even more overwrought Homer furnishes complementary material on the phenomenon.

West also renders Homer's inner condition visible through images of flooding that closely resemble the liquid-based figurations Theweleit isolates as a prime component of the fascist male's imaginary repertoire.[49] For example, after getting out of the tub, Homer feels emptied out; after bathing he is more "washed out than usual" (273). Extricating himself physically from the water is here a trope for the need he experiences to get rid of the tumultuous drives that flood through his psyche. "His [Homer's] emotions surged up in an enormous wave, curving and rearing, higher and higher, until it seemed as though the wave must carry everything before it. But the crash never came. Something always happened at the very top of the crest and the wave collapsed to run back like water down a drain, leaving, at the most, only the refuse of feeling" (273). The surging waves are translations of unconscious desire, of the pleasurable urges that the character fears will inundate and engulf him if he fails to rid himself of them successfully. (Though the visual figures are part of the narrative discourse, they may be attributed to the character as an indication of how he conceives of his mental condition.)

Psychic maintenance is achieved through figures of corporeal and mental fortification. To give in to his desires would cause a disastrous inferno, would lead to the immolation of his ego. "When the days passed and he [Homer] couldn't forget Faye, he began to grow frightened. He somehow knew that his only defense was chastity, that it served him, like the shell of a tortoise, as both spine and armor. He couldn't shed it even in thought. If he did, he would be destroyed." No longer utilizing free indirect discourse, the narrator comments: "He was right. There are men who can lust with parts of themselves. Only their brain or their hearts burn, and then not completely. There are others, still more fortunate, who are like the filaments of an incandescent lamp. They burn fiercely, yet nothing is destroyed. But in Homer's case it would be like dropping a spark into a barn full of hay" (290). The turn toward images of bodily and psychic shielding is indispensable as a means of preventing the kind of overexcited state that would result in the explosion of the subject. But these images are in addition indispensable material for the critical analyst seeking to comprehend the inner condition of potentially dangerous persons, of the kind of individual capable of being swept into a fascist movement. For West male fantasies offer a promising basis for incisive political inquiry.

(A misprint in the recent Library of America edition of the novel substitutes "armor" for "amour" in the comic dialogue between Tod and Claude commented on above. What "the barber," the typical film spectator, wants, Claude explains in the mistaken version, "is armor and glamor" [256]. In an odd way the mistake is faithful to an aspect of the novel's social critique: it is not love but defense against wild passion or the productive flow of unconscious desire that someone like Homer requires for psychic maintenance. Tod's subsequent rejection of his diagnostic reliance on a "metallizing" trope is also pertinent here. Late in the novel, he realizes he has fooled "himself into believing . . . with an image" that Homer will in fact benefit from Faye's presence, "as though a man were a piece of iron to be heated and then straightened with hammer blows" [330]. Here, West presents the beginnings of an epistemological critique of precisely the kind of images that fascist discourse utilizes to maintain orderly subjects.[50])

Rather than comment directly on the political ramifications of the subjective phenomenon he examines, West chooses instead in *Day* to satirize the condition while hinting at its socially determined causes. The novel suggests that Homer's predicament can be linked to the mechanization of the work process. If he hasn't slaved "at tedious machines of all sorts" as have the savage and bitter persons that form the rushing crowd outside the movie premiere at the novel's end, his twenty-year stint as a hotel bookkeeper has left him, like the others, without "the mental equipment for pleasure" (380). His job keeping track of numbers may also have contributed to his obsessive/compulsive behavior, to his development of a "complicated tic" ("But I can't help it . . . I have to do it three times"), which Tod finds horrifying because of "its precision" (359). While Miller was writing about his search for a way to escape "the automatic process" that had transformed him into a killer ("I was like a puppet in whose hands society had placed a Gatling gun"[51]), West was busy inventing ways to satirize the effects of this process. For Miller, the solution was to become a desiring machine that writes, was to reinvent himself as the producer of grotesque autobiographies. West's strategy was to deploy the grotesque to construct parodic counterparts to the weapon-like men of steel and bronze the entertainment industry was rapidly manufacturing.

Superman and Doc Savage eliminate all traces of sexuality from their metallized flesh so that they may mete out punishment to those who deserve it. Their satisfaction comes from fighting not from the flows of unconscious desire. "He [Doc] had long ago made up his mind that women were to play no part in his career." (He also seems impervious to water. Despite being out in the rain, his "hair and skin showed not the least wetness."[52]) Homer too appears in the final pages of *Day* to have successfully subdued his passion and overcome his traumatic regression. Walking along "like a badly made automaton," "his features . . . set in a rigid, mechanical grin" (*Novels, Day*, 381), he ends up stomping a child (Adore) who has been taunting him. Taken as an ironic commentary on such ostensibly admirable superheroes, Homer's transformation from autistic child to murderous weapon makes the protofascist ambition to reconcile the body with the machine appear as the gruesomely ludicrous response to an unbearably shocking experience.

The description of characters through the use of machinic similes is in fact a comic compositional strategy West deploys frequently in the text. Like the hinges on the door to Homer's cottage in Pinyon Canyon, individuals are frequently figured in *Day* as if they were "made by machine," whether or not they "have been carefully stamped to appear hand-forged" (265). Earle Shoop's "two-dimensional face" for instance, is said to bear a strong "resemblance to a mechanical drawing" (299). Homer himself has previously been shown getting "out of bed in sections, like a poorly made automaton" (267). Falling ill, Harry Greener, the old vaudeville comedian and father of Faye, is "like a mechanical toy that had been overwound, something snapped inside of him and he began to spin through his entire repertoire" (279). And later he laughs with "a sharp, metallic crackle," the sound rising in pitch "to become a machinelike screech" (284). The materialist thesis the analogies argue is that human beings in urban-industrial modernity are constructed artifacts whose movements are programmed by external forces.

The most developed example of this rhetorical strategy occurs in the wake of Homer's emotional breakdown. After witnessing Faye having intercourse with Miguel (a parodic primal scene), Homer collapses. It is as if the scene brings back the "thing he was trying so desperately to avoid" yet that "keeps crowding into his mind" (268). This thing is the memory of a failed encounter with a drunken boarder at the hotel where he previously worked. His initial reaction to Miss Martin's advances is to label "his excitement disgust." Soon, however, "little waves of sensation moved along his nerves and the base of his tongue tingled" (269). Yet nothing happens, and he ends up feeling as if he had escaped a terrible fate (290). The later incident has more dire consequences. First, he manages to relate the story to Tod in a streaming flow of verbiage. "The lake behind the dam replenished itself too fast. The more he talked the greater the pressure grew because the flood was circular and ran back behind the dam again" (368). Once the gushing liberation of his discursive drives is over, language no longer leaping out of him "in a muddy, twisting torrent," he is reduced to being "like a steel spring which has been freed of its function in a machine and allowed to use all its strength centripetally. While part of a machine the pull of the spring had been used against other and stronger forces, but now, free at last, it was striving to attain the shape of its original coil." Recoiling at the sight of two people in bed, Homer deanimates himself. His reified condition resembles one Tod recollects having seen described in a "book of abnormal psychology" as "Uterine Flight," a simpler, infantile system in which feeding is "automatic" (372).

In that he tries to console Homer and has some analytical sense of his condition as a pathological one, it would seem that Tod is situated outside the problematic. That this is by no means the case becomes apparent in the final scene outside Kahn's Persian Palace Theatre – decreed "A PLEASURE DOME" by a hanging electric sign. What this scene clarifies is the degree to which Tod's expressive aesthetic is as much of a defense reaction to the unsettling flow of unconscious desires as are fascist reconfigurations of the body as an instrument of destruction.

The character's fascination with the lower-middle-classes has remained strong throughout the novel. When he spies individual members of this social group gathering outside the movie palace for a premiere, he decides to "kill some time by looking at the crowds" (378). But the behavior of this speedily growing entity soon provokes a perceptual agitation that (again through free indirect discourse) should be attributed to the would-be observer. The "dense mass" appears as a "demoniac" force whose movements, if it is offended, will only be halted by "machine guns." The crowd is now seen as a violently aggressive entity that may "grab and rend" whatever objects attract its attention. The similarity of this perspective to Tod's earlier impression of Faye as a threat to his bodily integrity suggests that the excited crowd may be, as she was, an embodiment of his chaotic emotions. It is therefore difficult to determine the objective accuracy of his speculations on what is driving this mob into an apparent frenzy. The persons constituting it may or may not be embittered and resentful and dependent on violently sensationalist fare "to make taut their slack minds and bodies" (381). In fact, the mood of the crowd seems to be a jumble of hysterical anger and festive delight. Many of the "rioters" are laughing and appear to be having a good time, while others, such as the young girl who is being molested by an old man, look to be on the verge of throwing a fit. We are on much safer interpretive ground when we take the ambiguities of the description as an indication of Tod's own uncertainty in relation to the masses.

As the event progresses, disobeying a policeman's orders, Tod moves closer to the preview watchers. Shortly thereafter, he gets caught up in what is tellingly figured as an uncontrollably flowing body of water. Terrified, he frantically struggles "against the tide" to no avail. Having ridden "the current" as best he can, he is nonetheless swept off his feet and carried along against his will to the point where he feels his ribs starting to crack. As the panicked observer is swept into the rushing crowd, he feels as if his physical frame is about to come apart. To avoid being "sucked back" in, Tod clings in desperation to the top of a driveway fence. He then finds it necessary in order to maintain his position of relative safety to lash out brutally at the clutching fingers of a sobbing woman. "Tod felt his fingers slipping from the rail and kicked backwards as hard as he could. The woman let go" (387). An act of violent aggression against a clinging woman turns out to be the only way the man can keep himself above the crowd.

That Tod's painterly endeavor is a psychic defense mechanism becomes fully apparent at this point in the novel. Experiencing intense agony, Tod turns to his artwork. "After his quarrel with Faye, he had worked on it continually to escape tormenting himself, and the way to it in his mind had become almost automatic" (387). What motivates the project is the affective combination of desire that Faye and the crowd induce in him. His expressive aesthetic is thus a means of maintaining control over a force that threatens him emotionally and physically. The burden of "The Burning of Los Angeles" is to differentiate the fraught artist from the carnivalesque entity that puts his autonomy at risk. An act of visual surveillance,[53] the character's painting is part of an effort to preserve his identity by framing this other and is comparable to the police's efforts outside the premiere to keep the fans from moving across an arbitrarily drawn line. The officers struggle to maintain control over the crowd by ramming its overflowing parts backward, which only causes "the bulge" to "pop out somewhere else." This is one kind of violent reaction to the refusal of an amorphous substance to stay put; fixing it in place in a work of art is another. Both amount to an attempt to beat the mass into submissive shape. What the law does with clubs the avant-garde artist does with his paintbrush. My point throughout this chapter has been that this rage to order is aimed as much at the chaos inside the male subject as it is at what lies outside.

In the end it is evident that Tod's terror of being absorbed extends from the feminine and the masses to the mechanical. Tod's tragic (in the sense of the term as Dahlberg uses it in "Ariel in Caliban") descent into apparent madness as the novel concludes evokes first the confusion and then the elimination of any firm distinction between natural and mechanically generated sounds. The police car "siren began to scream and at first he thought he was making the noise himself." After checking his lips to make certain that it is the car and not he who is emitting the sound, Tod begins "to imitate the siren as loud as he could" (389). Like one of Roger Caillois's insects, Tod fades into his mechanized background, becoming an indistinguishable part of his environment through an involuntary act of mimicry. In contrast to Edvard Munch's famous depiction of a screaming homunculus' attempt to project outward onto his environment the monadic subject's "inward feeling" of anxiety,[54] at the end of *Day* a traumatized Tod(ysseus) capitulates via imitation to the external cry of a mechanized siren.

In a letter dated February 14, 1939, West described his second novel, *A Cool Million*, as a book that "came out when no one in this country except a few Jeremiahs like myself, took seriously the possibility of a Fascist America" (*Novels*, 791).[55] I have been arguing that although he continued to take this possibility seriously while writing *Day* (which would be published a few months later), the focal point of his investigation shifted to the tormented inner world of a particular kind of male subject. And the later novel suggests that one of the ways such a subject defends himself from what he alternately fears and desires is to adopt a prophetic stance toward it. In other words, Tod's refusal "to give up the role of Jeremiah" in relation to those living on the periphery of the film industry in Los Angeles is symptomatic. The "strong feeling of satisfaction" he derives from the "dire conclusion" that his painterly labors have led him to is a protective gesture. By the decade's end, aesthetic and religious predictions of "doom and destruction" and the cognitive happiness these furnish had become for West symptoms of a male hysteria that might be laying the groundwork for a fascist future in the United States.

The critical thread that links the two radical inquiries is the author's sustained concern with the way charismatic bodies may serve as the basis of forming collective identities. The function of natural corporeal beauty (male or female) and one kind of reconciliation of the body and machine (the man of steel or bronze as efficient weapon of destruction) is to provide psychically and physically fatigued individuals with relief from their otherwise exhausting existence. In *A Cool Million*, West interferes with this process by satirically dismantling the type of attractive body Alger's dime-novel hymns to American capitalism had helped put into public circulation. At the same time, he demonstrates the way in which the fragmented body can be incorporated back into a system of ideological inscription; when used to tap into unconscious fears, the sight of somatic wreckage may compel persons to join organized political movements. The critical approach he takes in regard to the fascinating aspects of a more thoroughly modernized form of visual culture (Hollywood film) proceeds along different lines.

In *Day*, West repeatedly takes the reader, via Tod's strolls through the studio lots, behind the scenes to draw attention to the artificial *materials* that furnish the ultimately flimsy backgrounds against which the mirage of the film star's body stands out. Chapter 18 provides the best example. On his walk, he observes among other things a papier mâché sphinx, fiber lawns, cardboard food, a cellophane waterfall, celluloid swans, ostensibly stone porticos flapping in the breeze, not to mention the god Eros lying "face downward in a pile of old newspapers and bottles" (324–25). He then ends up famously at the "final dumping ground" of past productions. Here, amid the junked remnants of old sets, flats, and props one can see clearly the "plaster, canvas, lath, and paint" used to make dreams "photographic." "A Sargasso of the imagination!" (326). He then watches impassively as the unfinished set replicating Mont St. Jean falls apart. The "classic mistake" is to order "the cuirassiers to charge." "With their sabers in their teeth and their pistols in their hands," these elaborately costumed warriors (who wore steel breastplates) cause the hill to collapse under their weight. "The sound of ripping canvas was like that of little children whimpering. Lath and scantling snapped as though they were brittle bones. The whole hill folded like an enormous umbrella and covered Napoleon's army with painted cloth" (328). The illusory representation of nineteenth-century martial heroism clearly rests on unsteady grounds.

Tod's disavowal of the contrived dimensions of Faye's theatrical performances is another case in point. "Being with her was like being backstage during an amateurish, ridiculous play. From in front, the stupid lines and grotesque situations would have made him squirm with annoyance, but because he saw the perspiring stagehands and the wires that held up the tawdry summerhouse with its tangle of paper flowers, he accepted everything and was anxious for it to succeed" (292). Faye may be for the fictional subject a fetish that hides (and reveals) the constructive labor that goes into producing the spectacle of aesthetic beauty, but the reader is encouraged to register the mechanisms behind the masquerade. Much like the cheap façades of the houses in Pinyon Canyon, cinematic figures are precariously erected constructs.

West's interest in disclosing the human labor, mechanical equipment, and formal materials required to fabricate fascinating images of the body suggests a point of convergence between his writing and the painterly endeavor Thomas Hart Benton had completed two years before the book appeared in print. In *Hollywood* (1937; see figure 5), Benton shows the extent to which the alluring sight of the natural body in film has become the height of artifice. "The Burning of Los Angeles" falls short of this critical perspective, for it amounts to little more than a grotesque inversion of mainstream cinema. Tod merely sets an art of the ugly against Hollywood's mass reproduction of classical beauties. The character's phenomenological ambition to render the invisible visible, to manifest in sensuous form the anguished souls of his subject matter, falls far short of West's ironically materialist analysis of the soul as an effect produced by an illusory system of mirror images. Tod's aesthetic idealism prevents him from disclosing that the social function of mechanized leisure has become to provide spectators with the sense of being centered selves as compensation for the fact that mechanized labor is busy eliminating this feeling as part of everyday life. The motif of the automaton

Fig. 5 Thomas Hart Benton, *Hollywood*, 1937

in West is designed to disclose the truth mainstream movies obscure: that the reifying impact of work in urban-industrial modernity reduces persons to the status of spiritually empty, dead things. Like Cremonini's faces, as Althusser comprehends them, West's comically deformed lifeless characters are haunted by the absent structures that determine their existence.

Dos Passos makes it possible to extend our understanding of the process of giving and taking away souls to the intertwining of the military machine and imperialist spectacles. Here again the grotesque image of the mutilated body proves to be the pivot around which an act of Depression-era critical radicalism turns. And as Dos Passos directs his critical energies toward the way language determines subjectivity, it becomes evident that deformation is disfiguration.

4

Militarism and mutilation in John Dos Passos

Suppose I'd been horribly burned, like that girl, disfigured for life. (John Dos Passos, *Manhattan Transfer*)

To the dismemberment of the body corresponds a dismemberment of language. (Paul de Man, "Phenomenality and Materiality in Kant")

In "Into the Night Life," Henry Miller goes on a dream journey that leads to a terrifying sight of physical mutilation. Arriving at a box factory, which turns out to be "The Morgue," he looks down from a window into a courtyard at a collection of to him seemingly unknown dead persons.

None of the cripples have feet, few have arms; their faces are covered with soot. All of them have medals on their chest.

To my horror and amazement I slowly perceive that from the long chute attached to the wall of the factory a steady stream of coffins is being emptied into the yard. As they tumble down the chute a man steps forward on mutilated stumps and pausing a moment to adjust the burden to his back slowly trudges off with his coffin.[1]

It is as if the victims of military combat have become laborers in an industrialized graveyard, their designated task to bury themselves. The condensation in Miller's psyche of the worker and the soldier is presumably overdetermined by the corporeal damage each experiences. At any rate, the next installment of *Black Spring* clarifies the significance of this disturbing scene. At the end of "Walking Up and Down in China" he fondly recalls the friends of his youth but then notes sadly that they all "had their heads blown off or their guts bayoneted" in the First World War. The "boys from the north side and the boys from the south side – all rolled into a muck heap and their guts hanging on the barbed wire. If only one of them had been spared" (*Black Spring*, 210). The seemingly anonymous cripples of "Into the Night Life" can retroactively be recognized as the particular individuals Miller goes on to name. If the shocking death of the boys he grew up with has traumatized the speaker, autobiographical writing is the means through which he works through his private, though historically inflected anguish. Repressed materials must be brought forth from the unconscious so that mourning can proceed.

Three years later, Dalton Trumbo set before the public an equally distressing reminder of the war; and one wonders whether the fictional protagonist of *Johnny Got His Gun* (1939) is better or worse off than Miller's friends. Joe Bonham has "been spared," yet he has survived in severely truncated form. Waking up on a hospital bed in France, he realizes to his horror that he has become a faceless torso. All four limbs have been amputated, and there is nothing but a hole where his face once was. "He had no legs and no arms and no eyes and no ears and no nose and no mouth and no tongue."[2]

After enduring much anguish, Bonham establishes contact with the outside world by in effect transforming what is left of him somatically into a component of a telegraph.[3] He discovers that he can communicate with others by pounding his dismembered body against his bed in Morse code. Mimicking a mechanical apparatus, the "wireless set" he had when he was a kid, "the stump of a man" repetitiously taps away, determined to continue doing so until someone finally picks up his transmission. "He would continue the tapping just as you turn on a machine and it continues to operate after you have gone away" (*Johnny*, 238). Finally a nurse grasps the significance of his physical gestures and soon he is receiving messages as they are tapped onto his wrecked body. The body thus becomes its own prosthetic device, artificially compensating for its sensory deprivation. The deficiencies of a body without perceptual organs are overcome as the torso replaces the eyes and ears. In semiological terms, the devastated body becomes the means of producing signifiers that can be graphically transcribed as dots and dashes and then translated into a signified.

Having opened up lines of communication with those who are caring for him, the soldier makes a surprising request. What he desires is to be presented to the public as a carnivalized attraction. Recalling the assorted venues at which human oddities are put on display, Joe states his wish to become such an exhibit. "Take off my nightshirt and build a glass case for me and take me down to the places where people are having fun where they are on the lookout for freakish things. Take me in my glass case to the beaches and the country fairs and the church bazaars and the circuses and the traveling carnivals" (288). Not only would this allow him to become financially self-supporting, the government could even turn a profit on the enterprise. After all, "People were always willing to pay to see a curiosity they were always interested in terrible sights and probably nowhere on the face of the earth was there any living thing quite so terrible as he was" (284).

> You could do a wonderful business with me I could pay you for the trouble. You could give them a good spiel. They've heard of the half-man half-woman. They've heard of the bearded woman and the thin man and the midget. They've seen the human mermaids and the wild men from Borneo and the meat-eating girl from the Congo throw her a fish and watch her snap for it. They've seen the man who writes with his toes and the man who walks on his hands and the Siamese twins and those little rows of unborn babies pickled in alcohol.
> But they've seen nothing like this. This will be the goddamndest dime's worth a man ever had. This will be a sensation in the show world and whoever sponsors my tour will be a new Barnum and have fine notices in all the newspapers because I am something you can really holler about. I am something you can push with a money back guarantee. I am the dead-man-who-is-alive. I am the live-man-who-is-dead. (289)

As an exemplary freak of war, a pedagogical display, the soldier will bring the awful truth of military combat home to civilians. The gruesome entity would serve a cautionary, didactic function. He would show what modernized weaponry can do to the fragile human body:

> He would be an educational exhibit. People wouldn't learn much about anatomy from him but they would learn all there was to know about war. That would be a great thing to concentrate war in one stump of a body and to show it to people so they could see the difference between a war that's in the newspaper headlines and liberty loan drives and a war that is fought out lonesomely in the mud somewhere a war between a man and a high explosive shell . . . he would have a sign over himself and the sign would say here is war and he would concentrate the whole war into such a small piece of meat and bone and hair that they would never forget it as long as they lived. (287–88)

He wishes to become the corporeal referent of an anti-war discourse. A politicized attraction, the sight of the repulsive entity would be a shocking demonstration of the effects of engaging in armed combat. "See that red gash there with mucus hanging to it? That was his face girls" (293). His public appearance in the brutalized flesh has the potential to counteract the persuasive impact of patriotic discourses that rely on conceptual abstractions and encouraging slogans derived from popular tunes – like the one used ironically as the title of the book. Insubstantial verbiage has been the object of an earlier critique. "For Christ sake give us things to fight for we can see and feel and pin down and understand. No more highfalutin words that mean nothing like nativeland," or like "liberty or freedom or democracy or independence or decency or honor" (147).

Though the rhetoric of nationalism cannot be pinned down semantically, its effects can be somatically devastating when deployed as a recruiting tool.

What the soldier has learned is that only those who have passed away can say for sure whether the sacrifice that they made was genuinely valuable. "Nobody but the dead know whether all these things people talk about are worth dying for or not. And the dead can't talk. So the words about noble deaths and sacred blood and honor, and such are all put into dead lips by grave robbers and fakes who have no right to speak for the dead" (150). War propagandists are to his mind thieves and liars who are guilty of a linguistic subterfuge; they propose to supply information that they do not really possess. The impression they leave their listeners with, that the propagandists have access to and are expressing the convictions of military casualties, is a false one. The speaker's protest indicates that the duplicitous enterprises in question are produced by the use of prosopopoeia. The ideologists of patriotism create pernicious illusions by misleadingly using figurative language to attribute to the dead a power only the living possess: speech. He alone, the protagonist feels, has had an authentic experience of death, and he therefore occupies the uniquely privileged position from an ontological standpoint of being a person who has actually acquired knowledge that others illegitimately claim to have. Only this devastatingly wounded soldier can justifiably assert that he has the inarguable ability to carry on a conversation from beyond the grave. "He was a dead man with a mind that could still think. He knew all the answers that the dead knew." "He could speak for the dead because he was one of them . . . Nobody could dispute with him" (153).[4]

Overcoming his muteness by the conversion of his body into a mechanical apparatus turns out to be a wonderful achievement that renders the fragmented body whole once again. His lost limbs and detached organs come back to him. "His legs that were smashed and gone got up and danced. His arms that were rotted" now swing "free at his sides" and "the eyes they had taken from him looked up from the garbage heap they had been consigned to and saw all the beauties of the world. The ears that were shattered and full of silence rang suddenly with music. The mouth that had been hacked away from his face and now was filled with dust returned to sing" (276). His damaged parts repaired and reattached, the physically resurrected solider feels he is now free to "tell all the secrets of the dead" (277). Unfortunately, yet predictably, his request is denied on the grounds that it is against regulations. So he is condemned by the authorities to decay in a military hospital. Drugged to keep him "quiet" and kept out of sight, the soldier's wish to body forth the gruesome but unofficial "truth" of the recent war remains unsatisfied. As partial compensation for this (fictive) act of censorship, we have a narrative representation that posits itself as the augmentation of an inaccessible oral discourse. Unable to show itself, the thing may still communicate insofar as writing functions as a prosthetic supplement to speech, extending the range of the absent voice.

The unique aspects of the *U.S.A.* trilogy can now be brought into focus. In sharp contrast to Trumbo's affecting yet traditional method of politicizing literature, John Dos Passos' political aims led him to seek to release writing from its customary servitude to the spoken word. His anti-mimetic and non-expressive endeavor was to radicalize American literary practice by establishing the novel as the site of critical endeavors. His aim was to impede the flow of competing discourses (such as lyric poetry and print journalism) by unsettling their representational claims. Repeatedly undermining as well the authority of the speaker in the process of developing a rhetorically enlightened method of writing, his achievement was in part to dissolve the distinction between writing and critical reading. Correlatively, one of the mainsprings of this linguistically rigorous enterprise was the negation of persuasive figures of speech, the taking apart of compelling tropes.

Because in the end his disfigurative operation makes striking use of an image of violent physical mutilation to make itself visible, I character-ize Dos Passos' text as a kind of rhetorical hybrid: a grotesque allegory. *1919*, the second volume of the trilogy, culminates in an act of criti-cal resistance directed at the post-war administration's epistemologically duplicitous manipulation of the shattered corpse of an unknown soldier for explicitly ideological purposes. Grasping the imaginative transfor-mation of a dead individual into a national monument as a linguistic undertaking, Dos Passos, in "The Body of An American," struggles to bring the symbolic icon back down to its material conditions of origin. As the critical procedure runs its course and arrives at the repulsive remains of the mortally wounded soldier, we arrive at a figure for the effects of an act of disfiguration. To the blasted decaying corpse corresponds a blasted, decaying trope.

That Dos Passos' main Depression-era enterprise was the product of the interaction between literature and American amusement is not as immediately apparent as it has been in the cases dealt with previ-ously in this study. It was not difficult to demonstrate that Dahlberg and Miller drew a considerable amount of their aesthetic energies from carnivalized entertainments. West's attitude toward forms of modernized fun was certainly more mixed, yet his writing clearly emerges out of an ongoing engagement with these. Dos Passos' approach seems at first glance to resemble West's. Each sets out to ironize commercial culture in the hope of generating an awareness of the ideological power of such practices to shape subjectivity. West's critical priorities led him to eliminate almost entirely the distance between literature and amusement, for the latter, in addition to providing him with the subject matter he analyzed, also supplied him with the compositional models his parodic endeavors required to come into existence. Dos Passos' even more ambitious critical aim was to subsume the novel's many "others" (including print journalism, advertising, popular song, and lyric poetry) in the hope of re-grounding the genre's political authority on the far side of mimetic representation and aesthetic pleasure. Nevertheless, a closer look reveals that Dos Passos, like Dahlberg and Miller, took some compositional cues from mechanized recreation. This partial reliance can be glimpsed in Dos Passos' fairly obscure 1925 review of a recent dramatic production.

In "Is the 'Realistic' Theatre Obsolete?" Dos Passos praises the stage as being "among the last survivors of what might be called the arts of direct contact."[5] His assessment would seem to evince a nostalgic preference for traditional as opposed to technologically mediated culture in that he sees the threat to this dying art coming from "the movies and radio and subsequent mechanical means of broadcasting entertainment and propaganda." But Dos Passos' point is that the modern theatre must discover ways to compete against its new challengers, something mainstream drama has failed at miserably, largely because of its capitulation to the expectations of an audience that respects "the idiotic schism between Highbrow and Lowbrow."[6] If "the theatre is going to survive, it has got to find for itself a new function." It must, for instance, abandon the attempt "to convince the audience" that "they have strayed into a West Virginia mining town in the middle of an industrial war." Lawson's at times "crude and comic and grotesque" play stands as a desirable alternative to the conventionally realistic theatre because it rejects "the invisible fourth wall" and seeks instead to "put on a show," as "burlesque, musical comedy, and vaudeville" have been doing most recently.[7] What is needed then is a kind of "theatre of attractions" in Gunning's sense of the term.[8]

That such a theatre is by no means incompatible with the kind of thrilling effects generated by mechanized amusements becomes evident at the end of the review. To characterize the "horror and consternation" with which Lawson's admirable effort to "climb wholeheartedly out of the blind alley of realism" was met, Dos Passos compares the outraged audience to "a maiden aunt who has been unwillingly coaxed by a small boy to ride on a roller coaster. They felt sick and held on desperately and prayed that it would stop. But as a trip to Coney Island on a Sunday afternoon will show you, there are a great many people in New York who are crazy to ride on roller coasters."[9] No doubt it is to these people, those who are not "pathetically afraid of being moved either in space of time or in their feelings," that the novel Dos Passos had just published would appeal – a novel named after a New Jersey railway station: *Manhattan Transfer*. Kinetic writing was to reproduce the disorienting sensations of riding mechanical amusements.

This priority also informed his next major literary project – *U.S.A.* – though by this time a different mechanical amusement had emerged as a touchstone for the experience of being emotionally unsettled and intellectually jostled: the newsreel.[10] What Dos Passos borrowed from this sensationalized entertainment was its montage format as well as the technique of extracting and arranging sequentially fragmentary materials from other cultural sources. Despite this compositional debt, Dos Passos had minimal interest in affirming that the bits and pieces of news he inserted into his textual construct offered accurate information or perceptual glimpses of world events. Rather, he utilized the minor film genre as a means of undermining the "naive" reader's faith in reportorial and other discourses. A cinematic method of juxtaposition became the basis of an ironic tactic whereby the critically oriented writer adopted the stance of a film editor in order to generate in the minds of those who lacked it a linguistic self-consciousness.

The distressing consequences of the widespread failure to achieve rhetorical enlightenment were for Dos Passos most evident in the damage done to individual bodies in modernized warfare. The inability to resist the persuasive force of propagandistic discourses was one of the preconditions for the widespread experience of somatic pain and death. If Dos Passos' commitment to political dissent in the twenties and thirties crystallized around the corporeal suffering of the American soldier,[11] his concern was as much with the disciplinary and ideological procedures that compelled persons to submit willingly to their own destruction as it was with combat. In addition, the physical and psychic subjection demanded by the military ended up providing Dos Passos with a model for understanding existence in modern society. What army training did to soldiers was not much different from what the mass media did to civilian bodies and minds. To combat the automation of movements and programming of thoughts, Dos Passos labored to reinvent the novel as an aggressively critical practice. The violent mutilation of texts was to serve as a means of battling against the militarization of everyday life.

MILITARY AUTOMATONS

"It's the discipline. I'm tellin' yer, it gits a feller in the end," said Happy. (John Dos Passos, *Three Soldiers*)

The regimentation and mass-production of soldiers, to the end of turning out a cheap, standardized, and replaceable product, was the great contribution of the military mind to the machine process. (Lewis Mumford, *Technics and Civilization*)

In "The Drama of the Machines," an essay published in *Scribner's Magazine* in August 1930, Lewis Mumford proposed that the effort of the machine to entrench itself in modern society might be staged as a military struggle between the human and the mechanical. The first victory has been won by the "army of the machines" which has established itself "as a central force in Western civilization." Notably, the "chief incentive to mechanical contrivance has come, he notes, "from the institution of warfare." It was the "application of a deadly earnestness to the slaughter of men" that inspired technological invention. For instance, "the internal combustion engine – bullets propelled by gunpowder – was a product of warfare." As martial combat became increasingly lethal, metal workers necessarily developed their art, initially responding to the demand to manufacture steel armor, then muskets, then cannons, and, finally, armored battleships and armored tanks. Advances in mining and smelting also followed from the need to supply greater amounts of weaponry to fighting forces, which caused those with "skilled minds" to attend to "technological processes" with greater rigor than before. Technical ingenuity was utilized to make the war-process more efficient, to improve through rationalization the economy of mass destruction.[12]

In measuring the "gains that the machine has brought" while balancing these "against the losses," the negative effects are predominant. Much of the drudgery of labor has been eliminated, but the products of the machine have wrought "wholesale destruction" against the forests, have "depleted the country side" and "brought into existence" "irredeemable misery" due to the "constant threat of universal annihilation by mechanized warfare."[13] The critic can therefore be forgiven for looking "forward to a shrinkage of the total area occupied by the machine," to the day when the animate reasserts its rights and rediscovers its power over the inanimate. After all, "the central fact of life is not mechanism but life."[14] Assuming one is still determined to specify the positive contributions of the machine to human existence, one must necessarily pursue this task without a naive faith in the notion that "all change is progress and all progress is beneficial."[15]

The task Dos Passos undertakes with *U.S.A.* is to invert the existing power relations between human beings and technology, to master the machines that have achieved the status of oppressors over mankind. Only by becoming self-conscious of the significance of the machine may this task be accomplished, may technology be subordinated to the human and the invented once again be under the control of the inventors. Several years before, in "Homer of the Trans-Siberian," a critical appreciation of the French poet and novelist Blaise Cendrars, Dos Passos had asserted a comparable outlook on this topic.[16] After recalling a visit when a small child to one of the "brand-new" train cars on exhibit at the Paris Exposition Universelle of 1900, Dos Passos goes on to reflect on the physical pain caused by our dependence on mechanized systems of transportation and accompanying addiction to travel. Today "our bodies are tortured," for as we "run across the continents" we are overwhelmed by the mechanical, which penetrates us by way of the senses. We are "always deafened by the grind of wheels, by the roar of airplane motors, [we] wallow in all the seas with the smell of hot oil in our nostrils and the throb of the engines in our blood."[17] The virtue of the French writer's epic work is that it has a soothing effect. Cendrars is "a kind of medicine-man trying to evoke the things that are our cruel and avenging gods." These include "turbines, triple-expansion engines" and "navigation, speed, flight, annihilation."[18] Situated at the end of a stage of great technological achievement, he reflects back on this heroic period of industrial development, interpreting it through narrative, transforming action into knowledge. "As the old earth-shaking engines are scrapped one by one, the myth-makers are at work," composing "hymns of the railroads."[19] "In this age of giant machines and scuttle-headed men it is a good thing to have a little music. We need sons of Homer going about the world beating into some sort of human rhythm the shrieking hullabaloo, making us less afraid."[20] Historical cognition will relieve the tension produced by physical and mental immersion in the technological, our courage restored to us and our superiority re-established once we grasp the machine's meaning as a sociocultural phenomenon.

Dos Passos' first important critical encounter with the disciplinary pressures of machine culture occurs in *Three Soldiers* (1921), his second novelistic engagement with the First World War, the historical event that sparked much of his radical fury throughout the twenties to the early thirties. It is the homologies he perceived between army and civilian existences in the early twentieth century that make this novel a solid point of departure for an inquiry into Dos Passos' politicized response to the coercive forces of machine culture. For him, everyday life inside and outside the military was a highly regimented, standardizing experience. From the perspective of their effects on the (manufactured) subject, the military and entertainment industries performed nearly identical tasks. Both were factories manned by drilled bodies and designed to reproduce trained minds.

In depicting the trajectory of three unfortunate members of the American armed forces during and after the First World War, Dos Passos, in *Three Soldiers*, repeatedly tropes the military as a mechanized force, one systematic function of which is to engage in the "hideous farce of making men into machines."[21] According to the figures the novelist consistently employs, the work of the army involves the breaking down of natural bodies and reshaping of them into artifacts, a form of institutional tyranny that degrades a living human being to the status of inanimate construct, a mere "piece of machinery" (92).[22] Dos Passos' characterization of the process of preparing men for combat as the manufacturing of soldiers out of raw corporeal material is unmistakably apparent in the headings of the six parts of the book. "Making the Mould" "The Metal Cools" "Machines" "Rust" "The World Outside" "Under the Wheels." And the minimal narrative tension the book produces comes when the most autobiographical of its three protagonists, John Andrews, goes AWOL, fleeing the constraints of the disciplinary apparatus in the hope of recovering in the natural environment his physical and spiritual humanity. Yet his desertion is the exception to the rule of the book, which is to show that from basic training forward the military is an aggressive force that brutally eliminates the living being's intellectual and bodily spontaneity, that takes away the freedom to think and move as one pleases. The summary effect of the drills, the repetitious marching back and forth, the line-ups, and the multitude of regulations that prescribe behavior at the level of the minute details of everyday life is, metaphorically, to fashion metallic, iron things. The "grinding discipline" aims at "the harsh constriction of warm bodies full of gestures and attitudes and aspirations into moulds, like the moulds toy soldiers are cast in" (22).

The coercive insistence on conformity in thought and action appears as violence enacted on the bodies and minds of recruits. If in the army a "lithe body" is thrown into a mold to be made the same as other bodies, and "the quick movements" are "standardized into the manual at arms," so too will "the inquisitive, petulant mind" be "battered into servility" there (415). The violent aspects of the process of eradicating difference in the name of a calculated, measurable similarity are condensed in the recurrent image in the book of the soldiers' legs as "all being made the same length on the drill field" (22). The "helpless" soldier who gives up "his will power" (31), who submits to his transformation into an exact copy of everyone else, becomes an easily and efficiently maneuverable part of the system, a mobile weapon whose instantaneous reaction to commands is now predictable. Made docile in mind and body, the automated soldier is prepared for his tactical deployment as a force of destruction.

Dos Passos doesn't alter his imagery when dealing with injured soldiers. Since they are replaceable cogs in a machine, they may be tossed aside when they break down. If Andrews while in the hospital is a "piece of hurt flesh" (200), as he surveys the room he sees "discarded automatons, broken toys laid away in rows" (201). (Dos Passos will return to this figurative motif in Camera Eye [42] where a group of "casuals," given the task of dragging "scrapiron" off of flatcars, are conflated with the objects of their labor. The men are "spare parts no outfit wanted to use / mashed mudguards busted springs old spades and shovels entrenching tools twisted hospital cots a mountain of nuts and bolts of all sizes."[23]) The psychic condition of the wounded may also be troped as mechanical obsolescence; Andrews' mind is said to contain "superannuated bits of machinery" (*Three Soldiers*, 221) while he sits with the other patients. Internal and external damage cease to be the painful experiences of suffering subjects; soldiers are constructed things that eventually fall to pieces. The reifying effects of the military as a disciplinary practice are persistent. Andrews' "leaden" limbs and mind are weighed down not by his wounds but by "the stagnation of the life about him that he felt sinking into every crevasse of his spirit, so that he could never shake it off." Surrounded by "dusty ruined automatons that had lost all life of their own, whose limbs had practised the drill manual so long that they had no movement of their own left," Andrews sits "limply, sunk in boredom, waiting for orders" (216). Devastated by the routines of his daily existence, the soldier has lost the power to animate himself. He can no longer think and act on his own.

Dos Passos also registers the centrality of a literally mechanical device to military operations. On several occasions it is clerks sitting in front of typewriters who are shown to exert the greatest control over soldiers; the "click click" of the contrivance determines the movement of bodies. Who gets discharged or transferred and which assignment a person receives are in the hands of men who process information by tapping on keyboards. Not only do typewriters and typists control the network of internal communications and therefore manage the immediate destiny of the soldier; they also compile the records that govern his future fate. On a visit to a military office building Andrews realizes his helplessness in relation to the complicated system this new storage technology has generated. From every door comes, he supposes, "an imperious clicking of typewriters, where papers were piled high on yellow varnished desks"; "where the four walls were covered from floor to ceiling with card catalogues. And every day they were adding to the paper, piling up more little drawers with index cards" (340). Sitting in a café after his intimidating encounter with the military bureaucracy, the character reflects that "Men seemed to have shrunk in stature before the vastness of the mechanical contrivances they had invented"; "would the strong figures of men ever dominate the world again?" (343). As the context suggests, one of these vast machines can fit on a desktop. The typewriter, a by-product of the American Civil War, and a device characterized by one recent commentator as "a discursive machine gun,"[24] has gained the upper hand in the dramatic struggle between human beings and technical media.

How then to alter the course of this ongoing conflict? Andrews proposes music as a feasible source of resistance. A piano player and composer (who thus plays on a keyboard), his artistic labors function as an analogy for the writing of Dos Passos. Author and character alike are committed to resisting oppressively mechanized systems of inscription. For Andrews musical composition is a way to make up for the mistake he made when he enlisted in the army (he was not drafted as were the other characters) in a quest for relief from the pressures of daily existence. No longer frightened by the need to choose his path through the world, he attempts to reassert himself and in so doing revolt against the military machine by composing a piece based on the figure of the Queen of Sheba out of Flaubert's *The Temptation of Saint Anthony*. The multiple allusions to the latter clarify the set of oppositions governing Dos Passos' text. The properties connected with the army include boredom, monotony, rigidity, hardness, ruthless brutality, mechanization, pain, death, exhaustion, physical and emotional deprivation and masculinity, and reason. In contrast, the attributes of art include excitement, change, suppleness, softness, warmth, luxury, gentleness, libidinous and attractive bodies ("grotesque as a satyr" that flames "with worlds of desire") and thus pleasurable excess (the "inexhaustible voluptuousness of life"), femininity, and imagination (224). Although Andrews eventually abandons this project, taking up a more radically oriented undertaking titled the "Soul and Body of John Brown," his use of the American abolitionist as a creative touchstone extends the conceptual and evaluative patterns in place in the novel.

While such humanist distinctions do structure *Three Soldiers*, they fail to capture the nuances of Dos Passos' emerging theory of writing as a critical activity. Brief glimpses of the latter, which will come into practical fruition a decade later, appear in Andrews' undeveloped speculations on what he hopes to accomplish as a composer. Though articulated as an appeal to self-expression, an aesthetic priority Dos Passos will refer to with disdain in the coming years, Andrews' concern to reproduce in art the repetitive "rhythm" of his intolerably dull existence foreshadows his inventor's future literary aspirations. While Andrews wants to "fix" his experience primarily to communicate it to others, to "make the ears of multitudes feel it, make their flesh tingle with it" (22), Dos Passos will stress representation of the elements of daily life in modernity as a means of transcending an unbearable predicament. This change in emphasis can be faintly detected near the end of the novel when a stammering Andrews restates his artistic goal. "If I could once manage to express all that misery in music, I could shove it far down into my memory" (411). The ability to put life down on paper, to write, will soon be conceptualized as the precondition of taking charge of history on a personal and collective scale, an achievement which amounts, as Dos Passos sees it, to a subordination of the machine to the ends of mankind.

An equally fleeting trace of the technique Dos Passos will fashion to accomplish this task appears when Andrews sits down at the piano. Reflecting back on his past wish "to express all the cramped boredom of this life; the thwarted limbs regimented together, lashed into straight lines," he now dismisses this aspiration as silliness. He then starts "to play snatches of things he knew, distorting them, willfully mutilating the rhythms, mixing into them snatches of ragtime" (243). This formal mutilation and mixing of disparate genres parallels Dos Passos' innovative method of critical writing in the Newsreel sections of *U.S.A.* The critical distortion or rearrangement of textual materials taken from elsewhere – fragments of things already known such as popular song lyrics, advertisements, and reportage – in these collage/montages remains his most essential contribution to American radical prose. Refining the experimental tactics pioneered by other avant-garde artists, Dos Passos' technique was imitated by numerous dissident writers in the thirties – Ruth McKenney's *Industrial Valley* (1939) being perhaps the most remarkable of the innovative texts that followed Dos Passos' compositional lead.[25] As virtually all his commentators point out, the purpose of his ironic manipulation of the discursive shards of mechanically reproduced culture is largely to combat the coercive role these tend to play in the formation of public opinion.

In *Three Soldiers* Dos Passos' denunciation of technologically mediated commercial entertainment is predominantly carried out thematically through frequent allusions to the misleading expectations war films generate in the minds of potential soldiers or via commentary on the mystificatory functions of cinematic experiences. For example, Fuselli, another main character and an avid filmgoer, eventually learns how foolish he has been to picture combat as a series of heroic adventures. Early on, when phrases like "entrainment" and "order of march" produce a "strange excitement" that starts him wondering "how it would feel to be under fire, memories of movies flickered in his mind" (*Three Soldiers*, 35). He will soon be disabused of his tendency to confuse the real and the imaginary; it will no longer be possible for "everything" to be "lost in a scene from a movie in which khaki-clad regiments marched fast, fast across the scene" (37). Similarly, Andrews must struggle to overcome the perniciously seductive effect of the "moving pictures":

Here and there a pair of eyes glinted in the white flickering light from the screen. Waves of laughter or of little exclamations passed over them. They were all so alike, they seemed at moments to be but one organism. This was what he had sought when he had enlisted, he said to himself. It was in this that he would take refuge from the horror of the world that had fallen upon him. He was sick of revolt, of thought. (26)

In Dos Passos' later work, comparable critiques are thus handled at the level of compositional method. Perceiving the effects on individuals of the war machine and mass recreation to be complementary (the one molding bodies, the other manufacturing minds), he sought in *U.S.A.* to counteract the disciplinary force of the culture industry by tactically rearranging its elements. Critical montage was to serve as a weapon in the fight against the modern army *and* contemporary entertainment's production of corporeally and cognitively docile persons. For Dos Passos, combat, labor, and leisure are all conducive of lethargy, reducing life to an unbearably quantified, monotonously repetitive sequence of physically and psychically numbing actions. Literature in turn is posited as a shocking force whose value lies in its capacity to shake up persons by putting mental and perceptual conventions in play. Yet the fact that his politicized technique of literary resistance derived formal inspiration from a popular amusement (the American newsreel) reveals that the latter was for him (as it was for West) a heterogeneous terrain. An agent of hegemonic social groups, mechanized entertainment also possessed the potential to function as the vehicle of radical protest against, among other things, militarism.

The significance of *U.S.A.* derives from Dos Passos' commitment to thinking his way through the conflict between bodies and machines along linguistic lines. To master the machine was for him to master language. Although he organized his textual enterprise around a set of correlated distinctions, all of these were grounded in the fundamental opposition between speech and writing. Passivity, delusion, and entertainment go together, as do activity, lucidity, and historical discourse. The distinction is gendered and corresponds to the difference between aesthetic style and epistemological rigor. Spontaneous speech, the poetic desire for self-expression is illusory and effeminate in relation to writing as a critical operation. Dos Passos' textual system was thus designed to sublate (negate yet conserve) speech, femininity, and the aesthetic by comprehending them as the duplicitous origins of faulty, untenable beliefs. In *U.S.A.*, the uncertainties precipitated by an encounter with technology coincide with a sexual and a linguistic anxiety. Women, mechanized entertainment, *and* figural language embody a combined threat to the male writer. These are the others against which Dos Passos defends himself in the fraught process of attaining the status of a masculine author.

"STRAIGHT WRITING"

Women and children blotted out   admits he saw floggings and even mutilations.
(John Dos Passos, "Newsreel VII," *The 42nd Parallel*)

A striking scene from *Manhattan Transfer*, the novel Dos Passos produced between *Three Soldiers* and the books that eventually came to constitute the *U.S.A.* trilogy, brings into focus several of the tensions in question. Here, Jimmy Herf, a reporter and partial surrogate for the author, dreams of engaging in an act of physical violence directed at his wife, Ellie, formerly a successful Broadway stage actress.

> He turned out the light, opened a crack of the window and dropped wooden with sleep into bed. Immediately he was writing a letter on a linotype. Now I lay me down to sleep . . . mother of the great twilight. The arm of the linotype was a woman's hand in a long white glove. Through the clanking from behind amber foots Ellie's voice Don't, don't, don't, you're hurting me so . . . Mr. Herf, says a man in overalls, you're hurting the machine and we wont be able to get out the bullgod edition thank dog. The linotype was a gulping mouth with nickelbright rows of teeth, gulped, crunched.[26]

Writing as typing appears here as a weapon that helps defend the male individual against a perceived threat of the combined forces of orality, femininity, and technology. The writer must strive to turn the functions of the machine to his advantage lest he be overwhelmed by its power, which is simultaneously the seductive power of the feminine (sensuality), the vocal, and commercial mass entertainment. The precondition of a masculine literary practice, what Dos Passos will term "straight writing" a few years later, is to take violent control over a gendered machine. Causing pain to the body of a machine/woman is a (sadistic) means of defense against the anxieties produced by new technological media, female sexuality, and mass entertainment. That the character can only fulfill this unconscious wish while sleeping indicates that he is destined not to achieve the position to which he aspires, a failure hinted at as well in his feminized name (*Herf*).[27] Dos Passos' *U.S.A.* is best understood as an (entrepreneurial) attempt to adjust to the mechanization of his medium by reinventing novel writing as an aggressive critical practice. This project required a reworking of the relation of the human and the mechanical rather than a repudiation of technology in the name of more natural creative enterprises. His most straightforward articulation of his decidedly heterosexist approach to novel writing appears in an essay he composed in the early thirties for a new edition of an earlier novel. It is in the "Introduction to *Three Soldiers*"[28] that Dos Passos sketches in the most illuminating manner the priorities underlying his then current literary project: *U.S.A.*

He begins the piece by fondly recalling the political excitement and aesthetic enthusiasms of the post-war period when it was possible to envision both radical reorganizations of society and the restructuring of the organs of the body. Not only was Lenin still alive, but "the Seattle general strike" appeared as "the beginning of the flood instead of the beginning of the ebb." Moreover, "Picasso was to rebuild the eye, Stravinski was cramming the Russian steppes into our ears, currents of energy seemed breaking out everywhere," and Charlie Chaplin dominated the movie screens. In retrospect it is evident that the optimistic anticipation of imminent revolutionary transformation at the level of sensory perception and collective existence was premature. Those who aspired to overcome the dichotomy between art and life have learned that they must accept assigned roles, that even would-be artists can be fixed into place in the symbolic or cultural order. "What was to have been a springboard into reality" has turned out to be "a profession" and "the organization of your life that was to be an instrument to make you see more and clearer turns out to be blinders made according to a predestined pattern."[29] Maturity comes with the realization of the limits external conditions impose on individual desires. The institutional dimensions of this heightened awareness involve recognizing one's position in the publishing industry as a producer of commodities. Dos Passos has also grown wary of the faith in the artistic as a prosthetic extension of the natural body. Whereas his generation had thought innovative art would enhance the power of their sensory organs, he has experienced art's constricting effects. The hope for corporeal supplementation, to see better, has resulted in something approaching organ mutilation, eye loss ("blinders").

To move beyond this impasse requires a reformulation of writing as a critical assault on the seductive pleasures of representational aesthetics. Dos Passos therefore posits his changed stance as a necessary response to the mechanization of language. Whereas in "the middle ages the mere setting down of the written word was a marvel," by the "renaissance the printing press suddenly opened up a continent more tremendous than America." And "now we have linotype, automatic typesetting machines, phototype processes that plaster the world from end to end with print" ("Introduction," 147). Dos Passos' evaluation of the results of this process are hardly original: the increase in quantity has come at the expense of quality. He also begins to frame the dilemma in typical fashion by employing gendered distinctions. The problem is "We're not men enough to run the machines we've made." To meet the challenge posed by technological improvements, the male writer will have to define firmly the purpose for which these potentially emasculating machines of reproduction were designed and built. Clarifying one's goals is the first step toward mastering the anxiety-inducing aspects of modernized cultural production. "A machine's easy enough to run if you know what you want it to do; that's what it's made for." The threat of mechanized commercial entertainment is not only gendered but generational. If "the girlishromantic gush about selfexpression" simply "won't do any more" it is equally the case that "making a living by selling daydreams, [and] sensations" is not "much of a life for a healthy adult" (147). The combined appeal of the machine and the feminine is to the vicarious experience offered by aesthetic illusion or artifice. Dos Passos' most explicitly stated condemnation of imitation or verisimilitude had appeared seven years before in his aforementioned review of Lawson's *Processional*. As Dos Passos disgustedly put it there: "The great triumph of the realistic theatre was when people put their umbrellas up coming out of *Rain*."[30] The allusion to "selfexpression" in the later essay helps establish that the broader target of his critical analysis is the specular relationship and accompanying imaginary substitutions that certain aesthetic forms encourage. Just as identification with a character in a dramatic setting – on stage or in a narrative fiction – should be renounced, the attraction of intimate, unmediated communication through lyric discourses must be rejected. Insofar as the Camera Eye both thematizes and formally solicits such pleasing yet unreliable substitutions, *U.S.A.* is designed to negate the function of the device. It should be apparent that this negation is also intended to serve as a defense against the danger of regressing back to behaviors deemed suitable only for women and children.

The most inclusive opposition governing Dos Passos' literary thought in the "Introduction" and his practice through the first two volumes of the trilogy is the opposition between speech and writing. (Though neither term is used in a strictly literal manner. In essence, "speech" conceptually encompasses what Dos Passos takes to be bad – expressive – practices of writing, whereas good – critical – practices fall into the category of "writing.") In his textual economy, the voice has the status of a naive faith in representational directness and writing is privileged as the instrument and outcome of the negation of the spoken word. Writing attacks oral discourse as the epitome of deluded uses of language. His unusual stance comes partially into view in the famous statement of purpose the "Introduction" contains. Acknowledging that the persuasive effect of any use of language is a matter to be taken into consideration, he asserts that there is a more fundamental reason for engaging in the activity of what he calls "straight writing." "What do you write for then? To convince people of something? That's preaching, and is part of the business of everybody who deals with words; not to admit that is to play with a gun and then blubber that you didn't know it was loaded. But outside of preaching I think there is such a thing as straight writing"

(147). (The analogy of writing as a firearm is worth underscoring.) He continues: "A cabinetmaker enjoys cutting a dovetail because he's a cabinetmaker." "The mind of a generation is its speech. A writer makes aspects of that speech enduring by putting them in print. He whittles at the words and phrases of today and makes of them forms to set the mind of tomorrow's generation. That's history. A writer who writes straight is the architect of history."

The switch from music to architecture (and cabinetmaking) as his principal analogy for writing also marks the development of Dos Passos' literary theory from the early twenties to the early thirties. Rather than seek to express himself, he commits himself to the negative task of clearing the ground for future construction, to dismantling pre-existing shapes, to leveling or tearing down standing figures. Writing ceases to be a supplement to memory, a derivative, secondary means of making speech permanent so that it may be preserved for posterity. By characterizing the novelist as architect *of* history, he attributes to writing the generative force of an origin or new beginning. The writer mutes the speech of others and in so doing becomes the primary source of power whose labors are the condition of possibility of social change, of historical development. The author may come after the spoken word and therefore be dependent on it, but only in the sense that the knowledge he provides stems from his analysis of and consequent silencing of those who wished to communicate immediately. Concrete speech, like sense-certainty in Hegel's *Phenomenology of Spirit*, gives way under the pressure of reflexive scrutiny; linguistic understanding dialectically arises out of a formalized experience of the limits (or abstraction) of spontaneous utterances. Writing is the self-consciousness of speech. In the process the nation as a whole is lifted up, the collective "mind" elevated by the critical reworking of past verbal materials.

To become a writer is also in this case indistinguishable from becoming a heterosexual male. Dos Passos goes on to define his notion of "straight writing" in relation to the threat posed by feminized forms of commercial entertainment. His conceptual conflation of a linguistic distinction with a sexual difference is strikingly apparent in the paragraph that follows the one quoted above. The author of *Ulysses* makes an appearance at this point as the father figure or ego ideal that the aspiring writer may identify with in the process of achieving literary manhood over and against the menace of the mechanized and feminized pleasures of American amusement. "What I'm trying to get out [the phrasing is apt, since what is at stake is the elimination or expulsion of an unwanted quality] is the difference in kind between the work of James Joyce, say, and that of any current dispenser of daydreams. It's not that Joyce produces for the high-brow and the other for the lowbrow trade, it's that Joyce is working with speech straight and so dominating the machine of production, while the daydream artist is merely feeding the machine, like a girl in a sausage factory shoving hunks of meat into the hopper. Whoever can run the machine runs it for all of us. Working with speech straight is vigorous ab-sorbing devastating hopeless work, work that no man need be ashamed of" ("Introduction," 148). To capitulate to mechanized leisure, to the imaginary fascinations of the "daydream," is to run the risk of castration, for the grinding up of "hunks of meat" resonates as a displaced figure for genital mutilation. The model of Joyce enables the would-be writer to overcome his attraction to a prohibited yet seductive object of desire: the illusory plenitude of a maternal/feminine speech. The oedipal passage toward a position beyond enchantment requires that one acknowledge the danger of corporeal damage that certain embarrassing transgres-sions may call forth. To avoid degradation and physical mutilation one must sacrifice immediate pleasures, deferring satisfaction in the hope of attaining the reward of phallic authority in the future.[31] Critical labor on speech is the process whereby one simultaneously achieves a norma-tive sexuality and a literary practice in which one may take pride. In sum, the authorial subject as writer comes into existence at the expense of infantilized and feminized bodies and selves, which he equates with orality or the spoken word. This "practice of division gives the textual artifact the energy of what it methodically eliminates."[32]

In the "Introduction"'s final paragraph (which Dos Passos omitted from a later version of the essay entitled "The Writer and His Tools"[33]), the analytical thrust of his critical project makes its presence felt. "These years of confusion," he states, "when everything has to be relabeled and catchwords lose their meaning from week to week, may be the reader's poison, but they are the writer's meat" (148). The mature writer feeds off what makes the innocent consumer sick. The current crisis of signification – the detachment of signifiers from signifieds, the need for renaming, the breaking of the bond between speaker and utterance – propels the writer (as critical reader) into action. Today "we can at least meet events with our minds cleared of some of the romantic garbage that kept us from doing clear work" in the past. "Those of us who have lived through have seen these years strip the bunting off the great illusions of our time, we must deal with the raw structure of history now, we must deal with it quick, before it stamps us out" (148). Despite the empiricist overtones, enlightenment follows in this instance not from an encounter with the substance of extra-textual reality but from an encounter with the foundations of language, the generative force of collective mystification. Writing discloses "the raw structure of history" as speech and in so doing makes social change possible.

To the degree that the writer as critical reader participates in the separation of signs from meanings, breaking the apparent bond between expression and expressed, he engages in an act of mutilation of a linguistic sort. Reacting to his fear of the feminized sphere of American entertainment as a corporeal danger, the male writer turns into a kind of linguistic slasher, violently assaulting the discourses he perceives to be a threat to his integrity, cutting into pieces what scares him in an apotropaic act of defense. Here this aggressive gesture of critical negation demands the rejection of an aesthetic priority: self-expression. The tactic is most visibly operative in the Newsreel sections of the trilogy, where Dos Passos' ironic tactic is to rearrange linguistic fragments torn from other discursive contexts. A maneuver that presupposes a semiological model of language, it is designed to maintain the distance between the author and the realm of the feminine and childish, which are encased in *U.S.A.* in the Camera Eye.[34] This is to say that within this text the function of the Newsreels is to negate the Camera Eye and in so doing pave the way for the writer's ascent to a more fully developed and stable compositional method: the biographies. If, as I intend to argue, the technique employed in the latter device can be described as allegorical, then it would seem that Dos Passos "was not without some sense of the comprehensive relationship between spoken language and script, which provide the philosophical basis of the allegorical."[35]

U.S.A. AS GROTESQUE ALLEGORY

from the upsidedown image on the retina painstakingly out of
colour shape words remembered light and dark straining
       To rebuild yesterday   to clip out paper figures to simulate
growth   warp newsprint into faces smoothing and wrinkling
              an unidentified stranger
              destination unknown
              hat pulled down over the   has he any? face (John Dos Passos,
Camera Eye (47), *The Big Money*)

Halfway through the final chapter of *Allegories of Reading*, Paul de Man shifts his attention from Rousseau's *Confessions* to his *Fourth Reverie*, noting that in it he recounts several episodes from the writer's past that seem inconsequential. These are "unpleasant stories of physical assault, bloody mutilation, and crushed fingers, told in such a way that one remembers the pain and the cruelty much better than the virtue they are supposed to illustrate."[36] Shortly thereafter, de Man asserts that these scenes of brutality "have to do with the threat of textual mutilation."[37] The machine in Rousseau's text is evidently the cause of these severe injuries, but neither the meaning of these scenes nor of the machine itself is immediately obvious. From a referential perspective the gruesome narratives are shocking, yet they seem "to be there more for the sake of allowing the evocation of the machine." For what reason do these descriptions of corporeal damage appear in the narrative? Initially the description of the machine itself seems excessive, a superfluous luxury with no necessary significance. But what it lacks in particular literal meaning at the level of denotation, the machine gains connotatively, emerging as a figure for the text in general. "The text as body, with all its implications of substitutive tropes ultimately always retraceable to metaphor, is displaced by the text as machine and, in the process, it suffers the loss of the illusion of meaning."[38] Establishing the machine as a reflexive trope for the literary work, the further implication of de Man's argument is that the semantic components of the text are unreliable because they are the effects of an operation not fully controlled by the author himself. Once it has been turned on the gratuitously improvisational machine is free to run or *perform* on its own, producing and destroying meaning in a ruthlessly overdetermined fashion beyond the intentions of the speaking subject.

This concept helps put us in a position to articulate the rhetorical structure and function of what I am calling a grotesque allegory. This strategy occurs when a writer – novelist or critic – makes the aggressive cutting up of the body serve as an emblem for the taking apart (disfiguration) of a figural construct, a trope.[39] Allegory in this narrowly defined context thus designates the turn in a given work away from the phenomenal world toward language. An epistemologically oriented process of negation, it empties the work of its referential plenitude by severing its contact with objective and subjective reality. Neither the imitative nor the expressive dimensions of the work survive the incorporation of the grotesque into the allegorical. A heightened awareness of the cognitive unreliability of figural language furnishes some compensation for this (extra-textual) loss. The reassurance such negative knowledge provides gives way, however, in extreme cases to an awareness of the process as a thoroughly mechanized event, one irreducible to the desire of an authorial subject inasmuch as it exceeds his or her intentions. When this happens, the virtually automated text performs as a critical machine, the principal function of which is to unsettle linguistic signification by generating alternately too much and too little meaning.

Explicating *U.S.A.* from this perspective enables us to gain access to the unique aspects of this literary undertaking, aspects that have for the most part eluded the eyes of Dos Passos' numerous commentators. My analysis of this text will focus primarily upon the interrelated functions of its three main formal devices: the Camera Eye, Newsreel, and biographical sections. Consequently, I will attend to the narratives in a more cursory manner, these having already received exhaustive, in-depth treatment from past commentators concerned with the more thematic elements of the three novels that together constitute the trilogy. Characterizing the text as a critical machine whose operation gets underway through the repetitious disfiguration of the tropological structures the text itself sets up, I argue that the mechanization of writing takes place here as the development of a politically subversive practice of critical reading.

Within the tradition of commentary on the trilogy, the Camera Eye protagonist is typically identified as the work's ethical, political, and aesthetic center, largely on the basis of his climactic articulation late in *The Big Money* of his firm commitment to radical dissent. As Barbara Foley puts it: "The Camera Eye presents the author's emerging class consciousness as not simply a theme, but an epistemological vantage point."[40] His denunciation of the rich and powerful who have betrayed the paternal speech of the nation is customarily taken as a closing of the narrative circle in that at the end of the third novel we seem to have reached the point presupposed at the beginning of the first. The converted speaker's loathing of those "strangers who have turned our language inside out who have taken the clean words our fathers spoke and made them slimy and foul" marks his adoption of the left-wing perspective governing *U.S.A.* and thus his transformation into its author.[41] The "I" that can finally say "we" provides a solid base from "which to judge the behavior portrayed in the narratives."[42] The passion and conviction of these famous passages of social protest notwithstanding, the linguistic priorities they support make it difficult to account for much of the text. In particular, the irony of the Newsreels often achieves its effect through a turning of "language inside out," through the manipulation and twisting of words, redirecting or perverting their original, ostensibly referential meanings toward something else. The rhetorical tactic employed in these sections of the text is often to appropriate the shards of ostensibly literal, denotative utterances and make them signify connotatively something other than what their producers intended. The apparent contradiction between compositional method and statement, between form and content, vanishes when one registers the decentered status of the Camera Eye protagonist relative to the tension-filled yet coherently structured textual system in its entirety.[43]

The way in which the Camera Eye is inscribed in *U.S.A.* as a by no means privileged point of view can be most efficiently grasped by attending to the early portions of *The 42nd Parallel,* the first novel in the trilogy. The first Camera Eye begins to make the device's association with representational illusion apparent thematically. In the autobiographical scene it recalls, the boy is shown running somewhere in Holland at the turn of the century with his mother, an angry crowd having mistakenly taken the two to be English. The frightened child is also worried about stepping "on the bright anxious grassblades," that he will harm "the poor" "green tongues" that shrink under his feet.[44] The anthropomorphic projection of human sensitivity onto the natural landscape is of course a familiar gesture in lyric poetry – in particular one thinks here of the sixth section of Whitman's "Song of Myself." Yet the rhetorical move has a distinctly reflexive significance here insofar as it employs the trope on which the device itself relies: prosopopoeia: the giving of a face to what lacks it. The appearance of a tongue implies the presence of a mouth, and were the figural chain given space to develop, ears, eyes, and a nose would surely follow. In fact these features are implicitly present within the device in that it continuously makes compelling appeals to the sights, sounds, tastes, smells, and tactile qualities of the child's changing environment. The figure of speech that the first Camera Eye thematizes in recording a childish consciousness' interaction with its surroundings is the same trope that the novelist utilizes in these highly stylized sections of the text. If the construction of a human visage is implicit in the process of recalling the subject's preceding responses to the flow of sensory data, the title of the device suggests that this retrieval is an act of reconstructive surgery. It is not a natural but a mechanical, prosthetic organ that serves as the means of recovering the past self.

The conclusion to this scene reinforces the stress on representational naiveté as the child and parent find shelter at a postcard shop. Safely hidden beneath the countertop, the boy, gazing at pictures of "pretty hotels and palaces," immerses himself in the watery world the shining images on the cards reproduce: "and the moonlight ripple ripple under a bridge and the little reverbères are alight in the dark under the counter and the little windows of the hotel around the harbor" (4). The textual system gets into motion as a critique of the imaginary confusion between illusory representations and things as well as the escapism that such confusions cultivate. The Camera Eyes generate the state of poetic mystification that Dos Passos intends to overcome. In the autobiographical aesthetic on which the cinematic device depends, words seem laden with the experience of consciousness, offering the reader the impression that he may gain unmediated access to the protagonist's interaction with phenomenal reality. Language, like film, appears to offer no obstacle to the reader, inviting the latter to perceive what the character remembers perceiving. The past flow of sensory data across the mind has been "mechanically" recorded and is now available for replaying or projection in a romantic "gush" of "selfexpression." The text is designed to supersede by canceling out novels conceived along the lines of new storage technologies (film) since the mainstream use of new media can be as aesthetically or representationally misleading as are commercial literary forms.

In its initial uses the device also conjoins early psychic, linguistic, and sexual "stages" of development. In regard to the former, although the visual, aural, and other senses are fully operative, the "I" of consciousness is not yet completely formed, or fixed in place. Throughout the ego is shown to be still in the process of being shaped and therefore relatively unaffected by external constraints. Correlatively, the poetic discourse, though it relies on grammatical categories, does not submit entirely to the formal rules of correct syntax, making it seem as if the speaker has only begun to grasp the limits on his verbal freedom that the existence of linguistic conventions entails. For example, the speaker utilizes the first-second-, and third-person singular as well as the plural of these forms interchangeably in the early Camera Eyes. The grammatical fluctuations reciprocate the fluidity of mental becoming; liberty in one register corresponds to ceaseless transformation in the other. Nor are the physical barriers between bodies firmly established in these portions of the novel. Such mingling is perhaps most apparent in Camera Eye (13) in which the protagonist undergoes a kind of sexual initiation ("afterwards you knew what girls were made like"). Left in the care of a young French governess, the child joins her in bed and listens as she tells him a frightening story about Loup Garou, which leads to erotic contact between the two: "rub against her and outside the wolves howled in the streets and it was wet there and she said it was nothing she had just washed herself / but the Loup Garou was really a man hold me close cheri a man howled through streets with a bloody snout that tore up the bellies of girls and little children" (*42nd Parallel*, 137). Fear and seduction go together in an atmosphere in which the individual has trouble distinguishing between real actions and fictive events, between personal experience and narrative legend.

In sum, the Camera Eye protagonist, at least through *The 42nd Parallel*, remains for the most part lodged within the mirror stage, self and other as well as words and things inadequately differentiated. Dos Passos demonstrates the character's narcissism and its consequences most tellingly in Camera Eye (14) where the boy sinks into the world depicted in Edward Everett Hale's *The Man Without a Country* – read to him by a Mr. Garfield – thoroughly identifying himself with the exiled protagonist of the story.

> And the Judge sentenced me and they took me far away to foreign lands on a frigate and the officers were very kind and spoke in kind grave very sorry reading voices like Mr. Garfield . . . and when I was dead I began to cry and I was afraid the other boys would see I had tears in my eyes. An American shouldn't cry he should look kind and grave and very sorry when they wrapped me in the stars and stripes and brought me home on a frigate to be buried I was so sorry I never remembered whether they brought me home or buried me at sea but anyway I was wrapped in Old Glory. (153)

The passage simultaneously registers the epistemological illegitimacy of the identification and implies that the self emerges from such a cognitively unreliable substitution. The child's impossible experience of his own death in this narrative representation illustrates what persuasive discourses can get away with; yet the undifferentiated "I," which here encompasses the speaker and the fictional character, may well be the precondition of a more stable identity. By introjecting an ideal, a masculine imago, the individual begins to gain a sense of self, though the act of internalizing an external model will subsequently be buried in his unconscious. The epistemologically aberrant alignment has in this case a disciplinary effect: the punishment the character in the novel receives for his traitorous behavior and his remorse serve to inculcate patriotic values in the story's youthful listener. Yet the overall purpose of this scene of reading is to remark critically upon all such illusory identifications, the nuances of their particular outcome notwithstanding. In this respect the device cautions thematically against the kind of substitution it cultivates rhetorically. The reader of the Camera Eyes is encouraged to take the place of the protagonist just as the latter slides into the mind and body of the anti-hero of the tale to which he listens. The content of the device warns against the coercive nature of its form.

The significance of the moving picture camera metaphor is greater than its function as an analogy for consciousness' interaction with its immediate surroundings. The subjectivized figure does more than provide a materialized image of the mind as a receptive surface on which impressions from the outside world are registered and saved. The trope inscribed in the device's title also gestures toward the possibility of conceptualizing the psyche cinematically as an optical and aural apparatus (which also appeals to the other senses as well), a principal function of which is to fabricate a sense of self. Lyric poetry, like the movies, participates in the mirroring process whereby the ego is formed through a sequence of exchanges or substitutions with the bodies of poorly perceived others. More provocative, however, are the implications of the fact that the operations of the device can be traced back to prosopopoeia. With this in mind it becomes possible to argue that the structure and function of certain figures of speech are as fundamental as cinema to an understanding of how the "ego" comes into existence. In other words, the device critically registers identificatory projection as a tropological phenomenon, clarifying in the process that the "me" that autobiographical reflection remembers has its origins in a linguistically grounded confusion of self and other.

The remarkable aspect of Dos Passos' undertaking is that he inscribes this process (in its technological and linguistic versions) at the bottom of the rhetorical hierarchy of his text. The Newsreels are meant to function as the critical negation of the expressive aesthetic employed in varying forms in a continuum of cultural practices extending from lyric poetry through Broadway theatre to Hollywood film (the latter is addressed thematically in the third installment of *U.S.A.*). The compositional tactic the device utilizes, a frequently ironic combination of collage and montage, has been correctly defined by numerous commentators on the trilogy, and a considerable number of particular Newsreels have been expertly analyzed.[45] What has received minimal attention, however, is the logical relationship of the Camera Eye and the Newsreel, one the dialectical contrary or antithesis of the other.[46] Thus the illusory depth of the poetic device, which approaches words as a transparent medium through which the reader may pass to gain access to the substance of the referent (as mind or external surroundings), is eliminated in the transition to the resistant, opaque surfaces of the reportorial one. As the rhetorical mode of the text shifts from expressive self-representation (the Camera Eye) to the re-presentation of material signifiers (the Newsreels), our impression of the sensuous particularity of the speaker disappears. The warmth of emotional affect, imagination, perception, and interiority are erased in the movement into the cold realm of material inscription. What replaces the lyrical "I" is an impersonal editor whose attitudes and feelings can be detected (or suspected) only by the way in which he manipulates a pre-existing archive by copying or re-citing selected portions of it. Moreover, in the switch from one device to the other, the impulse toward impassioned expression of private experience in a language relatively unencumbered by grammatical constraints (capitalization, punctuation, syntactical norms and rules) is canceled. For what is also at stake in the Newsreels is a critical analysis and negative infraction of the conventions that allow for coherent communication. Bracketing the referential appeal of the Camera Eye to a sensitive, lyrical consciousness, the Newsreels examine and subversively exploit the way in which changes in discursive context and fragmentation can remove or replace the significance of any given utterance.

An act of rhetorical disfiguration is implicit in the transition from the Camera Eye to the Newsreel. For one way to characterize the operation that leaves the reader staring at printed letters on the flattened surface of the page is as an act (repeated numerous times) of critical mutilation. In a sense, a prosthetic organ is forcibly removed, a figuratively constructed mechanical eye gouged out. Although the violent defacement (of a replacement part) occurs behind the scenes, the evidence remains in the collapse of the aesthetic construct, in the faceless impersonality of the critically oriented Newsreel editor who takes the place of the lyric artist. "Straight writing" as a way of "dominating the machine of production" proceeds initially as a ruthless cutting, as the aggressive destruction of a shaped entity. Wary of the tropologically produced ego, the "straight writer" engages in an act of self-mutilation. Though the "mutilation" is not shown (it will be put on stage in "The Body of an American"), grotesque imagery is still drawn upon to negotiate a critical operation: the negation of a figure of speech. And it is by (implicitly) figuring a linguistic procedure as a corporeal maiming that the text approaches the status of a grotesque allegory.

Traditional commentary emphasizes the ways in which, in *U.S.A.*, the devices fit perfectly together for the purpose of achieving a totalizing, panoramic representation of history.[47] Such spatializing interpretations miss the logic governing the text and the tensions driving it; the dynamic conflict between the devices is what keeps the machine in motion. Put differently, *U.S.A.* is, appearances aside, an allegory of the development over time of the writer from naive speaker to allegorist. This is autobiography to the second degree: not at the level of subject matter but at the level of compositional method. The text narrates (invisibly) the growth of rhetorical sophistication and technique beyond aestheticism, from self-expression (the Camera Eye) to ironic montage/collage (the Newsreels) to allegory (biographies).[48]

The critical slicing in question is carried in the Newsreels into the formalized sphere of grammar as well. The Newsreels – and this is rarely mentioned – consistently unsettle syntactical expectations by carving up sentences into pieces and then joining them to other similarly fragmented propositions, producing unstable linguistic assemblages that are at times nearly unreadable. One example of the breaking of previous syntagmatic chains and the forging of new linguistic links is Newsreel v, one of the shortest in *The 42nd Parallel*. Reproduced in its entirety, it is an example I have selected because parts of it evoke the literary operation under investigation:

> Bugs drive out biologist elopers bind and gag; is released by dog EMPEROR
> NICHOLAS II FACING REVOLT OF EMPIRE GRANTS SUBJECTS LIBERTY paralysis
> stops surgeon's knife by the stroke of a pen the last absolute monarchy of Europe
> passes into history miner of Death Valley and freak advertizer of Santa Fe Road
> may die sent to bridewell for stealing plaster angel
> *On the banks of the Wabash far away.*[49]

The partial combination of heterogeneous citations, the ripping of pieces of discourse from disparate sources and the reattaching of them to each other, engenders verbal monstrosities. In addition, the disruptive withdrawal of coherent signification through the violation of standard sentence structures shows the degree to which meaning rests on our willingness to obey the established laws of language. The rhetorical term that comes closest to naming the tactic employed in such passages is anacoluthon, the interruption of a given grammatical or rhetorical movement. A mode of discursive interference, such subversions of syntactical unity, while frustrating semantic expectations, also reveal, by mangling or refuting them, the formal codes and conventions that are the conditions of coherent communication. (For the most part Dos Passos confines his use of this tactic to the first two volumes of the trilogy; the Newsreel sections in *The Big Money* are less verbally subversive, yet they are also more incisively ironic.)

The manipulation of news items and other cultural debris transforms history into a text to be deciphered. Whereas the Camera Eyes promote a model of reading as the perception and recollection of personal

experience, the Newsreels insist that the reader adopt a skeptical standpoint toward a collective past, stressing the disparate perspectives available on any given event. The meaning of American history is to be
searched for thoughtfully rather than uncritically intuited or felt. The
highly crafted Newsreel I is a particularly illuminating case in point,
subtly weaving partial citations together to mock the appeal of turn-of-
the-century expansionist ideologies.

The Newsreel begins by quoting the lines of a popular tune glorifying
the United States military's efforts to suppress Filipino revolutionaries
against American rule in the Philippines. A set of spliced together news
reports follows: "black bear at large in Hyde Park Streets news of explorer
Perry ASKS LABOR TO CALL HALT Death of Oscar Wilde once famous
author dies in poverty in Paris Fierce Fight With Thugs" (*42nd Parallel*,
1; this portion of the Newsreel does not appear in the revised edition of
the novel). The running together of the last two items indirectly evokes
the Paris Peace Treaty of 1898 in which Spain, in the aftermath of the
Spanish-American War, ceded control to the United States of Cuba,
the Philippines, and other foreign lands. The reference to the battling
thugs suggests a harsh assessment of the two hostile world powers while
perhaps equating the victimized countries with the deceased, persecuted
poet. At any rate, the subsequent interpolation of an extended account
of a General Miles' tumbling off his steed while observing a parade
more decisively undermines the pseudo-heroic feats of American military
forces – infantry or cavalry. The epitome of military fashion, a magnificent image of power, bravura, and masculine virility while perched in
"gaudy uniform" atop a "spirited charger," the vain man tumbles to
the ground in an amusingly undignified manner during the spectacle,
his phallic authority temporarily undermined.[50] Drawing attention to
the embarrassing incident degrades the ostentation of the procession
and mocks in anticipation the content of another set of song lyrics in
praise of heroic American courage. *"And the Captain of Company B / Was
afightin in the lead / Just like a trueborn soldier he / Of them bullets took no
heed"*(*42nd Parallel*, 2). Dos Passos' aim here is to discredit the status of
the charismatic warrior as a desirable figure for the developing subject
to internalize as an ideal ego. In contrast, in the biographies, the radical
rebel will emerge as a suitable model for self-investment. To become an
admirable writer, one should identify with committed activists not with
military commanders.

To return to the Newsreel, a shift in thematic attention occurs next, the
significance of which only becomes apparent below. A headline referring

to moral corruption ("OFFICIALS KNOW NOTHING OF VICE") and civic disregard for public health ("Sanitary trustees turn water of Chicago river into drainage canal") join environmental and human filth together. Then the Newsreel returns to imperialist ventures, the citation of a song registering the effect of American geographical expansion – "*For there's many a man been murdered in Luzon*" – set alongside a headline asserting the permanency of conquest: "CLAIMS ISLANDS FOR ALL TIME." An excerpt from a banquet speech by Benjamin Harrison then tempers several optimistic salutes to the new century as the dawn of a new era. The ex-President and member of the Anti-Imperialist League, a coalition opposed to Senate ratification of the Paris Treaty, argues in favor of moderation in "territorial expansion," proposing instead that domestic development of our natural resources will enable us to match the economic strength "of the colonizing nations." After a couple of items dealing with the antics of high society and popular entertainers, Dos Passos inserts a portion of Senator Albert J. Beveridge's prediction, in stark opposition to Harrison's perspective, that what the coming century has in store for the rapidly modernizing nation is global domination. "The twentieth century will be American. American thought will dominate it. American progress will give it color and direction. American deeds will make it illustrious." Ignoring the kind of internal pollution alluded to above, Beveridge posits the developing United States as the salvation of the external decadent East, the possession of which will never be relinquished. "Civilization will never lose its hold on Shanghai. Civilization will never depart from Hongkong. The gates of Peking will never be closed to the methods of modern man. The regeneration of the world, physical as well as moral, has begun and revolutions never move backwards" (*42nd Parallel*, 3). Finally, the fourth repetition of the song dealing with annexation of territory outside the continental United States brings the Newsreel to an ominous end, drawing attention to the human suffering caused by empire building ("*There's been many a good man murdered in the Philippines / Lies sleeping in some lonesome grave*").[51] The summary effects are to present and satirize a variety of disparate opinions on foreign and domestic policy and to clarify that American military bravery abroad is often in the service of economic desires, in this case to keep trade opportunities in new markets open.

Dos Passos' ambivalence in regard to mechanically reproduced commercial entertainment and to the news media (the distinction between the two is tenuous) is unmistakable here. Such cultural products may degrade or mislead the American masses, yet when torn from their original contexts, these same products may be deployed in a new setting to indict systemic injustice, to protest, for instance, the politics of imperialism and governmentally sanctioned acts of military aggression. Reportorial, political, and advertising discourses as well as popular music (presumably through the mediation of the phonograph) may play a determining role in the shaping of the collective psyche, in the formation of national subjects. But it is from the historical archive these cultural practices constitute that the radical writer draws the material he manipulates to satirize public opinion and put prevailing wisdom into question. Notably, as he acknowledges, Dos Passos' redeployment of cultural debris, his subversive rearranging of bits and pieces of information and songs, resembles at the level of formal structure the procedures of a decidedly minor public amusement: the American newsreel.

While its name implies a commitment to journalistic standards, the principal allegiances of the assorted makers of the American newsreel were to show business.[52] Although it evolved historically out of film coverage of newsworthy events, the newsreel in the United States upon its emergence in 1911 was inextricably tied to the entertainment industry. Even in the 1920s and early thirties, when it reached its peak in popularity, the newsreel, roughly ten minutes in length and released twice a week, was distributed to exhibitors as part of a block-booked bill. Whereas there were a few theatres devoted exclusively to the showing of newsreels, they mostly appeared, like cartoons, travelogues, and other novelties, in film programs as support for a featured movie. Hence the stress in them on sensationalistic content. Rather than report the news in order to keep the public well informed, the newsreels sought to thrill and excite the spectator, avoiding whenever possible controversial issues. The customary focus of the newsreel was on the activities of celebrities and of criminals, humorous and scandalous incidents, sporting events, pageantry, celebrations, natural disasters, and, of course, social catastrophes like war. If Dos Passos mocks the banal, ephemeral content of much newsreel footage, he also takes its format – the rapid, serial display of loosely connected materials with little to no commentary on the significance of the cinematic clips – as the formal basis of one of his compositional methods. Politicizing the amusement, he converts it into a literary weapon, one that takes aim at the ideological function of the print media and political oratory as well as – mostly in *The Big Money* – advertising. Thus in addition to making the source of optical leisure the site of critical labor, the radicalized writer also assimilates the visual recreation as a critical tool: the Newsreels supply the model for satirical writing performances in which meanings are added and subtracted to pre-existing textual materials.

Such a polemical use of the products imposed upon persons by the dominant and social order, the cutting up and ironic juxtaposition of fragments of industrialized culture, corresponds to what Michel de Certeau has defined as a tactic in contrast to a strategy. An "art of the weak," tactics require that the *consumer* resourcefully take advantage of what is on hand, subversively manipulating available materials while situated inside the existing economic system. Insinuating himself into the space of the "other" (here mainstream journalism and popular music), the craftsman/editor of the Newsreels resists the media's tendency to colonize the psyche by shattering the significance of its verbal discourse. His active use of words dissolves the distinction between reading and writing while abandoning the novelist's claim to be the creative source of the language he employs. A performative use of language close to Austin's sense of the term in that Dos Passos is doing things with words, the critical maneuvers on display in the Newsreels disrupt the logical and rational imperatives that tend to govern speech-act theory.[53] While the significance of a given linguistic utterance is now located in the specific circumstances in which it is uttered, as opposed to the formal statement itself, the repetition of phrases in altered, aleatory contexts functions in this setting as a means of obstructing coherent communication. Unsettling grammatical conventions and ignoring orthodox syntactical patterns, the Newsreels open up the play of language by simultaneously dissolving old and wildly generating new meanings in an anarchic redistribution of semantic wealth. Such a disorderly practice of writing as reading disrupts the representational economy of the novel and reportage, as the irrational drive to construct "sentences that remain unpredictable"[54] overrides the sensible desire to transmit information clearly. Language thus emerges as the site of a struggle for cultural power; the radicalized slave's procedure of rearranging the lucid discourse of the master is motivated by the desire to seize control over or "dominate the machine of [ideological] production."

In *U.S.A.*, then, the analogy between film and literature functions not to reinforce the representational status of the novel but to establish it as a critical endeavor. Rather than a storage medium employing recording devices, literature is for Dos Passos an analytical enterprise aimed at revealing the naive narcissism of mimetic (expressively imitative) aesthetic discourses and the duplicity of the news media's claims to provide its readers with reliable information. The text is of additional interest in that it frames the distinction between aesthetic creation and linguistic criticism as an advance predicated on an understanding of the difference between words and things. This negative knowledge allows one to gain a measure of control over language, now comprehended as a system of signs, and such linguistic insight enables the subject to obtain a sense of the difference between men and women. Just as the male individual moves toward his sexual position by accepting the threat of castration, the artist moves toward the position of the writer by accepting the possibility of referential detachment.

The Newsreels, however, can only be partially satisfying to the writer who wishes to dominate the machine of production. For within the device the writer remains in a dependent position in relation to the news media and other culture industries. He can comment indirectly on political issues by twisting and mangling the materials these institutions furnish him; but the collage/montage method does not allow him to articulate his own opinions directly. Moreover, the way in which the Newsreels destroy and generate meaning exceeds in many cases the intentions of the author. There is a random, contingent element inscribed in the editorial tactic. It is as if the device were almost capable of running by itself, the kind of semantic havoc it wreaks at any given point often left to chance. If, as we will see, the biographies mark the author's attempt to regain control over his materials, and therefore constitute the next level in the rhetorical hierarchy the text seeks to erect, the narratives exhibit the predicament of those who cannot make the leap into linguistic self-consciousness.

The free indirect discourse Dos Passos uses in representing the lives of his various fictional characters makes it apparent that their thoughts and emotions come predominantly from elsewhere. The persons may think that they express private passions and direct their own actions, but it is evident to the reader that their ideas, feelings, and behavior derive primarily from outside influences. Language speaks through them. The machinery that generates current aesthetic, journalistic, and advertising discourses has the additional effect of fabricating minds *en masse*. One of the virtues of Jean-Paul Sartre's still valuable, existential interpretation of *1919* is that it frames the characters' common predicament simultaneously as a linguistic problem and as a dilemma of consciousness: "Dos Passos reports all his characters' utterances to us in the style of a statement to the Press. Their words are thereby cut off from thought, and become pure utterances." "It is as if there were a Platonic heaven of words and commonplaces to which we all go to find words suitable to a given situation."

For them [Dos Passos' characters], there is no break between inside and outside, between body and consciousness, but only between the stammerings of
an individual's timid, intermittent, fumbling thinking and the messy world of
collective representations.[55]

From this perspective the distinction between speech and writing can
be put in ontological terms. The characters, in essence speakers, are
condemned to an inauthentic mode of existence because they are not
the origin of their utterances. More important, they are unaware of
their condition. For Sartre, the intolerable state Dos Passos forces his
reluctant readers to recognize as their own should provoke them to try
and smash their preplanned destinies. Sartre does not, however, address
the specificity of what constitutes, for the American novelist, an effective
political intervention: the invention of a technique of *critical reading*.

An example of what Dos Passos deems to be a more or less obsolete
approach to radical activism can be found in the sympathetic representation of the labor organizer Ben Compton in *1919*. A politically admirable
and skilled "soapbox speechmaker," one who could "make people listen
to him," who "could talk and say what he thought and get a laugh or
a cheer out of the massed upturned faces" (*1919*, 433), he is ultimately
not much of a force in the class struggle. Near the end of the book, he is
arrested while speaking at a meeting in support of the Soviets; loses his
case in court; and the last time we see him he is on his way in handcuffs
to prison. Meanwhile, public delirium rages around him as the country
celebrates the armistice. The rewards of immediate oral communication may be palpable. "He'd hear his own voice enunciating clearly and
firmly, feel its reverberance along the walls and ceiling, feel ears growing tense." "Phrases like *protest, mass action, united workingclass of this country
and the world, revolution,* would light up the eyes and faces under him like
the glare of a bonfire" (440). Nevertheless, the voice was for Dos Passos
obsolete as an instrument of radical dissent.

The presence of the "straight writer" can be most strongly felt in
U.S.A.'s biographical narratives (all of which are of men until the portrait of Isadora Duncan in *The Big Money*). And though the claim seems
counter-intuitive, the rhetorical mode he employs in these narratives is
best defined as allegorical – in the traditional sense of a compositional
method that takes the relation between illustrative image and abstract
idea to be a conventional one. The biographies do not signal a lapse back
into historical prose, nor do they, as is often argued, indicate a retreat back
toward a Whitmanesque descriptive literalism. Rather, as the logical end
point of a developmental narrative, the authorial education that takes

place at the level of the formal devices as opposed to inside one of them (the Camera Eye), the biographies exemplify a rhetorical technique cleansed of aesthetic delusions. The seductive appeal of self-expression is superseded. The allegorist cannot appear in the Camera Eye but must emerge from *behind the device's back*; correlatively, the allegories do not seek to fulfill the reader's desire to recapture the referential substance (subjective or objective, of consciousness or the world) pre-existing the text. The biographies are like emblematic paintings of the medieval period, even if the intelligible concept Dos Passos intends to convey is infrequently registered in the title of the work. Whereas in the frescoes in the Arena Chapel in Padua, Giotto materially inscribes the meaning of the allegorical image he has painted, Dos Passos customarily leaves it to the reader to decipher the moral or ethical significance of the "portraits." It is therefore a mistake to approach the biographies as straightforward, mimetic representations of actual persons, even though each figure has a living or dead counterpart in historical reality.

In a 1967 talk, appropriately given in Rome, Dos Passos looked back to an experience he had while serving on the Italian Front in the First World War as a pivotal one in regard to the writing technique he subsequently developed:

Aside from the excitement of the architecture . . . there was the painting. I mention it because I am sure that the great narrative painting of the thirteen and fourteen hundreds profoundly influenced my ideas of how to tell a story in words. Padua between airraids: when we looked, peeping through the sandbags, at Giotto's frescoes in the Arena Chapel the intensity of their homely narrative was immensely heightened by the feeling that perhaps we were the last men who would ever look on these masterpieces; and the feeling too that perhaps, perhaps, Giotto's gospel tales might be the last thing we would experience on this earth.[56]

In an interview from the following year, he makes much the same point in direct response to a question about the biographies. "Its [the visual art of the thirteenth and fourteenth centuries] tableaux with large figures of saints surrounded by a lot of little people just fascinated me. I tried to capture the same effect in words."[57]

Priority in representation can therefore be said to go here not to the events of the historical individual's life but to an intellectual decision the writer has made, to the idea he has chosen to communicate to his reader. Dos Passos' selection of public personages may have been determined in each case by the suitability of the life as the vehicle of the meaning he hoped to convey. Yet the "portraits" still must be shaped in accordance with the conceptual abstraction he intended to render.[58] His purpose was to tell stories involving modern saints (Eugene Debs, Randolph Bourne, Bill Heywood, Robert La Follette, John Reed, Wesley Everest, Joe Hill) and sinners (Minor Keith, Theodore Roosevelt, Andrew Carnegie, J.P. Morgan, Woodrow Wilson). Other figures (Paxton Hibben, Thomas Edison, William Jennings Bryan, and Steinmetz) fall somewhere in the middle of the ethical spectrum, their behavior neither wholly evil nor purely good. Successfully resolving the psychic and linguistic tension inscribed in the text in the conflict between the Camera Eyes and the Newsreels, the allegorical biographies amount to a pedagogical strategy designed to provide moral instruction. The numerous figures that appear here are thus all paternal representations, ideal or disgraceful models, good or bad fathers – though the basis of evaluating their spiritual suitability for identification is political rather than religious. Given that these allegorical portions of the text constitute its rhetorical peak, it would seem that Dos Passos went backwards in art or literary history to move beyond romantic lyricism and realist reproductions of the visible world.

The telos of "straight writing" is a self-consciously figurative mode that does not constitute a representational regression to the expressive imitation of lived experience. The critical movement of *U.S.A.* leads from an expressive aesthetic style based on a faith in the phenomenality of the linguistic sign (Camera Eye) through a semiological tactic (Newsreel) to an allegorical (in the traditional sense) compositional strategy. The relatively deluded starting point (the belief that language can make the invisible visible) is consistently encompassed categorically as a form of speech. This is fitting since its determining figure enacts a tropological procedure – the giving of a face – that includes the positing of a mouth, the precondition of the voice. The negation of this trope of autobiography, which is seductive in that it generates the illusion that the expressive language of the text is rooted in the experiences of a highly particularized consciousness, may be thought of as a mutilation or defacement. Although this act of linguistic violence takes place behind the scenes, or in the editing room, its traces are easily detected. The flattened discursive surfaces of the Newreels are the consequences of the elimination of the impression of depth the Camera Eyes convey; the eradication of figuratively constructed features paves the way for a mode of writing in which linguistic fragments drawn from an available archive are provocatively rearranged.

It is this aggressive process of cutting, the ceaseless disfigurations, that allows for the adoption of a more politically viable form of allegorically instructive *writing*: the biographies. At the summit of *U.S.A.*'s rhetorical hierarchy a narrative dimension is recovered. The temporal limitations of the Newsreels, which are spatial constructs despite their historical allusions, are overcome when the author reaches the enlightened, rationalized standpoint that allows him to construct a series of representational tableaux. This is an ascent that none of the personages in the biographies negotiate successfully, and their enduring commitment to oral discourse is what marks the historical limits of the political horizon of even the most radicalized of these figures. In this regard the criterion of judgment has little to do with individual sincerity and personal integrity. The firm conviction behind Reed's left-wing journalism that "words meant what they said" (*1919*, 15), Joe Hill's songs that set "rebel words to tunes" (422), Debs' powerful affirmation of his working-class identity, and Bourne's radical essays are on a par with Bryan's misguided "silver tongue" (176) and Wilson's often hypocritical public addresses. The latter's desperate "talking to save his faith in words" at the end of his life until a stroke silences him may be a more pathetic or pernicious gesture than that of the others. Yet it is not only this son of "a teacher of rhetoric in theological seminaries," the father a lover of "correct syntax" (241), who lacks the requisite skills to become a radical writer in the sense of the term still being defined.

The assorted devices of the trilogy thus combine to constitute a textual machine whose principal function is to fix the male subject in place at the expense of the childishly naive "I" who also retains traits associated with the feminine. From this perspective, however, Dos Passos' textual strategy seems to fall short of the critical rigor attributed to (grotesque) allegory amid its rehabilitation by American deconstruction. For the biographies do not demonstrate the epistemological intensity characteristic of the device (the Newsreel) the biographies logically follow. Instead, the device would seem to signal the overcoming of the aggressive impulse to engage in acts of rhetorical disfiguration. Firmly fixed in place, the subject as radical Author should not need to remain on the defensive. Yet the actual organization of the text, with its incessantly disruptive shifts back and forth between the assorted devices (not to mention the various narrative fictions) suggest an alternative perspective. In contrast to the logical hierarchy or hidden structure of the text as I have been describing it, the disruptive surface arrangement of *U.S.A.* most closely resembles that of the Newsreels: on both levels, the demand on the reader is to negotiate ceaselessly between discrete systems of representation or signification. It is as if the authorial entrance to the social order cannot be permanently guaranteed, as if the precariously constructed masculine subject finds it necessary continuously to protect against falling back into the grip of imaginary delusions and behaving like a child or a foolish woman. What *U.S.A.* ultimately manifests is, then, the obsessive-compulsive aspects of the critical drive, the writer repeatedly compelled to draw a (straight) line between himself and his others in the endlessly deferred effort to set firmly in place his sexual and authorial identity.

The interest of *1919*'s explosive finale, the "prose poem"[59] titled "The Body of an American," is that it accomplishes its critical task without relying on a securely positioned, phallic subject. Recognizing that the political oration delivered in the course of erecting a public monument to commemorate the dead of the First World War serves to reinforce a patriotic nationalism, Dos Passos directs in conclusion his critical energy toward this war memorial: the Unknown Soldier. As the grotesque anatomization of a body occupies the center of the literary stage, the writer's aggressiveness turns inward. The sadistic impulse to fragment others gives way to a masochistic capitulation to the shattering of the self. For in the destructive excess of this last scene the authorial subject the text has labored to set up is put at risk. The radical passion of the dissident writer causes him to give up control over the literary invention he had built (partly with *ironic* components) in order to dominate the machine of production. By imaginatively inhabiting the mutilated body of a corpse in a scene of rhetorical and referential carnage, Dos Passos allowed himself to become the victim of his own epistemologically driven technique of rhetorical analysis.

THE RHETORIC OF PATRIOTISM

It has been my privilege to witness, the incident which(possibly more than any other) revealed to me those unspeakable foundations upon which are builded with infinite care such at once ornate and comfortable structures as La Gloire and La Patriotisme. (E.E. Cummings, *The Enormous Room*)

No more arresting emblems of the modern culture of nationalism exist than cenotaphs and tombs of Unknown Soldiers. (Benedict Anderson, *Imagined Communities*)

> We soldiers of all nations who lie killed
> Ask little: that you never, in our name,
> Dare claim we died that men might be fulfilled.
> The earth should vomit us, against that shame.
> > James Agee, "We Soldiers of All Nations
> > Who Lie Killed"

In his introduction to *The Unknown Soldier Speaks*, a collection of poems
by George Jarrboe, published in 1932, Jack Conroy appropriates this
symbolic figure as a radical icon. "Every year since the World War" we
discover, he writes, "fresh evidence of the diabolical betrayal of the soldiers and sailors who went to France presumably to end autocracy and
industrial tyranny as well." Since this time millions of veterans "have
roamed the streets," thousands gathering at the nation's Capitol only to
learn that "the imperialists require a younger crop of cannon-fodder"
and that therefore the still living "unknown soldiers and sailors" are of no
interest to the "fat man in the White House."[60] The significance Conroy
attaches to the figure of the unknown soldier is of course in direct competition with the ostensibly patriotic motivations lying behind the post-war
administration's ceremonial interment at the Arlington, Virginia cemetery of a randomly selected corpse. For the left-wing writer the icon
connotatively encompasses the fate of the deceived and then discarded
men who were told they were being sent abroad to represent and protect
the ideals for which their country stands. The government's purpose in
paying tribute to those who have fallen in the service of the country,
however, was to ease the internal social tensions that had emerged in
the aftermath of the nation's entrance into the European conflict. For
by the time the war had come to an end, the involvement of the United
States was widely perceived as having been determined by the financial
interests of large-scale capitalists. It was the economic ambition to maintain control over foreign markets and protect the massive loans issued
to the Allies that caused mass suffering. It was thus under the aegis of
honoring the dead that the State hoped, to paraphrase Donald Pease, to
reconstitute "a unified national identity out of diverse constituencies."
The Unknown Soldier was designed to help facilitate the "the construction of a new consensus."[61] The officially sanctioned act of mourning
simultaneously screens out the unpleasant facts of a historical event and
works to suture together a divided populace; a politicized, spectacular performance of collective grief stifles a lingering awareness of mass
victimization.

William March's innovative 1933 anti-war novel, *Company K*, is composed of 113 brief narratives, each told from the perspective of a different
American soldier, most of them privates, all of them members of the same
infantry company. "The Unknown Soldier," the eighty-third narrative, is
the only one that does not bear as its title the name of a specific individual.
In this piece, the speaker, caught on barbed wire after being struck by
machine gun fire, thinks back to the speech his town mayor delivered

in his annual address at the local Soldiers' Cemetery. Fragments of the speech float through his mind: "These men died gloriously on the Field of Honor!" They gave "their lives gladly in a Noble Cause!" "What a feeling of exaltation was theirs when Death kissed their mouths and closed their eyes for an Immortal Eternity!"[62] Having "listened enraptured to the speech and believing every word of it,"[63] he now lies whimpering in the field of battle on the threshold of death. When a German sentry approaches him, the American soldier articulates his despair upon realizing not only that he has been tricked but that he is now "more a part of" this system of duplicity than "ever before." For when the war has ended his body will be transported back home to the same cemetery, and there "will be a brass band and speech making and a beautiful marble shaft with my name chiseled on its base." And the same mayor will shout the same "meaningless words about glorious deaths and fields of honor" to a new set of enchanted boys. Desperate to avoid this fate, the character pulls his identification tags off and throws them away. He then gets rid of all his personal belongings, tearing up letters and photographs, and then tosses his helmet aside so that his identity can not be guessed "from the serial number stamped on the sweatband."[64] Feeling exultant, he proudly proclaims that he has "beaten the orators and the wreath layers at their own game." "Nobody will ever use me as a symbol. Nobody will ever tell lies over my dead body." Pleading with the sentry to shoot him, the American dies happy, convinced he has "broken the chain" and "defeated the inherent stupidity of life."[65] The poignancy of the scene stems from the fact that, as the chapter title indicates, the soldier's efforts have ironically led to his becoming an even more powerful national icon, a generalized figure encompassing all those who have fallen in military service to their country. By eliminating all traces of his particularity he rendered himself more vulnerable to the government, which transformed him after his death into an especially resilient link in the ideological chain of patriotic nationalism.

Dos Passos' aim in "The Body of an American" is to do decisive damage to this political discourse by exposing the epistemologically flawed assumptions on which the coercive icon in question (one that has become a tourist attraction) depends in order to function properly. His key insight, which becomes apparent as the prose poem unfolds, is that the structure and function of the national monument resembles the structure and function of a particular figure of speech: synecdoche.[66] The literary piece in which this tropological entity suffers an epistemological critique amounts to a condensed version of what I have been calling a grotesque allegory. Conjoining elements of the three major devices to perform a critical task, "Body" is an assemblage of technical components. The political thrust of this heterogeneous machine is what remains to be determined.

In *1919*, shortly before "Body," Dos Passos recounts the story of Wesley Everest, a working-class martyr. A decorated war veteran and logger, Everest becomes a proponent of "industrial democracy," joining the Industrial Workers of the World despite the fact that in "the summer of 1919" it was worse to "be a red" than it was being "a hun or pacifist in the summer of 1917." And on Armistice Day in 1919 parading vigilantes raid the Wobbly's new union hall in Centralia, Washington, the previous one having been destroyed on Memorial Day in 1918 by "the boys of the American Legion" (457). As they are about to lynch the IWW secretary, Everest manages to draw the "brave patriots" off by fleeing into the woods. The mob gives chase, captures him, bashes "his teeth in with the butt of a shotgun," cuts "his penis and testicles off with a razor," and then hangs him from a bridge (460). The narrator informs us that after the coroner's inquest the "mangled wreckage" of his body was hurled "into a packing box and buried" (461). Its referential accuracy notwithstanding, the biography raises Everest's status to that of a radical folk hero (the piece is titled "Paul Bunyan"). In this allegory of heroic sacrifice, the grotesque imagery of physical maiming is literal, the gruesome depiction of the physical torture of the man included as a way to intensify the effect of the victim's persecution. In the more rhetorically complex "Body," however, the imagery of corporeal mutilation functions literally and as a figure for the destruction of a pre-existing trope.

Here Dos Passos takes critical aim at the State's efforts to resolve domestic tensions and reunite the nation by erecting a symbolic icon. The political spectacle at which this icon was initially unveiled took place in Arlington, Virginia on Armistice Day, November 11, 1921 – paying tribute to the Unknown Soldier – and is a glaring example of such an ideological procedure.[67] The political pageant, an act of collective mourning, though one not without "a touch of color," nor one devoid of "beautiful" music, is lucidly understood by Dos Passos as a strategic attempt to forge a new mass consensus via the cynical manipulation of the corpse. An internally divided nation is to come back together, to coalesce, around the wounded corpse of an American soldier. To resist this process, the radicalized writer must expose the assumptions underlying it, and this is the purpose of his citation of the concluding portion of President Harding's eloquent address at the Memorial Amphitheatre:

> *We are met today to pay the impersonal tribute;*
> *The name of him whose body lies before us took flight with His imperishable soul . . .*
> *As a typical soldier of this representative democracy he fought and died believing in the indisputable justice of his country's cause . . .* (470)

The reverential tone notwithstanding, the "impersonal" quality of the eulogy is debatable given the ideological function it has been designed to perform, for it is in the interest of the current administration, as it was for the one preceding it, to rally the nation around a single collective identity. The context of course renders the quote ironic; yet its insertion gestures toward one of the fundamental premises Dos Passos is intent on contesting: that an invisible substance unifies the otherwise heterogeneous citizens of the United States. For President Harding this "typical" soldier's faith in and support of "his country's cause," his patriotic spirit, is what motivated him to sacrifice himself.[68] The assumptions underlying this aspect of the politician's discourse may be conceptually clarified by adopting a linguistic perspective and employing a more rhetorical terminology. His totalizing supposition rests on the formal structure of a particular figure of speech: a metaphorized synecdoche. Just as the trope assumes the inextricability of the part and the whole on the grounds that the two necessarily partake of the same fundamental essence, Harding takes it for granted that the individual members of the nation coalesce organically because they share the same basic spiritual convictions and values. And it is this axiomatic conviction that facilitates the identification of the living with the dead as well as the substitutability of one for the other, processes that in turn solidify affiliations among those who have survived the military crisis. The damaged body of the individual soldier is the central mediating point of a persuasive system of rhetorical exchanges that serves to suture the rent body politic back together.

As Dos Passos realized, Harding's speech is intended in part to produce what it presupposes as being already there: a collective commitment to military endeavors deemed necessary by the country's leaders. The writer's response to the ideological gesture was to disclose the tenuous nature of several of its claims. Thus, after opening the piece by quoting without much spacing a portion of the congressional resolution that brought the dead soldier "wholosthislifeduringtheworldwarandwhosei-dentityhasnotbeenestablished" (467–68) to Arlington, Dos Passos goes behind the scenes of the imaginary spectacle. Returning to France to the place where the rotting corpse was being kept, he reconstructs the selection process in order to mark the racist and ethnocentric priorities determining the otherwise arbitrary choice of the particular body that will serve as a general figure.

> In the tarpaper morgue at Chalons-sur-Marne in
> the reek of chloride of lime and the dead, they picked
> out the pine box that held all that was left of
> > enie menie moe plenty other pine boxes
> stacked up there containing what they'd scraped up of
> Richard Roe
> > And other person or persons unknown. Only one
> can go. How did they pick John Doe?
> > Make sure he aint a dinge, boys,
> > Make sure he aint a guinea or a kike,
> > How can you tell a guy's a hundredpercent when all
> you've got's a gunnysack full of bones, bronze buttons
> stamped with the screaming eagle and a pair of roll
> puttees?
> > . . . and the gagging chloride and the puky dirt-
> stench of the yearold dead . . . (468)

The "typical soldier" is shown here to stand for only a specific segment of the population. Whether it is due to the attitudes of the men sent to pick the corpse or, more likely, a result of orders from their superiors, the task is to choose an "authentic" ("a hundredpercent"[69]) or Anglo-Saxon person, difficult in this case given the lack of visible skin. The point would be to draw attention to the degree of ideological misrecognition that the act of identifying with the fallen hero involves for ethnic and racial minorities. For many, to see oneself in the Unknown Soldier is to overlook their social exclusion and to remain blind to the material conditions that perpetuate existing inequalities, all of this outside the purview of patriotic fervor. If the imaginary relation the symbolic icon facilitates thus also generates a questionable vision of collective unity, it does so, from a rhetorical perspective, on the basis of its metaphorical appeal. The supposition is that differences can be put aside in favor of similarities because all those involved in the system or chain of exchanges share an inherent property that makes the process work. Consequently, Dos Passos stresses the metonymic origins of the figure. That there is an arbitrary (though not random) element in the selection of the corpse clarifies its initial status as a floating signifier. The government then assigns a signified to the corpse by placing it in a discursive setting. The dead body is invested with meaning as it is moved out of the filthy morgue and into the hygienic arena of political spectacle. In this respect, the State employs without admitting it the same compositional strategy that the radical writer openly uses in the Newsreels as a critical tactic, albeit for a different purpose. And while the State uses corpses as the raw material of its signifying practice, whereas the writer relies on verbal archives, the formal methods are comparable. If the status of language as an active force in the world, as a means of exercising power over others, becomes fully apparent here, its performative effectiveness is shown to hinge on its success at presenting itself as a cognitively reliable, constative proposition. Propagandistic discourses masquerade as statements of knowledge to achieve their goals.

The counter-narrative of the soldier's death that Dos Passos offers should therefore be understood less as an effort to present a truthful version of the incident, one that corrects the State's false report, than as a means of establishing the event as the site of conflicting interpretations, as a text. By collapsing multiple protagonists into his alternative story of the character's life before induction into the army (468–69), Dos Passos attributes to his unofficial tale a competing degree of typicality. The fate suffered by the hapless protagonist of "Body of an American" is arguably as representative an account of what happened to soldiers in combat as is the official narrative. Upon entering the army, one is subject to an objectifying examination process that in effect reduces the "essence" of the human being to a set of marks on paper and integers stamped on a piece of metal. Weighed, measured, his penis squeezed to check for clap, his anus explored for piles, his teeth counted, eyesight, heart, lungs, and intelligence tested, and urine charted, the soldier is then given "a service record for a future (imperishable soul) and an identification tag" (470) with his serial number. The manufacturing of soldiers requires the reduction of individuals to the basic level of statistical persons, and the imposition of an abstract identity, an American soul, is a product of such disciplinary procedures.

The passive protagonist's subsequent physical molding in basic train-ing parallels the shaping of his consciousness by the hodge-podge of discourses, many patriotic, which have been swirling around him since childhood. The perceptually receptive, fully embodied youth has internalized the norms of his society through his senses. "John Doe had a head / for twentyodd years intensely the nerves of the eyes the ears the palate the tongue the fingers the toes the armpits, the nerves warmfeeling under the skin charged the coiled brain with hurt sweet warm cold mind must don't sayings print headlines" (471). The self is a composite of among other things religious guidelines, educational lessons, war propaganda: "Thou shalt not the multiplication table long division" and "Suppose a hun tried to rape you're my country" (471). In depicting the soldier's experiences in France, Dos Passos focuses on the character's terror and incontinence ("Cant help jumpin when them things go off, give me the trots them things do" [471]), as well as his sense of disorientation. His confusion is conveyed by variations, which get more impassioned with each repetition, on the following refrain: "*Say buddy cant you tell me how I can get back to my outfit.*" Scared and lost and devoid of any strong commitment to his military duty, the soldier lies down to rest in the sun and is subsequently torn apart and killed by shrapnel when a shell with "his number on it" falls nearby.

Whereas in Harding's commemorative speech the soldier's death is comprehended as a noble, sacrificial act, Dos Passos' diametrically opposed narrative presents the unidentifiable protagonist as the victim of an accidental, meaningless stroke of bad luck. The effect is to draw the reader's attention to the hypothetical nature of the President's assertion that he possesses knowledge as to the state of mind of the loyal soldier before he was killed. Yet the exhibition of the military icon as a nationalist symbol, its display as a solid figure, rests on the flawed notion that we can be certain about the soldier's emotional condition at the time of his death. Dos Passos insists on what the government's account represses: that in the absence of witnesses there can be no reliable interpretation of what happened. According to Agee's post-Second World War soldier: "We died. None knew, few tried to guess, just why, / No one knows now, on either side of the grave."[70] The problem for Dos Passos is that the government is among the few that try to guess, ignoring the fact that the noble and ignoble versions of the incident are equally plausible, that without proof there is no way to adjudicate between the two contradictory interpretations. The only empirically verifiable fact in this case is that the corporeal remains of an American soldier were found in a pine box in a morgue in France.

This allows for a double reading of the depiction of the mutilated soldier Dos Passos places in the text immediately after the explosion:

> The blood ran into the ground, the brains oozed
> out of the cracked skull and were licked up by the
> trenchrats, the belly swelled and raised a generation of
> bluebottle flies,
>> and the incorruptible skeleton,
>> and the scraps of dried viscera and skin bundled
> in khaki
>> they took to Chalons-sur-Marne
>> and laid it out neat in a pine coffin
>> and took it home to God's Country on a battleship
>> and buried it in a sarcophagus in the Memorial
> Amphitheatre in the Arlington National Cemetery
>> and draped the Old Glory over it (472)

This representation of a shattered and decomposing organism may be taken as an example of the kind of negative imagery that aestheticized political spectacles screen out. The grotesque portrait, which degrades "the imperishable soul" with an image of "the incorruptible skeleton," brings into view the carnage, the bloodshed of military combat that the State has a vested interest in veiling. The fragmented, putrid remains can also be taken as a way of making visible the critical endeavor Dos Passos pursues in the closing section of the text. From this angle, one observes here in condensed form the anatomical dissection of a symbolic icon (one made available for imaginary investments) that "Body" as a whole allegorically enacts. In both readings, the wrecked, mangled body is at the forefront. From a representational point of view, the displayed body has an extra-textual referent in the form of an American soldier who died on the field of battle in the First World War; from a reflexive standpoint, it figures an inter-textual act of rhetorical dismantling. The violence inherent in the critical procedure is brought out by comparing it to the physical experience of being brutally torn apart by the detonation of a charged projectile shot from a cannon. The radicalized writer ruthlessly attacks a political icon structured like a figure of speech and designed to function as a memorial to nationalist sentiments, as a monument to the ideology of patriotism. Benjamin has argued in a different literary historical context that martyrdom "prepares the body of the living person for emblematic purposes," that characters in the baroque *Trauerspiel* die because it is only "as corpses that they can enter into the homeland of allegory."[71] At the end of *1919*, the organic body of a soldier is painfully destroyed so that a new meaning may be picked up from his fragmented remains. Entering the "homeland of allegory," the blasted soldier becomes an emblem of what is left behind once the process of disfiguration in the rhetorical sense has run its critical course. The shattered corpse is an image of a dismantled linguistic entity and its decomposing condition corresponds to the decay of the patriotic passion that the State's figure had been erected to preserve.

One final victim of the iconoclastic endeavor under investigation has yet to be identified: the radicalized writer. As Dos Passos realized, the government's persuasive figuration pivots around the act of renaming the dead soldier. To call the unknown the Unknown is a reassuring way to overcome an initial lack of knowledge. A cognitive loss at the level of particular identity is compensated for by the general meaning the icon embodies: it does not matter who exactly the individual was insofar as he stands for all of us as patriotic Americans – soldiers and civilians alike. Naming the nameless in this manner gives him exemplary status.[72] To avoid participating in this dialectical recovery Dos Passos does not in "Body" employ the term the Unknown Soldier, designating the abstracted person instead through the interchangeable use of either John Doe or Richard Roe, two less comforting ways of designating an anonymous person. The consequence of the repeated appearance of John Doe, however, is especially disruptive since its sound closely approximates the first two syllables of the author's proper name. As the material signifier that serves to guarantee the status of the person as a unique individual is broken down into its component pieces, the soul of the author departs. Bringing the particular and known (John Dos Passos) into contact with the general and unknown (John Doe) undermines the integrity and specificity of the former. The punning insertion of the author into the text in this manner encourages the reader to associate the writer with the mortally wounded protagonist of the piece. Whether an intentional, self-conscious identification or the result of mere happenstance, the authorial subject is in effect torn to pieces. (There is a good deal of evidence that Dos Passos knew exactly what he was doing here in that parts of "Body" echo passages from the autobiographical Camera Eyes. For example, in Camera Eye [29], the speaker examines himself after "swimming in the Marne," noting "the limits of the hard immortal skull under the flesh a deathshead and skeleton" rests "inside the new khaki uniform inside my twentyoneyearold body" [72]. Similarly, in "Body" we are told that the soldier is "twentyodd" and that he has lost his identification tag while "swimmin' in the Marne" [471]). The physical blasting apart of the soldier corresponds to the rending of authorial identity amid the (self-)destructive effects of material letters. The overdetermined violence of mechanized warfare merges with the overdetermined violence of mechanized word play. Much as the unpredictable fate of the soldier is a result of his being in the wrong place at the wrong time, the mutilation of the name of the author is sealed by the contingent yet explosive collision of two names that happen to sound alike. The decomposition at the phonemic and graphic levels of the proper name – a whole signifier – blocks any final appeal to the authorial consciousness of the grotesque allegorist as the stable signified of the text. The critical apparatus the writer has constructed ends up disfiguring its inventor alongside the main targets of its critical undertaking. The unpredictable play of the textual machine short-circuits the fantasmatic identifications that the government promotes in order to maintain control over the nation *and* dismembers the critical novelist. In both cases, it is the name that is shown to be the most vulnerable cornerstone of the private and the public construct.

"The Body of an American" is, I have been arguing, an attempt to demonstrate (and resist) the government's efforts to encourage the crisis-ridden national subject to participate in a collective funeral rite as a form of protection against the cracks and flaws in the discourse of patriotism. The erection of the monument encourages individuals to indulge in an act of political fetishization. Accepting the Unknown Soldier as a symbolic icon serves as a means of defending oneself against a troubling uncertainty, a haunting lack of knowledge that the icon paradoxically also preserves by virtue of its existence. The figure both conceals and reveals the gaps in the country's traditional affirmation of military heroism as the destiny plotted out for its male subjects – gaps that the horrifying results of the recent world war had brought sharply into focus. We might say then that the soldier's corpse is a repulsive "piece of the real" that has been appropriated and aestheticized – for the ceremony it has been draped in the decorative accoutrements of honor (flags, medals, flowers) – by the State to serve as meaningful support for the symbolic order. For the President's speech manipulates the remains of an individual, whose feelings at the time of his death are due to the circumstances permanently unavailable and therefore inexpressible, to produce the satisfying illusion that a meaningful, sacrificial gesture has taken place. To accomplish this task Harding relies on the formalized elements of a ceremonial, ritualized discourse, on the repeatable conventions or grammar (and the tropes) of mourning. In making figurative use of a dead thing to stitch back together a torn body politic, the President sought to perform an act of mass interpellation.

It is the force of this compellingly patriotic yet ultimately mechanical rhetorical maneuver that Dos Passos struggled to counter at the end of *1919*. He therefore transformed the political novel into an aggressive practice of grotesque anatomization, taking pre-existing figures of speech rather than lived experience as the raw material of his critical *undertaking*. He mobilized literature to generate insight into the duplicitous functions of the language of the American body; and one indispensable by-product of this negative process was that the distinction between writing and reading texts collapsed.

Postface: Discharges

> And when they talked it was more like thinking aloud than speaking for the purposes of communication. Clusters of emotion, dim accretions of instinct and tradition rose to the surface of their consciousness like dead bodies floating swollen upon a night sea.
>
> Richard Wright, *Lawd Today!*

Approaching a state of extreme mental exhaustion, his commitment to his documentary endeavor on the threshold of becoming a feverish obsession, James Agee decided, on a blisteringly hot Sunday afternoon, to go for a drive. Gazing out his car window, he experienced a strange temporal dislocation as his external environment appeared to him as a severely wounded body.

> It was like returning several thousand years after the end of the world, when nothing but the sun was left, faithfully blasting away upon the dead earth as it twisted up, like a drowned body and the exactitudes of those scars and lesions it had sustained in the course of its active life. But it was worse. For this was not the end of the world, it was contemporary, the summer of nineteen-thirty-six . . .[1]

Though momentarily projected into a post-apocalypse future, Agee managed to come to his senses and relocate himself in his present while staring in dismay at his catastrophic surroundings. Some sixty-five years later, our still mournful situation in relation to the corpse-like 1930s is a bit different. The decade's remains, at least as I have gathered them together, form a strange and no doubt undesirably monstrous, decomposing thing that we can only look back on as a genuinely troubling part of a collective past from which we are permanently detached.

Why the compulsive forcing of the vile and hideous aspects of the Depression era back to the surface of our literary historical consciousness? Why not leave the traumatic decade underwater, held down, as it has been previously, by the weight of its preceding definitions? For in truth, the thirties have been less the victim of disciplinary repression than the object of excessive yet insistently inadequate description and interpretation. Again and again, the decade has been reduced, with the help of formal or generic categories (realism, documentary, naturalism, modernism, proto-postmodernism), to the monumental status of a symbolically meaningful, comprehensible period in the history of twentieth-century American literature. To my (perhaps perverse) way of thinking, such ultimately defensive accounts serve to facilitate the insertion of an enigmatic phenomenon into a falsely reassuring tradition. It is essential today to register the grotesque dimensions of the body of radical writing in question for the simple reason that if we fail to do so we render invisible the quite remarkable cultural event that took place at this time.

The argument of this study has been that it is by re-exhibiting and examining closely the numerous images of corporeal mutilation or somatic fragmentation the decade's prose featured that we can begin to perceive the circulation from amusement to literature of aesthetic traits and festive energies. My guiding assumption has been that the grotesque body functioned as a kind of medium of exchange or relay system between textual and extra-textual practices. Figures of the disfigured body were the means whereby attributes derived from the vaudeville or burlesque stage passed over to the literary page, whereby the properties of modern carnival flowed from Coney Island amusement parks and Bowery dime museums into autobiographies and novels. In my opinion, it is by virtue of this complex, often ambiguous series of inter-medial transactions – and of the paradoxical combination of excitement and anxiety these induced – that the decade retains its posthumous legitimacy as an enduringly intriguing object deserving critical investigation.

One of the most elusive themes of my inquiry has been the notion that coming into contact with mechanized amusements as well as technological devices like the phonograph and the moving picture camera precipitated a reconsideration of writing on the far side of traditional organic analogies. I have attempted to demonstrate the extent to which the structure and function of language were reconceived in the years this study encompasses in terms of (difficult to operate) apparatuses. With this in mind, James Agee's exasperated description of the machinations of verbal discourses in *Let Us Now Praise Famous Men* is exemplary. After acknowledging their capacity to "do or tell anything within human conceit," which "is more than can be said of the instruments of any other art," he qualifies his comments by adding that words "are the most inevitably inaccurate of all mediums of record and communication" and they "come at many of the things which they alone can do by such a

Rube Goldberg articulation of frauds, compromises, artful dodges and tenth removes as would fatten any other art into apoplexy if the art were not first shamed out of existence" (236). Perennially on the verge of breaking down, linguistic constructs are as functionally inefficient and as haphazardly built as the amusing domestic contraptions the well-known cartoonist had been drawing for the pages of the daily newspapers since the turn of the century. Whether they intend to or not, literary artists are destined to "interfere with the reproductive function of technical machines by introducing an element of dysfunction."[2] In *Literature, Amusement and Technology* I have tried to show that the semantically and referentially frustrating play of the literary machine is by no means politically superfluous.

My ambition has been to measure up to the challenge this strange decade presents without taking recourse to conventional literary historical wisdom. To satisfy this desire it seems necessary in the end to admit that determining the significance in relation to our present circumstance of what happened in or to American literature during the Depression era is no simple task. In other words, and as if in response to the question Dahlberg posed in 1941 (the same year that Agee's documentary was finally published): No, these bones don't exactly seem to be living, but they don't appear to be resting peacefully in the morgue of literary history either. Worse, I'm not absolutely sure why. In other words, there is much that remains unfathomable about the literary corpus I have dissected and displayed in the hope of enhancing our understanding of the relationship between radical politics, grotesque aesthetics, and modern carnivals in the 1930s.

I too love everything that flows: rivers, sewers, lava, semen, blood, bile, words, sentences. (Henry Miller, *Tropic of Cancer*)

To end this study in a chronologically apt manner, I would like to move toward a passage from Agee's wonderfully bizarre documentary. Like the 1930s considered as a period of literary history, *Famous Men* has been characterized in several different ways: as a realistic documentary;[3] as a modernist masterpiece;[4] as "a quintessentially postmodern text;"[5] and as the progenitor of a new, mixed generic category, "postmodernist realism."[6] As with the decade in its entirety, the point is not to contest such evaluative assessments but to recover a sense of the strangeness that such judgments tend to obscure.[7]

The passage in which I am interested appears near the end of a section titled "(On the Porch: 2." Agee explains that he originally intended "On the Porch" as a whole (there are three parts) to serve, presumably in the form of a single continuous piece, as the preface to a much longer work. In the present, less expansive book, however, its functions are multiple: it is meant "as a frame and as an undertone and as the set stage and center of action, in relation to which all other parts of this volume are intended as flashbacks, foretastes, illuminations and contradictions" (*Famous Men*, 245). Despite his assertion of its centrality to his project, "On the Porch" has received relatively minimal attention from past commentators on *Famous Men*. It has been noted that the epistemological rigor of "(On the Porch: 2" is severe enough to put the representational claims of the documentary enterprise into question, yet there is much in this exceptionally speculative portion of the book that has yet to receive the critical scrutiny it deserves. Take, for example, his startling declaration that "human consciousness" is nothing but an infected "wound" or "sore." To convey a sense of "essential human frailty" in relation to the world we inhabit, Agee tropes the mind as a somatically traumatized body. This painful predicament is a general one from which we all perpetually suffer; consequently, all ontology becomes pathology. "The prime generic inescapable stage of this disease is being. A special complication is life. A malignant variant of this complication is consciousness. The most complex and malignant form of it is human consciousness." Correlatively, cultural accomplishment in philosophy, art, and religion are reduced to the status of defensive reactions an already injured psyche adopts to protect itself from experiencing further damage. The "most intangible reaches of thought, deduction and imagination" as well as "the deity the race has erected to shield it from the horror of the heavens" are, like "the skull that scabs the brain," hardened crusts of blood raised to cover an otherwise open sore (229).

Shortly thereafter, Agee produces a description of the natural landscape in which all traces of the human vanish as the environment manifests itself as a wounded and wounding giant. The passage begins by referring literally to a nearby creek but quickly develops into an elaborate figuration of a physical entity, a river, as a flowing monstrosity. The first appearance in the passage of this trope, Agee's use of the verb "smiled" to describe the merging of the creek into a stronger stream, is unremarkable. But the grotesque quality of the imagery quickly becomes noticeable as he addresses the erosive force of flowing water as it comes into contact with the earth. "The surface of a continent, condensed here and there by chance into the serious infant frowning of mountain systems, is drawn away by the action of water into an enormous and unnaturally slender vine" (250). It is worth underscoring the fact that Agee figures this natural process as the disfiguration of a face, for when the passage returns to this image later, it will be mingled with the act of writing. The grotesque emerges even more dramatically two sentences later; now two immense, ancestral bodies are shown interacting with one another, no sharp boundary lines closing one monstrously proportioned entity, the earth, off from the other, the river:

> ... this eternal, lithe, fingering, chiseling, searching out the tender groin of the land that the water in a river system is carrying on in ten million parts of a face of earth at once, so that in the least creasing of the land sucked into scars between two stalks of corn you are seeing an organic part of the great body of the Mississippi River. There is no need to personify a river: it is much too literally alive in its own way, and like air and earth themselves is a creature much more powerful, much more basic, than any living thing the earth has borne. It is one of those few, huge, casual and aloof creatures by the mercy of whose existence our own existence was made possible; and at the very least as much as it is good to hear the whining of dynamos, the artifacted hearts of our civilization, it is well to hear, to become aware of, the operations of water among whose spider lacings by chance we live ... (251–52)

Agee imparts a sense that the exchange between the two bodies is both erotic and violent. The "chiseling" and "searching out" of "the tender groin," which is followed by a "creasing" that sucks the land into scars, evokes an act of penetration which harms the undoubtedly gendered (female) body of the earth.[8] In this instance, the naturally destructive process, as crucial to existence as human technology, leads to renewal: the water's powerful actions produce the energy necessary for the growth of the season's corn. Agee's figuration (though he insists upon its "literality") would seem to have a reassuringly integrative effect in regard to the relationship between human beings and the natural environment. The relationship may be hierarchical, one of dependency, but the embodiment of three of the four elements – air, water, earth – as living creatures appears to ease the sense of difference between the self and the external world. But Agee's intent, as the rest of the passage makes clear, is instead to provoke a feeling of human insignificance, to minimize the importance of persons relative to nature (though he realizes this is an impossible point of view to sustain: "we cannot bear, for any length of time, to carry in our minds in any literalness the fact of our small size and our youth" [247]).

The two sentences cited above (only partially) twist and turn as aimlessly as the object – the river – they describe, which is a clue that the landscape description can be read reflexively as an account of writing. Such sentential wandering also makes it difficult to cite Agee for the purpose of explication; his words digressively veer away from and back toward their meaning. For example, in the following citation the second sentence seems to alter its direction in midstream, almost reversing the evaluation presented in the first one:

> ... the crop it [the river] brings up, the destruction it is capable of, the dams and the helmeted brains of generators thrown across it and taking a half-hitch on its personal energy are small, irrelevant, not even noticed incidents in its more serious career which is by a continual sagging in all parts of its immense branched vine and by a continual searching out of weakness, the ironing flat and reduction to dead sea level of the wrinkled fabric of the earth. How beautifully then it has drawn our country into pleated valleys, in what language it has written upon the genius forehead of the earth the name and destiny of water, how handsome are the meanderings of its dotage through yellow flats across which is seen in the hard sunlight the broken and glass glistering of a city, are matters less truly important than the wrinkling open of a gully in a cornfield, the cellophane crackle of cold mountain branches, the twinkling spiral of sand that stands out of the heart of a spring, the sleeping and high-breasted sliding along of a milewide river, the great, final, digressive rectal discharge which beneath New Orleans yellows the Mexican Gulf: and the knowledge that such actions, going on intimately in every yard of thousands of miles of land beneath the hoverings and discharges of the sky, are all of one thing, one more than beast. (253)

In both passages I have cited a topographical shift from the high to the low takes place. In the first, Agee moves from the face to the groin, in the second from the forehead to the anus (by way of the breast). As any reader of Bakhtin knows, to degrade or debase an object or entity is, within the logic of folk symbolism, not simply to kill it but also to prepare its rebirth. The spatial trajectory the two successive descriptions follow from the upper to the lower regions of the body may be taken as a fall into a fertile grave, a reproductive zone. The excremental imagery and the apparent senility of the elderly body constitute one stage in what we are to take as an interwoven, endless process of "discharge" and reception. What the river releases the gulf takes in; what the sky drops the land absorbs. The important point is that negative events like defecation and aging always imply their positive, rejuvenating complements (though in this instance, the latter – the "wrinkling open of a gully," the upward thrust of the spring – are placed before the former).

While at first glance the allusion to writing appears merely to be a figurative embellishment, supplementing the grotesque landscape description, the passage can also be read as a reflexive account of the inhuman force of writing.[9] From the first perspective, the act of writing is merely a trope for a brutal natural process, our perception of what the river does to the earth sharpened (arguably) if we visualize it as the signing of a name upon a forehead. Yet reversing the figural and literal poles of the metaphor makes the reference to writing the only literal element in the entire description. From this perspective, the natural flow of the river becomes comprehensible as an extended figure, one stretching across the entire paragraph, the proper meaning of which has to do with a cultural practice (writing) and its complex effects. (Some support for this claim comes from the fact that Agee has twice used "sag" in a preceding critique of "naturalism" to describe the failure of words to reproduce satisfactorily the "real," this form of writing adding to the intended object a "weightiness" it "does not of itself have" [235]). Read allegorically, the passage furnishes an understanding of writing as both a gently nurturing and a cruelly destructive power, as a force of change that may be associated with the positive construction and with the negative elimination of features. If writing possesses the rejuvenating strength to push upward, to erect forms in space ("the twinkling spiral of sand that stands out of the heart of a spring"), the "heaviness" of writing as it ages, in its "dotage," also causes it to press down, to level shapes (253). For Agee, although the basis of "its more serious career" are the critical, reductive tasks it performs, these are "less truly important" than its capacity to breach barriers. Writing is crucial to existence (and difficult to bear) because, like water, the flow of prose alternately wrinkles and smooths, creases and decreases, forms and deforms. It is this double function of writing, the frequently violent interplay within it of creative figuration and critical disfiguration, composition and decomposition, that I have sought to examine as a politically significant phenomenon in the literature of the decade that Agee's marvelously peculiar performance brings to a fittingly monstrous close.

Notes

INTRODUCTION: DISFIGURATIONS

1 Dahlberg later changed the title of his critical history to *Can These Bones Live* to match the King James translation of Ezekiel (37:3). Djuna Barnes pointed out his mistake. Seeing Dahlberg out walking one day, she shouted: "'It's Can, Mr. Dahlberg! Can! Can!'" Charles DeFanti, *The Wages of Expectation: A Biography of Edward Dahlberg* (New York University Press, 1973), 148.

2 Edward Dahlberg, *Do These Bones Live* (New York: Harcourt, Brace and Company, 1941), 53.

3 Leslie Fiedler's characterization of Depression-era, left-wing fiction as a gothic "exhibition of social horrors" seems tame in comparison. *Love and Death in the American Novel* (rev. ed.; New York: Dell, 1966), 485.

4 Edmund Wilson, "Dahlberg, Dos Passos, and Wilder" (1930), *The Shores of Light: A Literary Chronicle of the Twenties and Thirties* (New York: Farrar, Straus and Young, 1952), 442–50.

5 D.H. Lawrence, "Introduction," Edward Dahlberg, *Bottom Dogs, From Flushing to Calvary, Those Who Perish, and Hitherto Unpublished and Uncollected Works*, ed. Harold Billings (New York: Minerva Press, 1976), 151.

6 *Ibid.*, 152.

7 For a valuable account of this dynamic in an earlier period of literary history, see Bill Brown, *The Material Unconscious: American Amusement, Stephen Crane, and The Economies of Play* (Cambridge, MA: Harvard University Press, 1996).

8 James Agee and Walker Evans, *Let Us Now Praise Famous Men* (Boston: Houghton Mifflin, 1941), 463.

9 Mark Seltzer, "Wound Culture: Trauma in the Pathological Public Sphere," *October* 80 (Spring 1997): 3–26.

10 On carnival festivity as an ongoing site of social conflict, see Joseph Roach "Carnival and Law," *Cities of the Dead: Circum-Atlantic Performance* (New York: Columbia University Press, 1996), 239–81. See also Mary Russo, "Female Grotesques: Carnival and Theory," *The Female Grotesque: Risk, Excess and Modernity* (New York: Routledge, 1994), 58–62.

11 Peter Stallybrass and Allon White, *The Politics and Poetics of Transgression* (Ithaca: Cornell University Press, 1986), 191–202.

12 For critical accounts of the function in the thirties of the grotesque other in relation to the formation of a middle-class or bourgeois identity, one might

read profitably Zora Neale Hurston's *Their Eyes Were Watching God* (1937) (New York: Harper & Row, 1990); Djuna Barnes' *Nightwood* (1936) (Normal, IL: Dalkey Archive Press, 1989); and Eudora Welty's stories "The Petrified Man," "Keela the Outcast Indian Maid," and "A Memory," collected in *A Curtain of Green, and Other Stories* (New York: Harcourt, Brace and Company, 1941).

13 Edward Dahlberg, "Ariel in Caliban," *Samuel Beckett's Wake and Other Uncollected Prose* (Elmwood Park, IL: Dalkey Archive Press, 1989), 3–8.

14 Neil Hertz, "Lurid Figures," *The Ends of Rhetoric: History, Theory, Practice*, ed. John Bender and David Wellbery (Stanford University Press, 1990), 100–24.

15 Paul de Man, "Aesthetic Formalization: Kleist's *Uber das Marionettentheater*," *The Rhetoric of Romanticism* (New York: Columbia University Press, 1986), 288–89. Michael Fried's *Realism, Writing, and Disfiguration: On Thomas Eakins and Stephen Crane* (University of Chicago Press, 1987) demands recognition here. To the degree that, as Fried puts it, his interpretive interests are keyed to "issues of writing as such" rather than to "language and rhetoric" (185), his study is not a primary theoretical determinant of mine.

16 On corporeal and mental fragmentation at the capitalist workplace, see Georg Lukács, *History and Class Consciousness* (Cambridge, MA: MIT Press, 1971), 88–89 and Fredric Jameson, *The Political Unconscious: Narrative as a Socially Symbolic Act* (Ithaca: Cornell University Press, 1981), 219–42. On carnival anatomizations, see Mikhail Bakhtin, *Rabelais and His World*, trans. Helen Iswolsky (Bloomington: Indiana University Press, 1984), esp. 347–52. On fragmentation and subjectivity, see Jacques Lacan, "The Mirror Stage as Formative of the Function of the I as Revealed in Psychoanalytic Experience" and "Aggressivity in Psychoanalysis," *Écrits*, trans. Alan Sheridan (New York: W.W. Norton, 1977), 4–5, 10–12. On the relation between technologies of printing or the mechanization of writing to psychical and physical disintegration, see Marshall McLuhan, *Understanding Media: The Extensions of Man* (New York: New American Library, 1964). Though there is some overlap between my study and Elaine Scarry's important work, *The Body in Pain: The Making and Unmaking of the World* (New York: Oxford University Press, 1985), in that we both focus on grotesque images of the body, her concern is more with *literal* representations of hurt bodies and the ethical stakes of attaching or detaching language from its extra-textual referent, of connecting or disconnecting verbal assertions from the material substance of the injured person's body.

17 For a Depression-era manifestation of authorial anxiety in relation to the use of grotesque representational strategies, see Tillie Olsen's aborted depiction of a mining accident in *Yonnondio: From the Thirties* (New York: Delta, 1974), 20–21. For a reading of this scene, see Constance Coiner, "Literature of Resistance: The Intersection of Feminism and the Communist Left in Meridel Le Sueur and Tillie Olsen," *Radical Revisions: Rereading 1930s Culture*, ed. Bill Mullen and Sherry Linkon (Urbana: University of Illinois Press, 1996), 158–59. On Olsen and the grotesque, see Paula Rabinowitz,

Labor and Desire: Women's Revolutionary Fiction in Depression America (Chapel Hill: University of North Carolina Press, 1991), 124–36.

18 On the statuesque giant as "one unifying element of the diverse phenomenon of proletarian poetry in the 30s," see Cary Nelson, *Repression and Recovery: Modern American Poetry and the Politics of Cultural Memory, 1910–1945* (Madison: University of Wisconsin, 1989), 141–47. On the "Third Period proletcult" use of "compensatory fetish images" of muscular (white) male torsos, see the profile of Hugo Gellert (a lithographer) in Walter Kalaidjian, *Revisionary Modernism & Postmodern Critique* (New York: Columbia University Press, 1993), 138–45.

19 Lauren Berlant, *The Anatomy of National Fantasy: Hawthorne, Utopia, and Everyday Life* (University of Chicago Press, 1991), 24.

20 Wallace Stevens, "Gigantomachia," *The Collected Poems* (New York: Random House, 1982), 289. On this topic, see Amy Kaplan, "Romancing the Empire: The Embodiment of American Masculinity in the Popular Historical Novel of the 1890s," *American Literary History* 2:4 (Winter 1990): 659–90; Linda Boose, "Techno-Muscularity and the 'Boy Eternal': From the Quagmire to the Gulf," *Cultures of United States Imperialism*, ed. Amy Kaplan and Donald Pease (Durham: Duke University Press, 1993), 581–616; Susan Jeffords, *The Remasculinization of America: Gender and the Vietnam War* (Bloomington: Indiana University Press, 1989), 11–22.

21 Berlant, *Anatomy*, 24.

22 *Nathanael West: Novels and Other Writings* (New York: Library of America, 1997), 238.

23 On the dialectical relationship of images of fragmentation and corporeal wholeness, see Bill Brown, "Science Fiction, the World's Fair, and the Prosthetics of Empire," *Cultures of United States Imperialism*, ed. Amy Kaplan and Donald Pease (Durham: Duke University Press, 1993), 125–66.

24 Hal Foster, *Compulsive Beauty* (Cambridge, MA: MIT Press, 1993), 136.

25 Cited in Helen Harrison, *Dawn of a New Day: The New York World's Fair, 1939/40* (New York: Queens Museum, 1980), 108.

26 Siegfried Giedion, *Mechanization Takes Command* (New York: Oxford University Press, 1948), 41.

27 Lewis Mumford, "The Drama of the Machines," *Scribner's Magazine* 83:2 (August 1930): 150–61.

28 Hart Crane, *The Complete Poems and Selected Letters and Prose of Hart Crane*, ed. Brom Weber (New York: Doubleday, 1966), 261–62.

29 Cited in Joseph P. Cusker, "The World of Tomorrow: Science, Culture, and Community at the New York World's Fair," *Dawn of a New Day*, 4. Cusker notes that Mumford addressed the fair planners at a dinner in 1935, imploring them to make up for the failure of past expositions to demonstrate the "social and historical significance" of technological innovation.

30 *Ibid.*, 6.

31 See Robert W. Rydell, *World of Fairs: The Century-of-Progress Expositions* (University of Chicago Press, 1993), 139.

32 Giedion, *Mechanization*, 22. On Marey, for whom the metaphor of the body as machine was indispensable, see Anson Rabinbach, *The Human Motor: Energy, Fatigue, and the Origins of Modernity* (New York: Basic Books, 1990), 84–119; and Mary Anne Doane, "Temporality, Storage, Legibility: Freud, Marey and the Cinema," *Critical Inquiry* 22 (Winter 1996): 313–43.

33 See Giedion, *Mechanization*, 27 and Brown, "Science Fiction," 140–51.

34 The quotes from Paul Moss (the city commissioner of licenses) and Mayor LaGuardia respectively, are cited in Robert C. Allen, *Horrible Prettiness: Burlesque and American Culture* (Chapel Hill: University of North Carolina Press, 1991), 255–58. In April 1937 five female dancers at Minsky's Gotham Theatre were prosecuted on the grounds that they had given an obscene performance by undressing to the accompaniment of "soft music and softer lights." The theatre's license was revoked.

35 On the conflation of the feminine and the technological, see Andreas Huyssen, "The Vamp and the Machine: Fritz Lang's *Metropolis*," *After the Great Divide: Modernism, Mass Culture, and Postmodernism* (London: Macmillan, 1986), 65–81.

36 On the continuity between industrialized work and mechanized recreation, see Theodor Adorno and Max Horkheimer, *The Dialectic of Enlightenment*, trans. John Cummings (New York: Continuum, 1944), 137. The theorists do, however, acknowledge that "in the grotesque," which they also refer to as "pure amusement," the possibility of "negation does glimmer for a few moments." Such negation is for them the "extreme role" of art (142). See also Walter Benjamin, *Charles Baudelaire: A Lyric Poet in the Era of High Capitalism*, trans. Harry Zohn (New York: Verso, 1973), 131–38.

37 See Charles Musser, *The Emergence of Cinema: The American Screen to 1907* (Berkeley: University of California Press, 1990), 48–54.

38 Rabinbach, *The Human Motor*, 87.

39 Kathy Peiss notes that along the streets of New York City, arcades were "crammed with slot machines, phonographs, muscle-testing apparatus, automatic scales, and fortune-telling machines" (*Cheap Amusements: Working Women and Leisure in Turn-of-the-Century New York* [Philadelphia: Temple University Press, 1986], 145). See also David Noble, *Going Out: The Rise and Fall of Public Amusements* (New York: Harper Collins, 1996), 120–34; David Robinson, *From Peep Show to Palace: The Birth of American Film* (New York: Columbia University Press, 1996), 12–51; and Musser, *The Emergence of Cinema*, 55–89.

40 Linda Williams, *Hard Core: Power, Pleasure, and the "Frenzy of the Visible"* (Berkeley: University of California Press, 1989), 51.

41 Mark Seltzer, *Bodies and Machines* (New York: Routledge, 1992), 108.

42 *Ibid.*, 109.

43 Robert Forsythe, "In Defense of the Machine," *Culture and Commitment 1929–1945*, ed. Warren Susman (New York: George Braziller, 1973), 258–60.

44 Cecilia Tichi, *Shifting Gears: Technology, Literature, Culture in Modernist America* (Chapel Hill: University of North Carolina Press, 1987), 216.

45 Henry Miller, *Tropic of Capricorn* (New York: Grove Press, 1961), 284–85.
46 See Brown, "Science Fiction," 129–63; Mark Seltzer, "Serial Killers," *Differences* 5:2 (Spring 1993): 98–99; Mary Anne Doane, "Technology's Body: Cinematic Vision in Modernity," *Differences* 5:2 (Spring 1993): 3; Hal Foster, "Prosthetic Gods," *Modernism/Modernity* 4:2 (April 1997): 5–38; Tim Armstrong, *Modernism, Technology and the Body: A Cultural Study* (New York: Cambridge University Press, 1998), 70–105; and McLuhan, "The Gadget Lover: Narcissus as Narcosis," where the extension of various parts of the body through modern technology is characterized as "a kind of auto-amputation." Embracing the machine numbs perception (*Understanding Media*, 51–56).
47 James Agee, "Introduction" (1946), Helen Levitt, *A Way of Seeing* (Durham: Duke University Press, 1965), vii.
48 John Dos Passos, "Introduction to *Three Soldiers*," *John Dos Passos: The Nonfictional Prose*, ed. Donald Pizer (Detroit: Wayne State University Press, 1988), 146.
49 On Johnson, see Robert Palmer, *Deep Blues* (New York: Viking Press, 1981), 124–31.
50 Robert Johnson, "Phonograph Blues," *King of the Delta Blues Singers, Vol. II* (Columbia 30034).
51 The phrasing is Friedrich A. Kittler's. See *Gramophone, Film, Typewriter*, trans. Geoffrey Winthrop-Young and Michael Wurtz (Stanford University Press, 1999), 56. For an equally interesting, Depression-era take on the intimacy between human beings and phonographs, see William Saroyan's "1,2,3,4,5,6,7,8." In the story, the device and the character are curiously conflated. "The phonograph was pretty much himself. He had gotten into the machine and come out of it, singing . . ." (*The Daring Young Man on the Flying Trapeze and Other Stories* [New York: Random House, 1934], 75).
52 Though there has been much scholarly debate about this shift, most agree that the Communist Party's elimination of the John Reed Clubs and adoption of Popular Front strategies were determining events. Another was the Works Progress Administration's support of the development of the Federal Writers' Programs (FWPs). See Walter Rideout, *The Radical Novel in the United States: 1900–1954: Some Interrelations of Literature and Society* (Cambridge, MA: Harvard University Press, 1956); Daniel Aaron, *Writers on the Left: Episodes in American Literary Communism* (New York: Harcourt, Brace and World, 1961); James Gilbert, *Writers and Partisans: A History of Literary Radicalism in America* (New York: John Wiley, 1968); Lawrence Schwartz, *Marxism and Culture: The CPUSA and Aesthetics in the 1930s* (Port Washington, NY: Kennikat, 1980); Eric Homberger, *American Writers and Radical Politics, 1900–39: Equivocal Commitments* (New York: St. Martin's Press, 1986), and James Murphy, *The Proletarian Moment: The Controversy Over Leftism in Literature* (Chicago: University of Illinois Press, 1991). On the FWPs, see Jerre Mangione, *The Dream and the Deal: The Federal Writers' Project 1935–1943* (Boston: Little, Brown and Company, 1972).

53 Alfred Kazin, *On Native Grounds: An Interpretation of Modern American Prose Literature* (New York: Reynal and Hitchcock, 1942), 371. In the chapter on thirties fiction titled "The Revival of Naturalism" Kazin approvingly cites Dahlberg's *Do These Bones Live*.

54 *Ibid.*, 492, 496.

55 See also William Stott, *Documentary Expression and Thirties America* (New York: Oxford University Press, 1973). For a reassessment of this Depression-era trend, see Paula Rabinowitz, *They Must Be Represented: The Politics of Documentary* (New York: Verso, 1994), 35–104.

56 Barbara Foley, *Radical Representations: Politics and Form in U.S. Proletarian Fiction, 1929–1941* (Durham: Duke University Press, 1993), viii.

57 *Literature at the Barricades: The American Writer in the 1930s*, ed. Ralph Bogardus and Fred Hobson (University of Alabama Press, 1982), 3–4.

58 Ferraro's essay, "Avant-Garde Ethnics," mainly deals with Roth and Henry Miller. See *The Future of American Modernism: Ethnic Writing Between the Wars*, ed. William Boelhower (Amsterdam: Vu Press, 1990), 1–31. See also Marcus Klein, *Foreigners: The Making of American Literature 1900–1940* (University of Chicago Press, 1981), 18.

59 Michael Denning, *The Cultural Front: The Laboring of American Culture in the Twentieth Century* (New York: Verso, 1996), 122. My interest is more in the *leisuring* of American culture in the thirties.

60 *Ibid.*, 229.

61 *Ibid.*, 201. As Denning notes, there is precedent for his insight in Alfred Kazin's *Starting Out in the Thirties* (Boston: Little, Brown, 1965), 12–13.

62 Denning, *The Cultural Front*, 121. See also Tim Libretti, " 'What a Dirty Way of Getting Clean': The Grotesque in Proletarian Literature," where the grotesque is said to function "as the central strategy of cultural resistance" (*Literature and the Grotesque*, ed. Michael Meyer [Atlanta, GA: Rodopi, 1995], 175).

63 In *Voices of Persuasion: The Politics of Representation in 1930s America*, Michael Staub argues that a "number of thirties writers, precisely because of their encounters with disinherited peoples, anticipated dilemmas that poststructuralist theory would identify: an awareness of the contestedness of historical truth, and the impossibility of representing reality without being complicitous in its distortion" (New York: Cambridge University Press, 1994), x.

64 Thus Karen Jacobs juxtaposes Fredric Jameson and West in *The Eye's Mind: Literary Modernism and Visual Culture* (Ithaca: Cornell University Press, 2001), 243–63.

65 Caren Irr claims that Dos Passos adopts a "proto-poststructuralist position" on history and national culture. *The Suburb of Dissent: Cultural Politics in the United States and Canada During the 1930s* (Durham: Duke University Press, 1998), 66.

66 Ishmael Reed, *Yellow Back Radio Broke-Down* (Normal, IL: Dalkey Archive Press, 2000), 34–35.

67 Tom Gunning, "The Cinema of Attractions: Early Film, its Spectator and the Avant-Garde," *Early Cinema: Space-Frame-Narrative*, ed. Thomas Elsaesser

and Adam Barker (London: British Film Institute, 1990), 56–62; and "An Aesthetic of Astonishment: Early Film and the (In)Credulous Spectator," *Art and Text* (Spring 1989): 36. See also Rosalind Krauss, "The Im/pulse to See," *Vision and Visuality*, ed. Hal Foster (Seattle: Bay Press, 1988), 51–78.

68 An alternative way of framing the present inquiry would be to say that it traces the adventures of the historical or anti-modernist avant-garde in the United States. Indeed, the American writers on whom I focus shared the formal and functional priorities of European movements like Dada and surrealism (as theorized by Peter Bürger) at the compositional levels of imagery (dreamscapes, corporeal fragmentation, automatons) and technique (collage/montage) and in terms of radical ambition (to integrate art into the praxis of everyday life and political existence). See *Theory of the Avant-Garde*, trans. Michael Shaw (Minneapolis: University of Minnesota Press, 1984). Put differently, if "in [Walter] Benjamin's work of the 1930s . . . the hidden dialectic between avantgarde art and the utopian hope for an emancipatory mass culture can be grasped alive for the last time," comparable aspirations were operative in Dahlberg's and Miller's, as well as (with critical reservations) West's and Dos Passos' Depression-era outputs. See Andreas Huyssen, "The Hidden Dialectic: Avantgarde – Technology – Mass Culture," *Great Divide*, 14.

1 DISINTERRING EDWARD DAHLBERG

1 Edward Dahlberg, *Do These Bones Live* (New York: Harcourt, Brace and Company, 1941), 28.

2 See *Edward Dahlberg: American Ishmael of Letters*, ed. Harold Billings (Austin: Roger Beacham, 1968) and *Edward Dahlberg: A Tribute*, ed. Jonathan Williams (New York: David Lewis, 1970).

3 In their wide-ranging accounts of the period, Barbara Foley, *Radical Representations: Politics and Form in U.S. Proletarian Fiction, 1929–1941* (Durham: Duke University Press, 1993) and Michael Denning, *The Cultural Front: The Laboring of American Culture in the Twentieth Century* (New York: Verso, 1996) mention Dahlberg only in passing.

4 James Agee, "Comedy's Greatest Era" (1949), *Agee on Film: Reviews and Comments* (Boston: Beacon Press, 1958), 6. For Henry Miller's brief appreciation of slapstick film, see "The Golden Age," *The Cosmological Eye* (New York: New Directions, 1939), 54.

5 Miller, "Golden Age," 7.

6 Andreas Huyssen, "The Vamp and the Machine: Fritz Lang's *Metropolis*," *After the Great Divide: Modernism, Mass Culture and Postmodernism* (London: Macmillan, 1986), 71.

7 Edward Dahlberg, *Bottom Dogs, From Flushing to Calvary, Those Who Perish, and Hitherto Unpublished and Uncollected Works*, ed. Harold Billings (New York: Minerva Press, 1976), 16.

8 Fredric Jameson, *Postmodernism; or, The Cultural Logic of Late Capitalism* (Durham: Duke University Press, 1991), 34.

9 See Lynne Kirby, "Male Hysteria and Early Cinema," *Male Trouble*, ed. Constance Penley and Sharon Willis (Minneapolis: University of Minnesota Press, 1993), 67–85 and Wolfgang Schivelbusch, *The Railway Journey: The Industrialization of Time and Space in the 19th Century* (New York: Berg, 1977), 113–23.

10 On the reductive figuration of human beings as puppets, marionettes, and automata as a grotesque strategy, see Wolfgang Kayser, *The Grotesque in Art and Literature*, trans. Ulrich Weisstein (Bloomington: Indiana University Press, 1963), 183–95.

11 Roger Caillois, "Mimicry and Legendary Psychasthenia," trans. John Shepley, *October* 31 (Winter 1984): 30–32.

12 *Bottom Dogs* is a modestly carnivalized autobiographical novel that examines the central role recreational pleasures played in the early decades of twentieth-century America in the daily life of inhabitants of marginal communities. I pass over it here because it concentrates on non-mechanized forms of commercial entertainment, whereas its follow-up, *From Flushing to Calvary*, takes up the corporeal implications of more technologically mediated amusements. The latter is thus the better point of access to the somatic and psychic ramifications of indulging in modernized pleasures.

13 Edward Dahlberg, *Samuel Beckett's Wake and Other Uncollected Prose* (Elmwood Park, IL: Dalkey Archive Press, 1989), 4.

14 No wonder Denning, who develops the category of the "ghetto pastoral" to account for the generic specificity of Depression-era "plebian" writing, ignores Dahlberg, who, from a sociological perspective, belongs in the category. See *The Cultural Front*, 230–58.

15 That Dahlberg fails to mention T.S. Eliot as a precursor here seems a textbook example of the anxiety of influence.

16 See Bill Brown, *The Material Unconscious: American Amusement, Stephen Crane, and the Economies of Play* (Cambridge, MA: Harvard University Press, 1996), 216 and Susan Stewart, *On Longing: Narratives of the Miniature, the Gigantic, the Souvenir, the Collection* (Durham: Duke University Press, 1993), 108–11. On the dime museum, see Brooks McNamara, "'A Congress of Wonders': The Rise and Fall of the Dime Museum," *Emerson Society Quarterly* 20 (1974): 216–32; Robert Bogdan, *Freak Show: Presenting Human Oddities for Amusement and Profit* (University of Chicago Press, 1988), 35–39; and Andrea Stulman Dennett, *Weird and Wonderful: The Dime Museum in America* (New York University Press, 1997).

17 Robert E. Snow and David E. Wright, "Coney Island: A Case Study in Popular Culture and Technical Change," *Journal of Popular Culture* 9 (1976): 960.

18 Henri Bergson, "Laughter," *Comedy*, ed. Wylie Sypher (Baltimore: Johns Hopkins University Press, 1956), 79. For a productive application of Bergson's theory to silent screen comedy, see Gerald Nast, *The Comic Mind: Comedy and the Movies* (2nd ed.; University of Chicago Press, 1979), 50–51. Dahlberg's

grotesque aesthetic might also be profitably juxtaposed with Freud's "The Uncanny" (1919). See Mary Russo, "Two Kinds of Grotesque: Carnival and Uncanny," *The Female Grotesque: Risk, Excess and Modernity* (New York: Routledge, 1994), 7.

19 Charles DeFanti, *The Wages of Expectation: A Biography of Edward Dahlberg* (New York University Press, 1973), 113.

20 Robert Toll, in whose *The Entertainment Machine: American Show Business in the Twentieth Century* I first encountered this photograph, remarks in its caption that "the 1890's phonographs began the revolution in home entertainment" (New York: Oxford University Press, 1982).

21 In *Bottom Dogs*, Dahlberg notes that the graphophone played songs while "colored still slides" were shown on "the white curtain" at a local movie house (*Works*, 170). Alexander Graham Bell named his version of the invention by reversing the syllables of Edison's machine. See David Nasaw, *The Rise and Fall of Public Amusements* (New York: Harper Collins, 1993), 120–21. Friedrich A. Kittler points out that the graphophone was also a Columbia brand name. He locates the origin of part of the analogical equation under investigation in the psychophysical work of Jean Marie Guyau, who, in "Memory and Phonograph" (1880) embraces "the phonograph as the only suitable model for visualizing the brain or memory" (*Gramophone, Film, Typewriter*, trans. Geoffrey Winthrop-Young and Michael Wurtz [Stanford University Press, 1999], 33, 55.)

22 Edward Dahlberg, "Graphophone Nickelodeon Days," *Samuel Beckett*, 306.

23 James Agee and Walker Evans, *Let Us Now Praise Famous Men* (Boston: Houghton Mifflin, 1941), 234. On the privileged representational status of the camera in Depression-era prose, see Alfred Kazin, *On Native Grounds: An Interpretation of Modern American Prose Literature* (New York: Reynal and Hitchcock, 1942), 489 and Miles Orvell, *The Real Thing: Imitation and Authenticity in American Culture, 1880–1940* (Chapel Hill: University of North Carolina Press, 1989), 198–239.

24 Kittler, *Gramophone*, 16.

25 I ignore the ambiguities of the minstrel show as a sociocultural phenomenon because the performance appears here as a wholly positive, joyous event. For a more complex account of the entertainment, see Eric Lott, *Love and Theft: Blackface Minstrelsy and the American Working Class* (New York: Oxford University Press, 1993). See "Carnival" in Langston Hughes' *Not Without Laughter* (1930) for a brief yet critically nuanced recollection of a minstrel performance (New York: Macmillan Publishing Company, 1969), 106–08.

26 Brown, *Material*, 143.

27 See Lewis Erenberg, *Steppin' Out: New York Nightlife and the Transformation of American Culture, 1890–1930* (Westport: Greenwood Press, 1981), 233–36.

28 Julia Kristeva, *The Powers of Horror: An Essay on Abjection*, trans. Leon S. Roudiez (New York: Columbia University Press, 1982), 5.

29 Edward Dahlberg, *From Flushing to Calvary* (New York: Harcourt, Brace and Company, 1932), 4.

30 Willie is operating a mutoscope, a device that improved upon the kineto-scope by enabling the viewer to control the flow of images by manually turning the crank. This less automated mode of projection increased the intimacy between patron and his mechanical source of pleasure. Nasaw, *Public Amusements*, 133.

31 For a while the x-ray machine was "all the rage" at amusement parlors until Edison's assistants learned that exposure to its radiation ulcerated human flesh, caused hair loss and death. *Ibid.*, 127.

32 In *Amusing the Millions: Coney Island at the Turn of the Century*, John Kasson notes, in the context of a discussion of Joseph Stella's "Battle of Lights, Mardi Gras, Coney Island," that mardi-gras night was a post-Labor Day celebration ([New York: Hill and Wang, 1978], 88–90). The painting, from 1913, strives to replicate the same "carnal frenzy" that Dahlberg would attempt to capture in literary form two decades later.

33 The phrases are Brown's, *Material*, 46. He is discussing a reporter's turn-of-the-century response to the pleasures of Coney Island's mechanical rides.

34 See Stewart, *On Longing*, 107–11. For a Depression-era impression of carnival freak show performers as the happily oblivious objects of the spectatorial gaze, see Thomas Wolfe's "Gulliver." "Each day the world throngs in to sit beneath the canvas top and feed its fascinated eye on their deformities, and they [the freaks] display themselves before that world and are not moved by interest, touched by desire, from what they see of it" (Thomas Wolfe, "Gulliver," *Short Stories* [New York: Penguin, 1947], 95).

35 Kenneth Burke, "The Philosophy of Literary Form," *The Philosophy of Literary Form: Studies in Symbolic Form* (1941; 3rd rev. ed.; Berkeley: University of California Press, 1973), 45. Notably, Burke asserts that such transference draws upon or corresponds to the attitude of the child to the parent.

36 Peter Stallybrass and Allon White, *The Politics and Poetics of Transgression* (Ithaca: Cornell University Press, 1986), 171–90.

37 Paul de Man, "Reading and History," *The Resistance to Theory* (Minneapolis: University of Minnesota Press, 1986), 68.

38 The incorrect citation is, as mentioned above (Introduction, note 1), from Ezekiel. Kristeva analyzes this and other Old Testament books in her essay on abjection. See *Power of Horror*, 90–112.

39 In contrast, for Walt Whitman, in the "Preface" to *Leaves of Grass*, the "great poet" drags "the dead out of their coffins and stands them again on their feet" (New York: Viking, 1959), 12.

40 Stewart, *On Longing*, 140.

41 Walter Benjamin, *The Origin of German Tragic Drama*, trans. John Osborne (London: Verso, 1977), 138–58.

42 On the tropological conflation of the linguistic and the anatomical, the grammatical and the skeletal, see Marjorie Garber, "Out of Joint," *The Body in Parts: Fantasies of Corporeality in Early Modern Europe*, ed. David Hilman and Carla Mazzio (New York: Routledge, 1997), 34–35.

43 That there is great deal at stake in the death of the mother is suggested by the striking swerve from biographical fact that occurs at this moment in the text. While her fictional surrogate passes away at the end of the novel, Dahlberg's actual mother (also nicknamed Lizzie) lived until 1946 (DeFanti, *Wages*, 158).

44 Friedrich Kittler, *Discourse Networks 1800/1900*, trans. Michael Metteer with Chris Cullens (Stanford University Press, 1990), 248.

45 On the performative dimensions of Olson's poetry and its relation to the thirties, see Michael Szalay, *New Deal Modernism: American Literature and the Invention of the Welfare State* (Durham: Duke University Press, 2000), 256–71.

46 Brown, *Material*, 241.

47 Given his dissatisfaction with his own innovations, it is not surprising that Dahlberg soon gave up on the novel. His last was *Those Who Perish* (1934), a hastily composed, anti-fascist narrative designed to take advantage of Dahlberg's notoriety after a Nazi beat him up while visiting Germany. The book does, however, depict a marvelously vicious game of Ping-Pong between two characters reportedly based on Dahlberg and Kenneth Burke.

48 See also Dahlberg's 1952 review of Lewis Mumford's *Art and Technics*. "The evil genius," Dahlberg writes, "of mechanical pastimes is very apparent. The American entertainments are no longer rustic or communal, a river picnic, the buggy ride, or Sunday in the park, but tend to be of a solitary character. Modern man gets his recreation from the electric devil-boxes, the radio, the television, and the movies. What a mournful people are the Americans, said Maxim Gorki, who have to get their entertainment out of mechanical amusements" (Dahlberg, *Samuel Beckett*, 288).

2 LAUGHTER AND DEPRESSION: HENRY MILLER AND THE EMERGENCE OF THE TECHNOCARNIVALESQUE

1 Henry Miller, *Tropic of Capricorn* (New York: Grove Press, 1961), 205.

2 Neil Hertz, "Medusa's Head: Male Hysteria Under Political Pressure," *The End of the Line: Essays on Psychoanalysis and the Sublime* (New York: Columbia University Press, 1985), 61–215.

3 On the affinities and differences between Bakhtin and Lacan, see Robert Stam, *Subversive Pleasures: Bakhtin, Cultural Criticism, and Film* (Baltimore: Johns Hopkins University Press, 1989), 4–6.

4 This set, from which Miller draws much of his rhetorical repertoire, consists of "images of castration, mutilation, dismemberment, dislocation, evisceration, devouring, [and] bursting open of the body," Jacques Lacan, "Aggressivity in Psychoanalysis," *Écrits*, trans. Alan Sheridan (New York: W.W. Norton, 1977), 11. On the masochistic dimensions of the drive to shatter the self, see Leo Bersani, "Sexuality and Aesthetics," *October* 28 (Spring 1984): 27–42.

5 For a reading of Miller's oeuvre in its entirety from this perspective, see John Parkin, *Henry Miller: The Modern Rabelais* (Lewiston, NY: Edwin Mellen Press,

Notes to pages 75–78

1990). On modern department stores as "refined Coney Islands," see William R. Leach, "Transformations in a Culture of Consumption: Women and Department Stores, 1890–1925," *The Journal of American History* 71:2 (1984): 324. On the association of shopping and femininity, see Rachel Bowlby, *Just Looking: Consumer Culture in Dreiser, Gissing, and Zola* (New York: Methuen, 1985), 18–35.

6 Mikhail Bakhtin, *Rabelais and His World*, trans. Helen Iswolsky (Bloomington: Indiana University Press, 1984), 367. In 1940 (one year after *Capricorn* was first published) Bakhtin submitted a version of his study as a thesis to the Gorky Institute of World Literature in Moscow.

7 In fact, Miller interpreted Freud's impact on the world through a carnival lens. In "An Open Letter to Surrealists Everywhere," his "contribution to the cause of human enlightenment" is characterized as "creative and anarchic"; Freud "turned the world upside down," though his disciples are "struggling to put the world back on its feet again." Miller, *The Cosmological Eye* (New York: New Directions, 1939), 168–69.

8 Mark Seltzer, *Bodies and Machines* (New York: Routledge, 1992), 95–97, 103–13, 155–62.

9 *Ibid.*, 108.

10 See Donna Haraway, "A Manifesto for Cyborgs: Science, Technology and Socialist Feminism in the Late Twentieth Century," *Simians, Cyborgs, and Women: The Reinvention of Nature* (New York: Routledge, 1991), 149–81; and Donna Haraway, "The Promises of Monsters: A Regenerative Politics for Inappropriate/d Others," *Cultural Studies*, ed. Lawrence Grossberg, Cary Nelson, Paula Triechler (New York: Routledge, 1992), 295–337. See also Matthew Brio, "The Man as Cyborg: Figures of Technology in Weimar Visual Culture," *New German Critique* 62 (Spring–Summer, 1994): 71–110.

11 By suggesting the positive interest Miller's writing might have for a feminist politics, I do not intend a polemical dismissal of feminist critiques of his work. My claim is that despite the overtly (thematically) misogynistic aspects of his enterprise, his writing has an intriguingly transgressive dimension when it comes to conventional gender distinctions and common notions of sexual/anatomical difference. Conversely, despite the possibility of reading Dos Passos as having made a progressive contribution to feminist thought in terms of characterization, I find his gendered understanding of writing as fundamentally masculine in need of serious scrutiny (see Chapter 4). On the "Phallic Miller" see *Critical Essays: Henry Miller*, ed. Ronald Gottesman (New York: G.K. Hall, 1992), 131–77, especially the excerpt from Kate Millet's *Sexual Politics*. For a more critical assessment than mine of "imaginary male femininity," see Andreas Huyssen, "Mass Culture as Woman: Modernism's Other," *After the Great Divide: Modernism, Mass Culture and Postmodernism* (London: Macmillan, 1986), 44–62.

12 Henry Miller, *Tropic of Cancer* (New York: Grove Press, 1961), 254.

13 Agee uses the phonograph as a directive for reading as a similarly masochistic experience. "Turn it as loud as you can get it. Then get down on the floor and jam your ear as close into the loudspeaker as you can get it." "If it hurts you, be glad of it," James Agee and Walker Evans, *Let Us Now Praise Famous Men* (Boston: Houghton Mifflin, 1941), 15–16. Like Miller, Dahlberg, and Algren, Agee's radicalism coincided with a commitment to a kind of aesthetic masochism, whereas, as we will see, for West and Dos Passos, politicizing literature required the development of more sadistic techniques of critical writing in which, ultimately, it was the body of other texts that was made to suffer.

14 On modernity and shock, see among many others, Mary Anne Doane, "Technology's Body: Cinematic Vision in Modernity," *Differences* 5:2 (Spring 1993): 6–15; and Ben Singer, "Modernity, Hyperstimulus, and the Rise of Popular Sensationalism," *Cinema and the Invention of Modern Life*, ed. Leo Charney and Vanessa Schwartz (Berkeley: University of California Press, 1995), 72–99.

15 On neurasthenia and modernity, see Anson Rabinbach, *The Human Motor: Energy, Fatigue and the Origins of Modernity* (New York: Basic Books, 1990), 153–63.

16 Antonin Artaud, *The Theatre and its Double*, trans. Mary Caroline Richards (New York: Grove Weidenfeld Press, 1938), 86.

17 On religious martyrdom or saintly penitence, which Miller's stance evokes, see Stephen Greenblatt, "Mutilation and Meaning," *The Body in Parts: Fantasies of Corporeality in Early Modern Europe*, ed. David Hilman and Carla Mazzio (New York: Routledge, 1997), 220–41. See also *The Grotesque in Art and Literature: Theological Reflections*, ed. James Luther Adams and Wilson Yates (Grand Rapids, MI: William B. Eerdmans, 1997).

18 On Dostoevski and the carnivalesque, see Mikhail Bakhtin, *Problems of Dostoevsky's Poetics*, trans. Caryl Emerson (Minneapolis: University of Minnesota Press, 1984), 106–80.

19 Michel Foucault, *Discipline and Punish: The Birth of the Prison*, trans. Alan Sheridan (New York: Random House, 1995), 65–69.

20 On modernist implementations of the rhetoric of "electro-vitalism" as a model for bodily processes, and – after Whitman – for "literary transmission," see Tim Armstrong, *Modernism, Technology and the Body: A Cultural Study* (Cambridge University Press, 1998), 13–41.

21 Classifying Miller as a late modernist tends to obscure his debt to mass amusements. See Jeffrey Bartlett, "The Late Modernist," *Critical Essays: Henry Miller*, 315–28; and Donald Pizer, *American Expatriate Writing and the Paris Moment: Modernism and Place* (Baton Rouge: Louisiana State University Press, 1996), 123–39.

22 Hart Crane, "The Bridge," *Complete Poems and Selected Letters and Prose of Hart Crane*, ed. Brom Weber (New York: Doubleday, 1966), 101–02.

23 For an appreciation of the "aesthetic significance of burlesk with a k," see E.E. Cummings, "You Aren't Mad, Am I?" This piece can be found, as

can two other mid twenties *Vanity Fair* articles on the therapeutic value of the circus and Coney Island respectively, in E.E. Cummings, *A Miscellany Revised*, ed. George Firmage (New York: October House, 1965), 126–31, 109–14, 149–53.

24 Leon Lewis, *Henry Miller: The Major Writings* (New York: Schocken Books, 1986), 104.

25 *Ibid.*, 109.

26 Henry Miller, *Black Spring* (New York: Grove Press, 1963), 163.

27 Miller's Depression-era achievement in its entirety was, however, made possible by the existence of an alternative mode of literary production. Without Jack Kahane and Obelisk Press, much of Miller's writing would doubtless have remained unpublished. See Hugh Ford, *Published in Paris: A Literary Chronicle of Paris in the 1920s and 1930s* (New York: Macmillan, 1975), 345–84.

28 In "The Universe of Death," Miller praises the contemporary avant-gardes for their "stress on humor" as "part of a conscious and deliberate attitude toward breaking down the old ideologies" but finds Swift to be a more "formidable Surrealist" than such "feeble iconoclasts." See Miller, *Cosmological Eye*, 130–31. On Miller and surrealism, see Gay Louise Balliet, *Henry Miller and the Surrealist Metaphor: "Riding the Ovarian Trolley"* (New York: Peter Lang, 1996) and Caroline Blinder, *A Self-Made Surrealist: Ideology and Aesthetics in the Work of Henry Miller* (New York: Camden House, 2000), and Miller's "Letter to Surrealists" where he recalls visiting an exhibition of surrealist painting, a "festival of the Unconscious" that provoked a nostalgia for "The Dime Museum," (Miller, *Cosmological Eye*, 172–73). European avant-garde and American amusement were for him associated because both brought grotesque images ("the organs of the human body," "the hungry, gnawing innards of man") up "from the depths" and incongruously altered these "hysterical phantoms" to fit other entities – hence Dali's "horse with the motorized sex organs."

29 That in the passage Miller mentions only Dreamland whereas the ride was actually at Luna Park is fitting given the stress on dreaming throughout "Fourteenth Ward." John Kasson notes that Dreamland featured a Lilliputian village with 300 midgets. Dreamland burned to the ground in 1911 and was never rebuilt (*Amusing the Millions: Coney Island at the Turn of the Century* [New York: Hill and Wang, 1978], 86, 110). On the Dragon's Gorge, see *Ibid.*, 64–65 and Kathy Peiss, *Cheap Amusements: Working Women and Leisure in Turn-of-the-Century New York* (Philadelphia: Temple University Press, 1986), 130. For a comparably nostalgic, Depression-era recollection of public amusement as stimulating magical experiences for children, see Thomas Wolfe, "Circus at Dawn," *Short Stories* (New York: Penguin, 1947), 32–37.

30 On the outraged responses in the United States to burlesque in the late 1860s, see Robert C. Allen, *Horrible Prettiness: Burlesque and American Culture* (Chapel Hill: University of North Carolina Press, 1991), 121–37.

31 Bernard Sobel, *A Pictorial History of Burlesque* (New York: G.P. Putnam's Sons, 1956), 53. See also Irving Zeidman, *The American Burlesque Show* (New York: Hawthorn Books, 1967), 218–35.

32 In *Cancer* Miller contemplates female sexual experience with some difficulty. "I find myself wondering what it feels like, during intercourse, to be a woman – whether the pleasure is keener, etc. Try to imagine something penetrating my groin, but have only a vague sensation of pain" (76).

33 *Letters to Emil*, ed. George Wickes (New York: New Directions, 1988), 155. For a review of burlesque at the National Winter Garden in the twenties, one that finds it superior to "the hideous, comic-supplement humors of uptown revue and vaudeville" and "the mechanical routine of Broadway," see Edmund Wilson, "Burlesque Shows," *The Shores of Light: A Literary Chronicle of the Twenties and Thirties* (New York: Farrar, Straus and Young, 1952), 274–81.

34 Jay Martin, *Always Merry and Bright: The Life of Henry Miller* (Santa Barbara: Capra Press, 1978), 284.

35 See also Henry Miller, *Hamlet Letters*: "If you are an artist, that means that you are denuding yourself more and more, that by the time you die you are stark naked and your bowels turned inside out," ed. Michael Hargraves (Santa Barbara: Capra Press, 1981), 152. This text, written in collaboration with Michael Fraenkel, consists of a series of critical letters loosely organized around Shakespeare's play.

36 For a later assessment of this performer, see Henry Miller, *Sexus* (New York: Grove Press, 1965), 468–89.

37 In *Low Life* Luc Sante mentions that one of the dime museum attractions was a machine designed to give customers electric shocks (New York: Random House, 1991), 100.

38 Gilles Deleuze and Felix Guattari, *Anti-Oedipus: Capitalism and Schizophrenia*, trans. Robert Hurley, Mark Seem, and Helen R. Lane (Minneapolis: University of Minnesota Press, 1983), 22.

39 *Ibid.*, 298. For a differently oriented critique of this remark, see Peter Stallybrass and Allon White, *The Politics and Poetics of Transgression* (Ithaca: Cornell University Press, 1986), 190.

40 Presumably, Moldorf's precursors include the medieval clown Bakhtin mentions under the names of Morolf and Marcolf. See Bakhtin, *Rabelais*, 20. On the incarnations of this figure in the English Renaissance, see Paul Semonin, "Monsters in the Marketplace: The Exhibition of Human Oddities in Early Modern England," *Cultural Spectacles of the Extraordinary Body*, ed. Rosemarie Garland Thomson (New York University Press, 1996), 80.

41 On the gruesome variant of the cultural institution, see Brooks McNamara, "'A Congress of Wonders': The Rise and Fall of the Dime Museum," *Emerson Society Quarterly* 20 (1974): 222–23. "Case after case," in these "museums of anatomy," "displayed gaping sores and hideous deformities attributed to various venereal diseases."

42 Georges Bataille, "Un-Knowing: Laughter and Tears," *October* 36 (Spring 1986): 90. Bataille's assessment of Miller's accomplishment is discussed by

Gilles Mayne in *Eroticism in Georges Bataille and Henry Miller* (Birmingham, AL: Summa, 1993).

43 *Capricorn* was a project Miller struggled to complete throughout the decade. In it he incorporates autobiographical materials he used previously in *Crazy Cock* and *Clipped Wings*. The first depicts his domestic experiences with June Smith; the second is a failed attempt to compose a Horatio Alger novel with Western Union Telegraph messengers as the book's protagonists.

44 Klaus Theweleit *Male Fantasies*, trans. Erica Carter and Chris Turner, 2 vols. (Minneapolis: University of Minnesota Press, 1987 and 1989), I, 229–300. Theweleit views Miller as a writer who does *not* close himself off to the flows of desire.

45 Cited in Gunther Barth, *City People: The Rise of Modern City Culture in Nineteenth-Century America* (New York: Oxford University Press, 1980), 199.

46 Allen, *Horrible Prettiness*, 183. As Allen sees it, the eventual assimilation of burlesque by vaudeville constitutes "another chapter in the history of the consolidation of the American bourgeoisie," 180–93. On vaudeville as an effort to mediate between high and low culture via an emphasis on purity and refinement, see M. Alison Kibler, *Rank Ladies: Gender and Cultural Hierarchy in American Vaudeville* (Chapel Hill: University of North Carolina Press, 1999), 23–55; David Nasaw, *The Rise and Fall of Public Amusements* (New York: Harper Collins, 1993), 19–33; and Albert F. McLean Jr., *American Vaudeville as Ritual* (University of Kentucky Press, 1965).

47 For the sake of my argument, Miller should have experienced his rebirth at Keith's New Boston Theatre, where the dynamo "rivaled the stage for attention." Upon entering this vaudeville house one passed down a marble staircase to the basement power station. In the reception hall a vast switchboard confronted the would-be vaudeville spectator. The visitor's gaze was then directed to the generators and engines in the main room, a "wondershop" of "swiftly moving steel," which to one observer surpassed all its rivals in terms of "elegance, utility, beauty, and artistic worth" (Barth, *City People*, 228).

48 Hal Foster, "Armor Fou," *October* 56 (Spring, 1991): 85; and Theweleit, *Fantasies*, II, 197–206.

49 Foster, "Armor Fou," 85.

50 My assessment of *Capricorn* hardly constitutes an exhaustive account of the manifestations of the monstrous in the text. See his hallucinatory description of a visit to Roseland dance hall (*Capricorn*, 104–09); and the passage that contains the following: "I see myself sitting before a table in the day, my hands and feet growing enormous, as though elephantiasis were over taking me at a gallop . . . my hands have become like the shapeless feet of the rhinoceros." "I am going to spread and spread until I fill the room with one solid mass of stiff jelly," (246).

51 Miriam Hansen, "Of Mice and Ducks: Benjamin and Adorno on Disney," *South Atlantic Quarterly* 92:1 (Winter 1993): 38, 42, 57.

52 Haraway, "Promises," 314.

53 The distinction between mechanization and machinism derives from Deleuze and Guattari. Machinism is for them a mode of unconscious production whereby parts are attached to other parts without concern for wholes. These temporary conjunctions are subsequently replaced by different connections, and it is in this manner that desires are satisfied. Mechanization in contrast involves closed systems made up of immobile sections. Here the crossing of systems or mixing of them together does not occur. Miller's method of plugging literature into a series of amusements, his conjoining of autobiography and various recreations, thus justifies a characterization of his body of writing as a machine assemblage. (Admittedly, my use of the term mechanization throughout the present study does not respect the conceptually rigorous distinction this note articulates.) See also Theweleit, *Fantasies*, I, 211.

54 Haraway, "Manifesto," 151.

55 Cited in David Gelertner, *1939: The Lost World of the Fair* (New York: The Free Press, 1995), 270.

INTERMISSION: VULGAR MARXISM

1 Meyer Levin, *The Old Bunch* (New York: Viking Press, 1937), 949.

2 *Ibid.*, 940.

3 Joe's aims are in line with a main trend in World's Fair statuary. See Burton Benedict, "The Anthropology of World's Fairs," *The Anthropology of World's Fairs: San Francisco's Panama Pacific International Exposition of 1915* (Berkeley: Scolar Press, 1983), 16–17, 34–35; and Bill Brown, "Science Fiction, the World's Fair, and the Prosthetics of Empire," *Cultures of United States Imperialism*, ed. Amy Kaplan and Donald Pease (Durham: Duke University Press, 1993), 140–51.

4 Levin, *Old Bunch*, 959.

5 Edward Dahlberg, *Do These Bones Live* (New York: Harcourt, Brace and Company, 1941), 51.

6 Kenneth Burke, "Revolutionary Symbolism in America," *American Writers' Congress*, ed. Henry Hart (New York: International Publishers, 1935), 87–94. On the contemporaneous reception of Burke's Marxism as the "discourse of excrement," see Frank Lentricchia, *Criticism and Social Change* (University of Chicago Press, 1983), 22.

7 Robert W. Rydell, *World of Fairs: The Century-of-Progress Expositions* (University of Chicago Press, 1993), 119.

8 This is from a journal entry Algren made while awaiting trial in a Texas jail after having stolen a typewriter. Bettina Drew, *Nelson Algren: A Life on the Wild Side* (Austin: University of Texas Press, 1989), 67.

9 Peter Stallybrass, "Marx and Heterogeneity: Thinking the Lumpenproletariat," *Representations* 31 (Summer, 1990): 69–95; Peter Stallybrass and Allon White, *The Politics and Poetics of Transgression* (Ithaca: Cornell University Press, 1986), chapter 3, esp. 129.

10 Georges Bataille, "The Psychological Structure of Fascism," *Vision of Excess: Selected Writings,1927–1939*, trans. Allan Stoekl (Minneapolis: University of Minnesota Press, 1985), 137–60.

11 Stallybrass, "Marx," 81, takes issue with Jeffrey Mehlman's competing interpretation of the lumpenproletariat in *Revolution and Repetition* (Berkeley: University of California Press, 1977) as a third term that subversively dislocates dialectical oppositions.

12 The italicized words are all etymologically legitimate meanings of fascism. See Bataille, "Structure of Fascism," 149.

13 Edward Dahlberg, *From Flushing to Calvary* (New York: Harcourt, Brace and Company, 1932), 86.

14 Albert Halper's *Union Square* (1933) begins with a serious rendering of such an event.

15 Edward Dahlberg, "From Flushing to Calvary," *Samuel Beckett's Wake and Other Uncollected Prose* (Elmwood, IL: Dalkey Archive Press, 1989), 221.

16 *Richard Wright: Early Works* (New York: Library of America, 1991), 866.

17 *Ibid.*, 865.

18 *Ibid.*, 867.

19 Richard Wright, "Introduction" to Nelson Algren, *Never Come Morning* (London: Neville Spearman, 1958), vii.

20 The citation that precedes the third part is well-known: "The 'dangerous class,' the social scum (lumpenproletariat), that passively rotting mass thrown off by the lowest layers of old society, may, here and there, be swept into the movement by a proletarian revolution; its conditions of life, however, prepare it far more for the part of a bribed tool of reactionary intrigue" (Nelson Algren, *Somebody in Boots* [New York: Thunder's Mouth Press, 1987]).

21 See also Algren's short story, "A Lumpen," *New Masses* 2 (July 1935): 19.

22 The original title was rejected because a presidential candidate was using it as a campaign slogan at the time (Drew, *Nelson Algren*, 83).

23 Wright's posthumously published first novel *Lawd Today!*, completed in the mid 1930s and submitted to publishers under the title "Cesspool," is indispensable in regard to understanding the Depression-era radical writer's complex attitude toward the American lumpenproletariat, the mind of which, the text's original title implies, is like an underground reservoir of waste.

24 On the combination of existentialism and naturalism in Algren, see James Giles, *Confronting the Horror: The Novels of Nelson Algren* (Kent: Ohio State University Press, 1989), 24–37.

25 Rydell, *World of Fairs*, 101–02.

26 Dahlberg, *Samuel Beckett*, 3.

27 The citations are from Georges Bataille, "The 'Old Mole' and the Prefix *Sur* in the Words *Surhomme* [Superman] and *Surrealist*," *Visions of Excess*, 36–37.

28 See Stallybrass and White, *Politics and Poetics*, 18–19, 52–53.

29 See Drew, *Nelson Algren*, 83.

30 Algren is presumably referring to the *Chicago Tribune*. In *The Lords of the Press*, George Seldes concludes that there exists "no newspaper which is so vicious

and stupid in its attack on labor" as the *Tribune*, "no paper so consistent in its Red-baiting, and no paper in my opinion is such a great enemy of the American people" (New York: Julian Messner, 1938), 47.

31 On the ideological fear of syphilis as a contagious mass that "produces another mass: a seething mound of rotting flesh," see Klaus Theweleit, *Male Fantasies*, trans. Erica Carter and Chris Turner, 2 vols. (Minneapolis: University of Minnesota Press, 1987 and 1989), II, 17. Algren consciously plays on such fears for radical purposes.

32 The juxtaposition of Sandburg and Algren was suggested to me by Carlo Rotella's discussion in *October Cities* (Berkeley: University of California Press, 1998) of the importance of the poem to Chicago's identity.

33 Carl Sandburg, "Chicago," *Chicago Poems* (New York: Henry Holt, 1916), 3–4.

34 See Lauren Berlant, *The Anatomy of National Fantasy: Hawthorne, Utopia, and Everyday Life* (University of Chicago Press, 1991), 27–28.

35 Rydell, *World of Fairs*, 9.

36 On the Depression-era technocratic faith in science as a progressive force, see Andrew Ross, *Strange Weather: Culture, Science, and Technology in the Age of Limits* (New York: Verso, 1991), 101–35.

37 On "ersatz or degraded carnivals" that serve primarily elite interests, see Robert Stam, *Subversive Pleasures: Bakhtin, Cultural Criticism and Film* (Baltimore: Johns Hopkins University Press, 1989), 92–121.

38 Bataille, "The 'Old Mole',"35.

3 FASCISM AND FRAGMENTATION IN NATHANAEL WEST

1 McWilliams later reported that he had been told by Cooper that he left the organization after realizing he had been misled into sponsoring it (apparently by William Randolph Hearst). See *Cinema Nation: The Best Writing on Film From the Nation, 1913–2000*, ed. Carl Bromley (New York: Thunder's Mouth Press, 2000), 109–14.

2 This is an allusion to Sinclair Lewis' somewhat hysterical, Depression-era bestseller, an anti-fascist novel titled *It Can't Happen Here* (1935).

3 The character was partially based on Marlene Dietrich, star of the Joseph Von Sternberg film, *The Devil is a Woman* that Dos Passos worked on – much to his displeasure. See Virginia Spencer Carr, *Dos Passos: A Life* (New York: Doubleday and Co., 1984), 339–40. On the appeal to "fetishistic scopophilia" in Sternberg's oeuvre, see Laura Mulvey, "Visual Pleasure and Narrative Cinema," *Narrative, Apparatus, Ideology: A Film Theory Reader*, ed. Philip Rosen (New York: Columbia University Press, 1986), 205–06.

4 Kenneth Robeson, *The Man of Bronze: Doc Savage* (New York: Bantam, 1964), 2–3, 34.

5 Klaus Theweleit, *Male Fantasies*, trans. Erica Carter and Chris Turner, 2 vols. (Minneapolis: University of Minnesota Press, 1987 and 1989), II, 150.

6 *Ibid.*, 162.

7 On West and the grotesque, see Ralph Ciancio, "Laughing in Pain," *Literature and the Grotesque*, ed. Michael Meyer (Atlanta, GA: Rodopi, 1995), 1–20; Dieter Meindel, *American Fiction and the Metaphysics of the Grotesque* (Columbia: University of Missouri Press, 1996), 178–84; Bernard McElroy, *Fiction of the Modern Grotesque* (London: Macmillan, 1989), 131–38; and John Clark, *The Modern Satiric Grotesque and its Traditions* (Kentucky University Press, 1991).

8 For another Depression-era effort to engage in social protest by critiquing the impact of an American amusement (the dance marathon), see Horace McCoy's *They Shoot Horses Don't They?* (1935; New York and London: Serpent's Tail Press, 1995).

9 Edward Dahlberg, *Do These Bones Live* (New York: Harcourt, Brace and Company, 1941), 155.

10 Two letters reveal that West admired Dahlberg's novels. See Nathanael West, *Novels and Other Writings* (New York: Library of America, 1997), 770–71, 777–78. For a comparison of the two writers, see Josephine Herbst, "Nathanael West," *Nathanael West: A Collection of Critical Essays*, ed. Jay Martin (Englewood Cliffs, NJ: Prentice-Hall, 1971), 21–23.

11 See also Caren Irr's discussion of the novel's critique as encompassing Depression-era left-wing narrative strategies (*The Suburb of Dissent: Cultural Politics in the United States and Canada during the 1930s* (Durham: Duke University Press, 1998), 192–212). On the "Chamber" as an "exact antitype" to the Chicago World's Fair, see Rita Barnard, *The Great Depression and the Culture of Abundance: Kenneth Fearing, Nathanael West, and Mass Culture in the 1930s* (New York: Cambridge University Press, 1995), 151.

12 On West and burlesque, see Jay Martin, "Nathanael West's Burlesque Comedy," *Critical Essays on Nathanael West*, ed. Ben Siegel (New York: G.K. Hall, 1994), 161–68.

13 A variation on this dramatic scene appears in *The Day of the Locust* in the newspaper clipping account of Harry Greener's vaudeville performance with the "The Flying Lings" troupe (*Novels*, 262–63).

14 Miriam Hansen, "Of Mice and Ducks: Benjamin and Adorno on Disney," *South Atlantic Quarterly* 92:1 (Winter 1993): 34.

15 Mikhail Bakhtin, *Rabelais and His World*, trans. Helen Iswolsky (Bloomington: Indiana University Press, 1984), 196.

16 For a good discussion of *A Cool Million* in the context of native, protofascist movements, see Jay Martin, *Nathanael West: The Art of His Life* (New York: Carroll and Graf, 1970), 225–43. For a critical overview of thirties right-wing organizations, see Stanley High, "Star-Spangled Fascists" (1939); for a sympathetic account of the phenomenon, see Lawrence Dennis, "Portrait of American Fascism" (1935). Both articles are contained in abridged form in *The Strenuous Decade: A Social and Intellectual Record of the Nineteen-Thirties*, ed. Daniel Aaron and Robert Bendiner (New York: Doubleday and Company, 1970), 326–54.

17 These citations are from "The Rhetoric of Hitler's Battle," Kenneth Burke's exemplary reading of *Mein Kampf* (*The Philosophy of Literary Form: Studies in*

Symbolic Form [1941; 3rd rev. ed., Berkeley: University of California Press, 1973], 201–03, 206). On the "aesthetic of fascism" as a "spiritual denial of an underlying economic disunity," see Burke, "Revolutionary Symbolism in America," *American Writers' Congress*, ed. Henry Hart (New York: International Publishers, 1935), 92.

18 Kaja Silverman, "Historical Trauma and Male Subjectivity," *Psychoanalysis and Cinema*, ed. E. Ann Kaplan (London: Routledge, 1990), 115.

19 On prosopopoeia as the means by which one's name "is made as intelligible and memorable as a face," see Paul de Man, "Autobiography as De-Facement," *The Rhetoric of Romanticism* (New York: Columbia University Press, 1986), 75–76. See also de Man, "The Epistemology of Metaphor," *Aesthetic Ideology* (Minneapolis: University of Minnesota Press, 1996), 46. A stunning scene in Tillie Olsen's *Yonnondio* makes it possible to understand the value rhetorical insights into the structure and function of this figure of speech may have for psychoanalytic examinations of psychotic behavior. In the scene, a deranged, hallucinatory miner, Sheen McEvoy, who lost his mind when his face was reduced to "a red mass of jelly" by a mine explosion, anthropomorphically imposes, as if in compensation for his lost features, a visage and voice onto the monstrous, inanimate entity he (mistakenly) holds responsible for his traumatic experience. "To him, the mine was alive – a thousand-armed creature, with ghosts hanging from the crossbeams, ghosts living in the coal.... Looking in the mirror at himself, he thought now some ghost in the coal was wearing it laughing." The narcissistic exchange generates the cognitively deluded impression of the mine as a devouring mother who has wounded the man because of her barrenness. "She only takes men 'cause she aint got kids." McEvoy therefore attempts to hurl the novel's female protagonist, Mazie, to the bottom of the mineshaft through the "hungry mouth" with which "she" (the mine) calls. Madness, which leads in this case to the attempted murder of a small child, is here tropologically determined – consciousness being structured like a language (*Yonnondio: From the Thirties* [New York: Delta, 1974], 10–11).

20 Louis Althusser, "Ideology and Ideological State Apparatuses," *Lenin and Philosophy and Other Essays*, trans. Ben Brewster (New York: Monthly Review Press, 1971), 174.

21 Michael Denning argues in *Mechanical Accents: Dime Novels and Working-Class Culture in America* that Alger wasn't a dime novelist proper but "a ventriloquist using the dime format in order to reform working-class reading and culture" (New York: Verso, 1988), 171–72, 203.

22 Robeson, *Man of Bronze*, 119.

23 *Ibid.*, 109.

24 Commenting on advertising aesthetics, Lauren Berlant argues that prosthetic bodies "ideally replace the body of pain with the projected image of safety and satisfaction commodities represent." See "National Brands/ National Body," *The Phantom Public Sphere*, ed. Bruce Robbins (Minneapolis: University of Minnesota Press, 1993), 178.

25 On the Alger hero as a type and on the ideological significance of his dismantling, see Jonathan Veitch, *American Superrealism: Nathanael West and the Politics of Representation in the 1930s* (Madison: University of Wisconsin Press, 1997), 101.

26 On West's activism in the thirties, see Martin, *Art of Life*, 257–60. The Communist Party shifted away from its Third Period call for proletarian revolution to the Popular Front strategy of expanding the constituency of the Left in 1935, partly in response to the growth of fascism in Europe.

27 West had already addressed the question of male hysteria and its relation to the mass media in *Miss Lonelyhearts* (1933).

28 Tod's figuration of these persons, "America's madmen," as a liquid substance, as the "cream" of a nation "rich in violence" (West, *Novels, Day*, 309) seems a less vulgar way of characterizing the lumpenproletariat – "scum" the more common appellation.

29 The phrase appears in a 1939 letter to the proletarian novelist Jack Conroy. West is justifying his exclusion "of the sincere, honest people who work in the city" and who "are making such a great progressive fight." Cited in Martin, *Art of Life*, 336.

30 Elsewhere Lacan extends his theory to encompass the child's history from day ten, when he first demonstrates an interest in "the human face" ("Aggressivity in Psychoanalysis," *Écrits*, trans. Alan Sheridan (New York: W.W. Norton, 1977), 18).

31 Susan Buck-Morss, "Aesthetics and Anaesthetics: Walter Benjamin's Artwork Essay Reconsidered," *October* 62 (Fall 1992): 37. She elaborates: "the significance of Lacan's theory emerges only in the historical context of modernity as precisely the experience of the fragile body and the dangers to it of fragmentation that replicates the trauma of the original infantile event (the fantasy of the *corps morcelé*)." See also Hal Foster, "Armor Fou," *October* 56 (Spring 1991): 65–97 (81–85).

32 It has been said "very often, and rightly" "that the cinema is a technique of the imaginary" and that "the spectator–screen relationship is a mirror identification." Christian Metz, "The Imaginary Signifier," *Screen* 16:2 (Summer 1975): 15, 18. A scene in John Fante's *Wait Until Spring, Bandini* (1938) is pertinent. When the autobiographical protagonist falls "under the spell of that celluloid drug," he (Bandini) becomes "positive that his own face bore a striking resemblance to that of Robert Powell." The actor then seems to lose "his identity" and become the character. Ultimately, however, the dejected character realizes "there really wasn't any resemblance at all," that "it was just a movie." (Santa Rosa: Black Sparrow Press, 1999), 78–80.

33 For Althusser's assessment of his debt to Lacan, see Louis Althusser, "Freud and Lacan," *Writings on Psychoanalysis*, trans. Jeffrey Mehlman (New York: Columbia University Press, 1996), 7–32.

34 Louis Althusser, "Cremonini: Painter of the Abstract," *Lenin*, 238–39.

35 On the painting/literature link, see Donald Torchiana, "*The Day of the Locust* and The Painter's Eye," *Nathanael West: The Cheaters and the Cheated*, ed. David Madden (DeLand, FL: Everett/Edwards, 1972), 249–82.

36 R.W.B. Lewis insists on the identity of character and author in regard to the vision of imminent apocalypse they share. See "Days of Wrath and Laughter," *Trials of the Word* (New Haven: Yale University Press, 1965), 213–18. Barnard tentatively equates the two, proposing that both the painting and the book contain "dialectical images," that the bleak, negative vision of the present they both express contains a positive element, a utopian insistence on "a revolutionary solution" (*Culture of Abundance*, 186–87). On the difference between Tod and West, see Tim Armstrong, *Modernism, Technology and the Body: A Cultural Study* (New York: Cambridge University Press, 1998), 236–39. For a good account of the stakes of the debate, see Thomas Strychacz, *Modernism, Mass Culture, Professionalism* (New York: Cambridge University Press, 1993), 185–206.

37 Leslie Fiedler, *Myths and Images of the Secret Self* (New York: Anchor Books, 1993), 295. See also Thomas Doherty, *Pre-Code Hollywood: Sex, Immorality, and Insurrection in American Cinema, 1930–1934* (New York: Columbia University Press, 1999), 295–318.

38 Martin, *Art of Life*, 312.

39 Doherty, *Pre-Code Hollywood*, 298.

40 William Carlos Williams, "*The Day of the Locust*," *Critical Essays*, ed. Jay Martin, 139.

41 Lacan, "Aggressivity," 11. Imago can mean either an introjected, idealized mental image (of another person or the self) or an insect in its adult, sexually mature, winged state.

42 If the dual, "pre-oedipal," imaginary intercourse with an alter ego is paradigmatically an exchange with the mother, then it is appropriate that when Tod tries to caress Faye she tears free, laughingly reproaching him with the threat that "Mama spank" (296). Couples dancing, which involves "the play of approach and rejection," figure in *Day* as imaginary transactions. On the ordered movements of two partners in an imaginary capture – sexual display or physical combat – as "dancity," see Jacques Lacan, "The Subversion of the Subject and the Dialectic of Desire in the Freudian Unconscious," *Écrits*, 305. Tod's lithographs are appropriately titled "The Dancers."

43 In an earlier version of the manuscript Claude was the first-person narrator of the novel; Tod was a late addition to the work. Martin, *Art of Life*, 312. Others might hear in Estee a reference to S. J. Perelman, West's brother-in-law, who wrote several Marx Brothers film scripts.

44 Constance Penley, "Feminism, Film, and the Bachelor Machines," *The Future of an Illusion: Film, Feminism, and Psychoanalysis* (New York: Routledge, 1989), 57–58. Later Penley quotes Jacqueline Rose: "The imaginary, of which the cinema may be the most privileged and efficient machine, is precisely a *machine*, an apparatus in which what is at stake is a repression or refusal of the problem or difficulty of sexuality," 62.

45 Henry Miller, "The Golden Age," *The Cosmological Eye* (New York: New Directions, 1939), 50.

46 In an interpretation of Aldous Huxley's representation in *Brave New World* (1932) of film production as a division of "Emotional Engineering,"

258

Peter Wollen asserts that a "carefully regulated new 'soul' is added to the new Fordized body, a kitsch soul for a machine body." See "Cinema/ Americanism/the Robot," *Raiding the Icebox: Reflections on Twentieth-Century Culture* (New York: Verso, 1993), 54. For a different yet convincing reading of the West passage, see Veitch, *American Superrealism*, 123–26.

47 See also Susan Edmunds, "Modern Taste and the Body Beautiful in Nathanael West's *The Day of the Locust*," *Modern Fiction Studies* 44:2 (Summer 1998): 306–30.

48 Gilles Deleuze and Felix Guattari, *Anti-Oedipus: Capitalism and Schizophrenia*, trans. Robert Hurley, Mark Seem, and Helen R. Lane (Minneapolis: University of Minnesota Press, 1983), 5.

49 See Theweleit, *Fantasies*, 1, 229–300. Though I claim West's novel antici- pates Theweleit's study, this dimension of *Day* became apparent to me only by reading *Male Fantasies*. Such hermeneutic circularity, which discloses what was already there but heretofore unseen, need not be confused with anachro- nistic projections of critical insights back in time. I offer the same defense for my study in its entirety.

50 Does not irony in West, and more so (as we will see) in Dos Passos, constitute a kind of linguistic armor against the amorphousness of sincerely expressive speech?

51 Henry Miller, *Tropic of Capricorn* (New York: Grove Press, 1961), 321–22.

52 Robeson, *Man of Bronze*, 79, 23.

53 That the act of staring is depicted inside the painting enriches but does not alter its function as a voyeuristically driven act of cognitive policing.

54 See Fredric Jameson, *Postmodernism; or, the Cultural Logic of Late Capitalism* (Durham: Duke University Press, 1991), 11–15.

55 Dahlberg was another such Jeremiah. See his essays "Hitler's Power Over Germany" (1933) and "Nightgown Riders of America" (1934), collected in Dahlberg, *Samuel Beckett's Wake and Other Uncollected Prose* (Elmwood Park, IL: Dalkey Archive Press, 1989), 16–28; "Fascism and Writers," a talk delivered at the First AWC; and his third novel, *Those Who Perish*. This is perhaps the place to note that several of the theoretical figures (Benjamin, Bataille, Kristeva, Deleuze and Guattari, de Man, and Theweleit), whose exemplary critical performances the present study in many respects mimes, formulated their ideas and (grotesque) aesthetics in direct response – implicitly and explicitly – to European fascism.

4 MILITARISM AND MUTILATION IN JOHN DOS PASSOS

1 Henry Miller, *Black Spring* (New York: Grove Press, 1963), 169.

2 Dalton Trumbo, *Johnny Got His Gun* (New York: J.P. Lippincott, 1939), 83.

3 See Tim Blackmore, "Lazarus Machine: Body Politics in Dalton Trumbo's *Johnny Got His Gun*," *Mosaic* 33:4 (December 2000): 13.

4 See also Katherine Anne Porter's 1939 story "Pale Horse, Pale Rider," in which the protagonist, near death, realizes that "soft carefully shaped words

like oblivion and eternity are curtains hung before nothing at all." (New York: New American Library) 157–58.

5 John Dos Passos, "Is the 'Realistic' Theatre Obsolete? Many Theatrical Conventions Have Been Shattered by Lawson's *Processional*," *John Dos Passos: The Nonfictional Prose*, ed. Donald Pizer (Detroit: Wayne State University Press, 1988), 75–78. *Processional* was composed by John Howard Lawson, with whom Dos Passos and three others would form the New Playwrights Theatre (1927–29) – a short-lived though important attempt to secure a popular audience for a cultural venture committed to revolutionary politics and to the use of avant-garde artistic techniques.

6 Dos Passos, "'Realistic' Theatre," 76.

7 *Ibid.*, 77.

8 Tom Gunning, "The Cinema of Attractions: Early Film, its Spectator and the Avant-Garde," *Early Cinema: Space-Frame-Narrative*, ed. Thomas Elsaesser and Adam Barker (London: British Film Institute, 1990), 56–62.

9 Dos Passos, "'Realistic' Theatre," 77.

10 *The Waste Land* may have influenced Dos Passos. Yet Hugh Kenner suggests in *The Mechanic Muse* that the impact of the rapid cutting from item to item in the newsreels probably furnished Eliot with a formal model. The two writers perhaps learned from the same media technology ([New York: Oxford University Press, 1987], 9, 34).

11 "The radicalism of Dos Passos simmered in the early twenties, boiled furiously between 1927 and 1932, and began to cool thereafter." Daniel Aaron, *Writers on the Left: Episodes in American Literary Communism* (New York: Harcourt, Brace and World, 1961), 361. On Dos Passos' complex political trajectory, see Robert Rosen, *John Dos Passos: Politics and the Writer* (Lincoln: University of Nebraska Press, 1981), 64–98; Melvin Landsberg, *Dos Passos' Path to "U.S.A.": A Political Biography 1912–1936* (Boulder, CO: Associated University Press, 1973); and Townsend Ludington, *The Life of John Dos Passos: Twentieth Century Odyssey* (New York: Dutton, 1980).

12 Lewis Mumford, "The Drama of the Machines," *Scribner's Magazine* 83:2 (August 1930): 151. On the inauguration and refinement of "a new systematic mechanisation of death" in "military killing machinery," and on its connection to Taylorized methods of industrial production, see Daniel Pick, *War Machine: The Rationalisation of Slaughter in the Modern Age* (New Haven: Yale University Press, 1993), 165–210. See also Michel Foucault, *Discipline and Punish: The Birth of the Prison*, trans. Alan Sheridan (New York: Random House, 1995), 135–46, 162–69. On the factory and the army as virtually interchangeable terms, see Lewis Mumford, *Technics and Civilization* (New York: Harcourt, Brace and Company, 1934), 84, 92.

13 Mumford, "Drama," 153.

14 *Ibid.*, 160.

15 *Ibid.*, 150.

16 This piece was first published in 1926 in the *Saturday Review of Literature* and later included in *Orient Express*, a collection of travel writings. On Cendrars

and Dos Passos, see William Dow, "John Dos Passos, Blaise Cendrars and the 'Other' Modernism," *Twentieth Century Literature* 42:3 (Fall 1997): 396–416.

17 John Dos Passos, *Orient Express* (New York: Jonathan Cape and Harrison Smith, 1927), 191, 204.

18 *Ibid.*, 201.

19 *Ibid.*, 192.

20 *Ibid.*, 204.

21 John Dos Passos, *Three Soldiers* (New York: George H. Doran Company, 1921), 331.

22 On the reduction of the soldier's body to the status of a "part of a multi-segmentary machine," see Foucault, *Discipline*, 164.

23 John Dos Passos, *1919* (New York: Harcourt, Brace and Company, 1932), 454.

24 See Friedrich A. Kittler, *Gramophone, Film, Typewriter*, trans. Geoffrey Winthrop-Young and Michael Wurtz (Stanford University Press, 1999), 191.

25 *Industrial Valley* (New York: Harcourt, Brace and Company, 1939) is a generic hybrid in that it mixes together without synthesizing documentary and novelistic elements. Part realistic fiction, part straight reportage on a historical event (the mid-thirties sit-down strikes in Akron, Ohio), McKenney's book is in addition a satiric commentary on the local news media's slanted coverage of this act of labor militancy. An inorganic and discontinuous text, *Industrial Valley* contains direct transcriptions of previously published newspaper articles, ironic summaries of these articles, and newly generated materials. The text constitutes, to play metaphorically on the title, a kind of valley between industrialized writing practices; it confuses with erasing the difference between creative and critical, fictional and factual modes of writing. Rendering traditional discursive oppositions obsolete, *Industrial Valley* may be considered grotesque not in terms of visual and pictorial imagery but in regard to its generically anomalous nature. This unclassifiable, heterogeneous text is a rhetorical freak.

26 John Dos Passos, *Manhattan Transfer* (Boston: Houghton Mifflin, 1925), 329.

27 Jimmy will later admit to being "stumped"when confronted with a phallic skyscraper from whose windows Ellie beckons "lifelike," 365.

28 I don't deal in this chapter with *The Big Money*, the trilogy's third volume. My reason for ignoring this text is my conviction that a decisive break, one with political and rhetorical implications, occurs in Dos Passos' career after 1932 (after the publication of *1919*). I thus use *U.S.A.* as a terminological convenience, admittedly obscuring the heterogeneity of the textual enterprise as a whole.

29 Dos Passos, "Introduction to *Three Soldiers*," *Nonfictional Prose*, ed. Pizer, 146.

30 Dos Passos, " 'Realistic' Theatre," 86.

31 In comparing Dos Passos unfavorably to Joyce, Marshall McLuhan seems to have missed the point, faulting the American novelist for not being "prepared to explore the interior landscape of the heart." "John Dos Passos: Technique vs. Sensibility," *Dos Passos: A Collection of Critical Essays*, ed. Andrew Hook

(Englewood Cliffs, NJ: Prentice-Hall, 1974), 148–61. Such "poetic" exploration was for Dos Passos the representationally naive starting point of his critically prosaic enterprise.

32 Michel de Certeau, "The Arts of Dying: Celibatory Machines," *Heterologies: Discourse on the Other*, trans. Brian Massumi (Minneapolis: University of Minnesota Press, 1986), 167. Notably, for de Certeau, the "essential characteristic" of a celibatory apparatus or writing machine, a category in which *U.S.A.* belongs, is that it is male and refuses to "express the feminine in writing," 166.

33 For the composite piece, see John Dos Passos, *Occasions and Protests* (Chicago: Henry Regnery Company, 1964), 5–15.

34 This imperative may have overdetermined his selection of materials in the Newsreels, for, as Janet Casey notes, "the Newsreels yield to an increasing emphasis on violence against women" (139). Casey, however, praises Dos Passos from a feminist perspective for his thematic rendering of the constraints of socially constructed gender roles and his examination of historically specific codes of sexual behavior. See Janet Casey, *Dos Passos and the Ideology of the Feminine* (New York: Cambridge University Press, 1998), 131–75.

35 Walter Benjamin, *The Origin of German Tragic Drama*, trans. John Osborne (London: Verso, 1977), 215.

36 Paul de Man, *Allegories of Reading: Figural Language in Rousseau, Nietzsche, Rilke, and Proust* (New Haven: Yale University Press, 1979), 290.

37 *Ibid.*, 296.

38 *Ibid.*, 298.

39 See also Anne Tomiche, "Writing the Body: The Rhetoric of Mutilation in Marguerite Duras's *L'amante anglaise*," *Thinking Bodies*, ed. Juliet Flower MacCannell and Laura Zakarin (Stanford University Press, 1994), 120–31.

40 Barbara Foley, *Radical Representations: Politics and Form in U.S. Proletarian Fiction, 1929–1941* (Durham: Duke University Press, 1993), 433.

41 John Dos Passos, *The Big Money* (London: Constable and Company, 1936), 450.

42 Donald Pizer, *Dos Passos' U.S.A.* (Charlottesville: University of Virginia Press, 1988), 207. See also Miles Orvell, *The Real Thing: Imitation and Authenticity in American Culture 1880–1940* (Chapel Hill: University of North Carolina Press, 1989): "The Camera Eye sections," he asserts "provide the implicit theoretical basis for the construction of the whole of *U.S.A.*, for they place at the center of the panoramic novel the creative consciousness of the artist." Thus the meaning of the device is "that the eye is prior to the word, that vision is a prelude to speech," 268. Arguing that Dos Passos' literary strategies were influenced by the Soviet filmmaker Dziga Vertov, Carol Schloss interprets the filmic trope (the Camera Eye) as an indication of the writer's faith in mechanized perception as an improvement on natural vision, as a supplement to "the unassisted eye" (*In Visible Light: Photography and the American Writer: 1840–1940* [New York: Oxford University Press, 1987], 161).

43 See Fred Pfeil, *Another Tale to Tell: Politics and Narrative in Post Modern Culture* (New York: Verso, 1990), 173.
44 John Dos Passos, *The 42nd Parallel* (New York: Harper & Brothers, 1930), 4.
45 See David Seed, "Media and Newsreels in Dos Passos' *U.S.A.*," *Journal of Narrative Technique* 14 (Fall 1984): 182–92; Charles Marz, "Dos Passos' Newsreels: The Noise of History," *Studies in the Novel* 11 (Summer 1979): 194–200 and Marz, "*U.S.A.*: Chronicle and Performance," *Modern Fiction Studies* 26 (Fall 1980): 398–416.
46 Stanley Corkin does stress the polarity of the two devices in his attempt to situate Dos Passos in relation to the intellectual tradition of Hegelian Marxism. See "John Dos Passos and the American Left: Recovering the Dialectic of History," *Criticism* 34:4 (Fall 1992): 597.
47 See, for instance, Cecilia Tichi, *Shifting Gears: Technology, Literature, Culture in Modernist America* (Chapel Hill: University of North Carolina Press, 1987), 210–16. Michael Denning's variation on this approach is to characterize *U.S.A.* as a failed attempt to do representational justice to a traumatic historical event: the Sacco-Vanzetti case. See "The Proletarian Sublime," *The Cultural Front: The Laboring of American Culture in the Twentieth Century* (New York: Verso, 1996), 192–99.
48 It is tempting to map the devices and the formal methods they embody onto the three classic "stages" – oral, anal, and phallic – in the subject's libidinal economy.
49 In preparing the revised edition of *The 42nd Parallel*, published in 1937, Dos Passos altered the appearance of certain Newsreels, presumably to make them more readable. In the process, he excised passages, making cuts in a text composed of clippings. On Dos Passos' altered attitude toward the Newsreels, see Pizer, *Dos Passos*, 34.
50 On the fraught process of producing masculinity through military display, see Norman Bryson, "Gericault and Masculinity," *Visual Culture: Images and Interpretations*, ed. Norman Bryson, Michael Ann Holly and Keith Moxey (Hanover: Wesleyan University Press, 1994), 228–49.
51 Shelley Fisher Fishkin interprets this same Newsreel in a comparable vein in *From Fact to Fiction: Journalism and Imaginative Writing in America* (Baltimore: Johns Hopkins University Press, 1985), 187–88.
52 Raymond Fielding draws this conclusion in *The American Newsreel 1911–1967* (Norman: Oklahoma University Press, 1972), 220–27. For a Depression-era denunciation of the Newsreel, see Henry Miller: "Have they shown us how our heroes won the war – and died for us? Have they shown us the gaping wounds, have they shown us the faces that have been shot away? Are they showing us what happens in Spain every day when the bombs rain down on Madrid? Almost every week there is another News Reel theatre opened up, but there is no news" ("The Golden Age," *The Cosmological Eye* [New York: New Directions, 1939], 59). On newsreel sensationalism in the thirties, see Paula Rabinowitz, *They Must Be Represented: The Politics of Documentary* (New York: Verso, 1994), 91–94. See also Laura Browder,

Rousing the Nation: Radical Culture in Depression America (Amherst: University of Massachusetts Press, 1998), 44.

53 J.L. Austin, *How to Do Things With Words* (Cambridge, MA: Harvard University Press, 1975).

54 Michel de Certeau, *The Practice of Everyday Life*, trans. Steven Rendall (Berkeley: University of California Press, 1984), 34–39.

55 Jean-Paul Sartre, *Literary Essays*, trans. Annette Michelson (New York: Philosophical Library, 1957), 93–95.

56 John Dos Passos, "What Makes a Novelist?" *Nonfictional Prose*, ed. Pizer, 269.

57 John Dos Passos, "An Interview with John Dos Passos," *Nonfictional Prose*, ed. Pizer, 283. Casey develops some of the implications of these late statements. See *Feminine*, 142–44.

58 This perspective renders superfluous questions as to whether or not Dos Passos was fair to the actual person. See Leo Gurko, "John Dos Passos' *U.S.A*: A 1930's Spectacular:" "His [Dos Passos'] scorn of Woodrow Wilson as a mouthpiece for the Morgan interests during the First World War is a gross oversimplification." *Proletarian Writers of the Thirties*, ed. David Madden (Carbondale: Southern Illinois University, 1968), 58.

59 Alfred Kazin, "Introduction," *1919* (New York: New American Library, 1969), xv.

60 Jack Conroy, "Introduction," *The Unknown Soldier Speaks* (Holt, MN: B.C. Hagglund, 1932), 3. On Jarrboe's poetry, see Cary Nelson, *Repression and Recovery: Modern American Poetry and the Politics of Cultural Memory 1910–1945* (Madison: University of Wisconsin Press, 1989), 154.

61 Donald Pease, "Hiroshima, the Vietnam Veterans War Memorial, and the Gulf War: Post-National Spectacles," *Cultures of United States Imperialism*, ed. Amy Kaplan and Donald Pease (Durham: Duke University Press, 1993), 559. See also Bill Brown on the recalcitrance of "the human corpse-as-image" to narratives "meant to heal a nation's trauma," *The Material Unconscious: American Amusement, Stephen Crane and the Economies of Play* (Cambridge, MA: Harvard University Press, 1996), 125–66.

62 William March, *Company K* (Tusacaloosa: University of Alabama Press, 1989), 179.

63 *Ibid.*, 180.

64 *Ibid.*, 181.

65 *Ibid.*, 182.

66 See Kenneth Burke: "The more I examine both the structure of poetry and the structure of human relations outside of poetry, the more I become convinced that this [synecdoche] is the 'basic' figure of speech, and that it occurs in many modes besides that of the formal trope. I feel it to be no mere accident of language that we use the same word for sensory, artistic, and political representation," "The Philosophy of Literary Form," *The Philosophy of Literary Form: Studies in Symbolic Form* (1941; 3rd rev. ed., Berkeley: University of California Press, 1973), 26.

67 Fielding notes that the contents of the first all-sound reel of *Movie Tone News*, released in 1927, included the Vatican choir performing at the Tomb of the Unknown Solider (*Newsreel*, 163).

68 Elaine Scarry has argued that "the idiom of 'heroism,' 'sacrifice,' 'dedication,' 'devotion,' and 'bravery' conventionally invoked to describe the soldier's individual act of consent over his own body is neither inappropriate nor false" (*The Body in Pain: The Making and Unmaking of the World* [New York: Oxford University Press, 1985], 112). My point, or Dos Passos', is that the epistemologically debatable claim to have knowledge of the sentiments of the dead serves as the cornerstone of perniciously ideological discourses.

69 Coined in 1921, a "hundred-percenter" is "a thoroughgoing nationalist" (*Webster's Dictionary*).

70 James Agee, *The Collected Poems of James Agee* (Boston: Houghton Mifflin, 1968), 160–61.

71 Benjamin, *German Drama*, 217.

72 On this memorial practice, see Thomas W. Laqueur, "Names, Bodies, and the Anxiety of Erasure," *The Social and Political Body*, ed. Theodore R. Schatzki and Wolfgang Natter (New York: Guilford Press, 1996), 123–41.

POSTFACE: DISCHARGES

1 James Agee and Walter Evans, *Let Us Now Praise Famous Men* (Boston: Houghton Mifflin, 1941), 381.

2 Gilles Deleuze and Felix Guattari, *Anti-Oedipus: Capitalism and Schizophrenia*, trans. Robert Hurley, Mark Seem, and Helen R. Lane (Minneapolis: University of Minnesota Press, 1983), 31.

3 See Fredric Jameson, *Postmodernism; or, The Cultural Logic of Late Capitalism* (Durham: Duke University Press, 1991), 10.

4 Miles Orvell, *The Real Thing: Imitation and Authenticity in American Culture, 1880–1940* (Chapel Hill: University of North Carolina Press, 1989), 272–85 and Peter Cosgrove "Snapshots of the Absolute: Mediamachia in *Let Us Now Praise Famous Men*," *American Literature* 67:2 (1995): 329–57.

5 Paula Rabinowitz, *They Must Be Represented: The Politics of Documentary* (New York: Verso, 1994), 46.

6 T.V. Reed, "Unimagined Existence and the Fiction of the Real: Postmodernist Realism in *Let Us Now Praise Famous Men*," *Representations* 24 (1988): 156–76.

7 See, however, Michael Denning who notes Agee's use of grotesque representational strategies (*The Cultural Front: The Laboring of American Culture in the Twentieth Century* [New York: Verso, 1996], 123); and Michael E. Staub, *Voices of Persuasion: The Politics of Representation in 1930s America* (New York: Cambridge University Press, 1994), who locates several "allegorical" passages in *Famous Men* (32–53).

8 One example among several: "Beneath the gulf lies dreaming, and beneath, dreaming, that woman, that id, the lower American continent, lies spread

before heaven in her wealth," *Famous Men*, 45. Agee's rhetorical strategy is to an extent to "feminize" existence in general (human and inhuman): he attributes unconsciousness, passivity, vulnerability, and penetrability to all organic entities. In turn he invests writing with the conventionally masculine qualities of consciousness, activity, and violent aggression. This produces a space for the male author to occupy apart from the devastatingly subjugated yet still desirable (and desiring) objects of the documentary venture.

9 I am tempted, pace Michael Fried, to argue that the linguistically reflexive tropes in evidence here rest on two hidden puns. The figure of the earth's face perhaps evokes the sur*face* of a piece of paper on which the writer as *water*, or author, signs its/his name.

Index

Note: Numbers in parentheses refer to pages where contextual information is found.

LaVergne, TN USA
25 September 2009
158976LV00003B/18/P

9 780521 120913

Guide to

DERECH ERETZ

Rabbi S. Wagschal

TARGUM/FELDHEIM

First published 1993

Copyright © 1993 by Rabbi S. Wagschal
ISBN 1-56871-022-4

Phototypeset at Targum Press

Printing plates by Frank, Jerusalem

Published by:
Targum Press Inc.
22700 W. Eleven Mile Rd.
Southfield, Mich. 48034

Distributed by:
Feldheim Publishers
200 Airport Executive Park
Spring Valley, N.Y. 10977

Distributed in Israel by:
Targum Press Ltd.
POB 43170
Jerusalem 91430

Printed in Israel